POLAR ~ EXTREMES

To Beeb *Poole from* Lincoln Ellsworth —
20 Oct. 1930.

POLAR EXTREMES

The World of Lincoln Ellsworth

Beekman H. Pool

University of Alaska Press

FAIRBANKS, ALASKA

For information contact:
University of Alaska Press
P.O. Box 756240
Fairbanks, AK 99775-6240
907-474-5831
fypress@uaf.edu
www.uaf.edu/uapress

Library of Congress Cataloging-in-Publication Data

Pool, Beekman H., 1909–
   Polar extremes : the world of Lincoln Ellsworth / Beekman H. Pool.
      p. cm.
   Includes bibliographical references (p. 287).
   ISBN 1-889963-43-7 (hardcover : alk. paper)
   ISBN 1-889963-44-5 (pbk. : alk. paper)
   1. Ellsworth, Lincoln, 1880–1951.   2. Explorers—United States—
Biography.   3. Polar regions—Discovery and exploration.   4. Arctic
regions—Aerial exploration.   5. Antarctica—Aerial exploration.   I. Title.
G585.E6 P66 2002
919.804´092—dc21   2002006411

Cover design by Mike Kirk
Text design by Rachel Fudge

This book is dedicated to Elizabeth Pool, my beloved wife.

Contents

List of Illustrations

14. Having made the world's first transpolar flight, the *Norge* crew posed with its leaders: (seated in front) Amundsen, Ellsworth, and Nobile, holding his dog Titina, who also made the trip.
15. General Umberto Nobile, 1885–1978.
16. Roald Amundsen, Richard E. Byrd, and Lincoln Ellsworth, celebrating their formation of the exclusive Polar Legion, whose membership comprised only those who had reached one of the Poles. While Scott and Peary were named members posthumously, Nobile was not invited to join this club.
17. Schloss Lenzburg, the castle in Switzerland that Lincoln inherited from his father and visited for the first time in June 1929.
18. Lincoln Ellsworth standing alongside the Lenzburg castle gate in 1929.

Following page 166
19. Tatiana, daughter of the czar of Russia. Although she was unattainable, Ellsworth was captivated by her charismatic beauty.
20. Mary Louise Ulmer and Lincoln Ellsworth at Lenzburg Castle, before they became engaged.
21. Lincoln Ellsworth and Mary Louise Ulmer on their wedding day in May 1933.
22. Invitation for Harold Clark to the christening of the submarine *Nautilus*, the vessel in which Sir Hubert Wilkins sought to explore the North Pole.
23. Ellsworth and Bernt Balchen aboard the *Polar Star,* built for Ellsworth by the Northrup Company for his first expedition to Antarctica.
24. Pilot Bernt Balchen, Lincoln Ellsworth, and Sir Hubert Wilkins.
25. Center, first row, Bernt Balchen, Lincoln Ellsworth, and Sir Hubert Wilkins with members of their crew.
26. The icebound *Wyatt Earp* on its voyage towards the Antarctic.

Following page 214
27. Taken by Ellsworth aboard the *Polar Star,* this photo shows the Eternity Range as it appeared on the first flight, November 21, 1935.
28. The *Polar Star* amid snow drifts.
29. The *Polar Star* snowed in at Camp III.
30. Out of fuel at Camp V on December 9, packed for departure and search for Richard E. Byrd's Little America.
31. Ellsworth, arriving at Little America on December 15.
32. Prepared for a celebration, Ellsworth carried these bottles of cognac across Antarctica. He and Hollick-Kenyon autographed the bottle at right.
33. National recognition was finally Ellsworth's when he was awarded a special gold medal by Herbert Hoover, June 16, 1936, for his flight across Antarctica.

Maps

Acknowledgments

The skill, knowledge, and commitment of Doreen Fitzgerald were integral to the production of this book. For steering the project to completion, I thank Jennifer Robin Collier.

For aid way beyond the call of duty, I am forever indebted to Rob Perkins.

And for her years of skill and patience in preparing the manuscript, I am deeply grateful to Judy Lessard.

My thanks to the following organizations for their generous responses to my requests for use of archival material:

American Geographical Society Collection, Golda Meier Library, University of Wisconsin; American Museum of Natural History; Byrd Polar Research Center, Ohio State University; Edison Institute, Archives and Library; Franklin Delano Roosevelt Library; Houghton Library, Harvard University; Johns Hopkins University Library; Eisenhower Library; Museo Storico-Aeronautica Militare; National Archives; National Geographic Society; Rockefeller Archive Center; Royal Geographic Society; Scott Polar Research Institute; Smithsonian Institution Archives; Stefansson Collection; Universitets Biblioteket i Oslo; Yale University Library.

For special help in handling foreign affairs, I thank:

Gertrude Nobile, Italy; Lars Melemseter and Ann-Christine Jacobsen, Norway; Sally Douglas, Australia; Monique Bordry, France; Timothy Hollick-Kenyon, Canada; Per Tryde, Denmark.

And on the home front:

John Bockstoce, Raimond Goerler, Louise Gordon, James Houston, Elizabeth Langby, Anne Lunt, Clare Prentice Neilson, Anna Maria Palmer, Daniel Pool, Sheila Rauch, Winston Ross, and Rob Stephenson.

Last, but far from least, heartfelt thanks to my daughter, Felicity, for her perspicacity and faith.

Introduction

BY 1930 LINCOLN ELLSWORTH was between projects and going through a period of despondency that would indirectly lead to my first encounter with the then fifty-year-old explorer. For three years he had vainly sought a new objective to satisfy his still-gnawing ambitions. Recent personal sorrows had added to his professional frustration.

Gertrude Hill Gavin, daughter of railroad pioneer J. J. Hill and a close friend of his from early days, had more than once been taken into Lincoln's confidence and was aware both of the sorrows and the need for pastures new. He wrote her in December 1929: "I should like to go on that Labrador trip and may yet, but that submarine trip looms big with me. I want to go back to the Arctic just once more. Wilkins returns from the Antarctic April first and then it is yes or no. Until then I must remain undecided."[1]

As it happened, Gertrude Gavin was my godmother, as well as being a close friend of Ellsworth's. She knew of my romantic idea of getting to Grand Falls in Labrador—a giant cataract so remote it had seldom been seen. Knowing of Ellsworth's need for a companion on "that Labrador trip," she suggested to him that he take me. Ellsworth and I had never met. He mulled the idea over, but not until spring did final word come, confirmed by a long letter to me that began, "I am looking forward to our trip together as I have never looked forward to a trip before."[2]

"Ellsworth to fly to Paris today on voyage to Canada. Explorer leaves Switzerland for 800-mile trip in canoe" read a headline in the Paris edition of the *New York Herald* in mid-June 1930. "Lincoln Ellsworth, Arctic explorer," said the article, "will fly from Bale [*sic*] to Paris

tomorrow to sail on the *Mauritania,* with plans for an 800-mile canoe trip to the unknown headwaters of the River St. John and Hamilton River in Labrador. Beekman Pool, a Harvard junior, will accompany him on his canoe voyage . . . 'My future plans must remain dark until autumn,' Ellsworth said. . . . 'If I go to the Arctic again it will be with Sir Hubert Wilkins on his projected submarine trip there.'"[3]

In 1930 Labrador was a land of loneliness and legend. Considerably more than a half-million square miles, it was known to the world, if at all, by Dillon Wallace's account of his companion Leonidas Hubbard's death from starvation during a canoe trip similar to the one we were planning. Undoubtedly this was an important credential, for Ellsworth wrote me that he had always wanted to see Labrador after reading Wallace's *The Lure of the Labrador Wild.*[4]

I first set eyes on my companion-to-be when we met in Quebec City on June 20, 1931. There flowed from him the same spirit of enthusiasm he had expressed in his letter. Of slight build, he had a friendly smile, graying crew-cut hair, and very blue eyes with crinkles at the corners. His nose was slightly crooked—the result, I later learned, of tumbling from a high-wheel bicycle when he was a youngster. He was dressed in an old-fashioned belted jacket with matching trousers. He had always wanted to see Labrador, he told me.

We traveled by coastal steamer to Sept Isles, our point of departure on the North Shore of the St. Lawrence River. Our gear consisted of camping equipment, provisions for sixty-five days, and two eighteen-foot, canvas-covered Labrador model canoes. Weighing ninety-five pounds each, they were described by the Chestnut Canoe Company of Fredericton, New Brunswick, as *"un canot pour les rapides et rivières tortueuses."*

On July 17 we started up the Moisie River with Charlie Vollant and Louis Riverin, two Montagnais Indian guides. The 1,500-foot ascent from sea level to the Height of Land entailed two weeks of backbreaking toil—paddling and poling hour after hour, lugging three loads apiece over each punishing portage. These demands provided deep satisfaction to Ellsworth, a man whose greatest joy, he once said, was to exert every muscle to the physical extreme.

Day after day, we drank in the beauty and variety of our surroundings: the ever-present music of rushing water; the beautiful, plaintive note of the whiskeyjack, or Canada jay; and northern lights flaring across the sky. Once we paused at an Indian burial place, its fifteen crude wooden crosses festooned with small humble offerings—a cluster of beads, a bottle of fly dope.

The first thirty pages of my diary are strewn thick with black flies, crushed between the pages. I wrote, ". . . it is misery to stop a minute on the trail for the flies torment you persistently, crawling down your collar, up your trousers, sleeves . . . [In late evening the flies would knock off work and] you can breathe without swallowing one—which was literally impossible today!"[5]

We were totally absorbed in the here and now, in our daily progress. Evenings we lay smoking pipes in our tent after supper at six o'clock, our bellies filled with the routine fare of beans or rice, content after another strenuous day. Flies pattered against the tent like rain. We talked, sometimes to the accompaniment of the river's quiet murmuring, sometimes above the roar of rapids.

"The country is getting flatter, with no hills, and we seem to be on the top of Labrador," notes my diary. As the country gradually flattened out, trees became more sparse, and portages easier. One day we came upon a phenomenon that even my widely traveled companion had never seen. He wrote: "For three hours we shoved, poled and pulled the canoes up an extremely shallow stream. At last the final rapid was passed, and into the muddy bottom of the lake Louis jammed his pole, so that only the top was sticking out above the water."[6] Other poles protruded above water, and twenty or thirty more showed beneath the surface. "The whole shallow lake bristled like a porcupine with abandoned canoe poles."[7] For generations, Indians passing the final rapids en route to their winter trapping grounds had thus disposed of their poles.

Two days later there was a beautiful clear stream running downhill. "August 2 . . . At last . . . on the headwaters of the Hamilton!"[8] The entry reflected jubilation, but not complacency. Although we had traveled a great deal faster than we had thought possible, much could happen in the remaining 500 miles. The route could be unexpectedly difficult to find. Wind on the great lakes might delay us for days—even weeks. The land was unforgiving; serious accident could delay us until freeze-up, resulting in the slow starvation such as Leonidas Hubbard had experienced.

Two more weeks went by. At first we passed through small ponds and made short portages. Then came vast lakes. At Lake Menihek, a hundred miles long, we were compelled repeatedly to retrace our course when the search for an outlet led only into a dead-end bay. More than once we experienced the wind's violence—once it kept us shorebound for thirty-six hours. And once, while we were impatiently waiting, it hurled one of the canoes into the water from fifteen feet up on shore. But finally came a magic evening when we heard, far off, the muffled sound of the Grand Falls.[9]

Another day's travel "and then we could see the mist hanging low over the woods like smoke from a forest fire."[10] Hours later we stood beside the falls, literally feeling the solid rock shake under foot. The roar, the tumult, the overarching mist were mesmerizing, smothering all sensation beyond awareness of the cataract's enormous strength.[11] Lincoln found it a "sublime spectacle," and was proud to note that "few white men have ever been enterprising enough to go and see [it]."[12]

So overwhelming was the sound, so stupendous the power, that we could well understand the Indians' unwillingness to visit this haunted site. Their lore tells of two maidens who, while collecting firewood near the falls, were lured to the brink and drawn over by the evil spirit of the place. Ever since, dwelling beneath the falls, they have sought to draw any mortal who ventures close. Perhaps this was why Charlie Vollant, a Montagnais of the Moisie band, stayed in camp, whereas Louis, from a different band further west, decided to accompany us.

The day after leaving the falls we loaded and unloaded the canoes nine times to portage and cross small lakes—some undoubtedly the very ones found by John McLean, in 1841, when he, too, was anxiously searching for a way around the falls and the raging rapids below.

There was no mistaking the Big Hill Portage when we did find it. "Down, down, down went the trail, steeper than the Grand Canyon's worst, 700 feet in one-half mile."[13] Then we were on the home stretch—less than 200 miles to go—aided by racing current, exciting rapids, and the stimulus of watching the food supply approach vanishing point.

Six days later we heard "far, far off, the 'put-put' of a motor boat. Our joy cannot be imagined!! Everyone laughing, and wondering how soon it would happen." We paddled an hour longer. "Then at last we saw it, going for shore. Suddenly it turned directly toward us . . . 'Hello,' the first man we'd seen for forty-five days. 'Hello,' he yelled back."

It was over, the journey Ellsworth recalled as "in some ways as interesting as any I ever made."[14]

In November 1930, Lincoln wrote me a letter from Coronado Beach, California. It was dated the twenty-third, by happenstance—or had my godmother told him—my birthday. "All I can dream of," he said, "is great lakes with the wind blowing across them, the call of loons, and northern lights shedding their radiance beyond the tread of human feet. Even 'black flies' are better than all this stuff. I mean New York, for it's wonderful out here with the great ocean rolling in and the sound of the surf forever in one's ears. When the call of the wild gets you, you are lost forever. And I guess that means you as well as myself. It's the companionship, I guess, as much as anything else."[15]

Polar Extremes is the story of this shy mystic, whose innate daring, beyond the seeming bounds of prudence, led him to become a major twentieth-century American explorer, advancing the frontiers of polar exploration in the air and beneath the ice, as he searched for the unknown.

≈ I ≈

The Long Road North

IN 1926, LINCOLN ELLSWORTH received a letter from Mabel Dunlop Grouitch, who had lived in the Ellsworth home when he was a boy:

> My dear Lincoln:
>
> I should perhaps say Mr. Ellsworth to one so mature and famous as you have become through adventure and courage of the rarest. . . . I remember you so vividly, in appearance too fragile to support the hard studies and hard games of other boys of whom you were always ahead in all that called for imagination and an attempt to achieve or provoke the marvelous, one feared you were an Elf Child. . . . To your practical and scientifically-minded father there was matter for anxiety in this love of the improbable on the part of his only son. . . . You were born for the 'Quest.'[1]

Her observation must have been mostly hindsight, for the only quest Lincoln could recall was looking under the bed for intruders before he could go to sleep at night. His early boyhood memories were mostly unpleasant. In delicate health, he suffered from colds, had no playmates except his sister and some cousins, and had few interests. His younger sister Clare was afraid of nothing, and she adored him. In turn, he was so devoted that he willingly played dolls with her until he was ten or eleven.[2]

Lincoln was born on May 10, 1880, in a house on Ellis Avenue on Chicago's South Side, and there he spent his early years. Clare, his only sibling, was born in Chicago on November 5, 1885. His father,

James W. Ellsworth, was a wealthy businessman and banker whose family was from Hudson, Ohio. His mother, Eva Frances Butler, married James on November 4, 1874.

When Lincoln was only eight, Eva became seriously ill. He could remember his father, pale with anxiety, dashing into the house with an oxygen tank, without noticing Lincoln, who stood nearby. When the boy sat beside his dying mother's bed, he took her hand. Certainly in distress, and perhaps unconscious, she drew her hand away, a gesture the child did not understand. This hurt him terribly; he thought the world had ended.[3] The loss of motherly comfort and understanding at an early age precipitated feelings of loneliness and insecurity that were to plague Lincoln for the rest of his life.

After Eva's death in 1888, the children were sent to live on the family farm in Hudson, Ohio. There, cared for by a housekeeper and a nurse, they spent the next two years. They rarely saw their father. Deprived of Eva's companionship, James immersed himself ever more deeply in business affairs, augmenting an already comfortable fortune. It was an era of expanding railroads, and he early recognized their insatiable need for coal from a readily accessible location. In 1890 he started assembling some 15,000 acres of coal mining property in Washington County, Pennsylvania, thirty miles south of Pittsburgh.[4]

Lincoln's room at the farm contained a large revolving globe of the earth, which stirred his imagination. He pictured himself sitting on the edge of the moon gazing down at the world. What better way of getting there, he thought, than persuading the government to undertake the project? Lincoln wrote to Congressman Benjamin Butterworth of Ohio, a family friend who sometimes visited the farm, suggesting that a trip should be made to the moon in a balloon, and venturing the hope that he might be taken along as a passenger.[5] Butterworth replied that the idea was commendable but beyond the resources of the government.

Lincoln preferred the farm to Chicago, mostly because it afforded opportunity for exercise, and physical endurance was already becoming his ideal. A stream flowing through a meadow fed a small pond where he could swim or skate. He took pride in long bicycle trips, and the cinder-packed driveway offered a good place for running. But what he remembered as the "abomination" of school darkened those days, as it did his entire youth. Unable to concentrate, he regularly fell behind. His marks were deplorable, both at the village primary school and at Western Reserve Academy, which he later attended as a day student.[6] His sister Clare remained one bright star in this rather forlorn childhood, offering support and encouragement that was to continue into adulthood.

James Ellsworth became engrossed in developing his mining property and founded the town of Ellsworth, Pennsylvania, with visions of making it a model. In Chicago he was a major force in promoting the Exposition of 1893, and he also found time to build a mansion on Michigan Avenue. The whole house was a veritable museum, and included an art gallery to house his collection of paintings and Chinese porcelains. In 1892 the children were brought to Chicago to share the new home, just in time for a grand event.

The 1893 Columbian Exposition was known popularly as the Chicago World's Fair. Despite the nationwide depression and financial panic of the early 1890s, its sponsors spared no expense, for they were determined to change Easterners' condescending opinion of their city, which was gaining a reputation as the "hog butcher for the world." The fair's spectacular setting centered around a half-mile-long lagoon. This splendid centerpiece, 250 feet wide, was surrounded by sparkling white buildings, some topped with golden domes. Along with industrial and agricultural displays and art exhibits, attractions were offered for every taste: a gigantic Ferris wheel capable of carrying 440 people at one time in thirty-six glass-enclosed cars; an Eskimo village; a Boone and Crockett log cabin attended by a long-haired hunter.[7] "Not since Noah's Ark and the Tower of Babel, had such oddly incongruous objects been collected in one spot on the globe," wrote historian Page Smith.[8] It is little wonder that an estimated 27 million people visited the exposition during the summer of 1893. When the fair closed, James Ellsworth purchased many of these objects—debris, Lincoln called them—and brought them to the Ellsworth farm in Hudson. When Lincoln visited the farm, the Boone and Crockett cabin directed his thoughts toward frontier life.

During the World's Fair, the Ellsworth mansion was frequented by distinguished visitors. Among the guests, for example, were painters George Inness and Frank D. Millet, poet Eugene Field, and pianist Ignace Paderewski, who usually played for the company after dinner. Lincoln recalled seeing streams of such notable guests, who were attracted to Chicago by the exposition. Those were apparently the happiest days of James Ellsworth's life, but they did not inspire his son.[9]

In April 1895, when Lincoln was fifteen years old, his father remarried, surprising all who knew him. Under the headline "A Millionaire's Quiet Wedding," the *New York Times* reported James Ellsworth's marriage to Mrs. Julia M. Fincke.[10] Their union proved to be a mysterious liaison. Neither Lincoln's diaries nor his father's memoirs contain any glimpses of family life together, although the marriage lasted twenty-six years, until Julia's death in Florence, Italy, in November 1925.

After the wedding, Lincoln was sent off to the Hill School in Pottstown, Pennsylvania. The original circular for this boarding school defined as undesirable anyone "who is not accustomed to the restraints of moral principle and a ready obedience to authority."[11] The school represented all the qualities cherished by James Ellsworth, particularly the conviction that nothing is "accomplished in our country but has begun with a puritanical spirit."[12] The headmaster, John Meigs, was a forbidding man with profound religious faith, penetrating educational vision, and an indomitable will—characteristics James applauded. Attendance at Bible classes, prayer meetings, and Sabbath worship was mandatory. Meigs and his wife conveyed to the adolescent boys the idea that sexual purity was the vital test of proper religious and moral training. Tennyson's Galahad, the young man with biceps and Bible, symbolized ideal purity.[13] This repressive credo must certainly have inhibited a reticent young man like Lincoln, whose emotional ties would remain enigmatic throughout his life. He was guarded, even secretive—a characteristic he shared with his future friend and fellow explorer, Roald Amundsen.

Starting in the third form, Lincoln was soon dropped to the second, when his scholastic difficulties became apparent. Away from home and alone for the first time, he grew homesick. "Dear Papa," he wrote, *"please* come and see me so the other boys will know I have a papa." Years later, when Lincoln's widow found piles of such pleas, "really *tragic* letters," she said she couldn't bear to keep them and destroyed them all.[14]

Papa did not visit. He was struggling with mightier matters, as a crisis threatened his reputation in the business world. At the urging of a close friend, he had accepted election to the board of directors of the Union National Bank of Chicago, only to learn that the bank was on the verge of closing. Industrialists Marshall Field and Philip D. Armour warned him to stay out of the mess, that the bank must close its doors. James Ellsworth replied that the bank would not close, if it broke his back.[15] He kept the bank open, but he had no time for his son.

How did the "elf child" fare with the other young men in a boys' boarding school? Lincoln remembered school life as a sort of nightmare. Nicknamed "Nelly," academically inept, and burdened with frequent remedial sessions, he might well have surrendered to self-pity. He lacked the companionship of friends, and alienated classmates with rough practical jokes, such as balancing pitchers of water over half-open door-ways. A photo of the track team, on which he was a distance runner, shows a dejected face above a thin body. However, he retained his ideal of physical endurance during his five years at the school, and by the time he graduated, had built his body into a solid core of muscle.

School records indicate how great an effort Lincoln must have made to earn even such faint praise as "a normal individual who earned his share of demerits during the middle years he was at the school."[16] He sang in the choir and the glee club, became class secretary and treasurer, and was active in the drama club. Formal debating was compulsory for all, and Lincoln recalled winning four gold medals for public speaking. Perhaps he did, but a school friend later said that Lincoln was one of the quietest boys he ever knew, and always read verbatim from a manuscript.[17]

Lincoln graduated two years later than average. The headmaster, writing to his father afterwards, described Lincoln's "patient and tireless devotion to his work" as "an inspiration to us [that will be] a sustaining memory to our hearts when the achievement [*sic*] of the facile and brilliant minds have been forgotten."[18] Thirty years later, the sustaining memory was refreshed by the declaration of a school holiday when Lincoln was honored by Congress. In school days it was clear that Lincoln had learned little from books. Following the path of one of his heroes, Theodore Roosevelt, he had worked at building muscle and endurance into a frail body. Sensitive and lonely, he detested routine pursuits.

The West Beckons

The turning point in Lincoln's early life came just after his graduation in 1900, when his father financed a pack trip for him in Yellowstone

National Park, with one of the Hill School teachers. From that western summer he brought back "a head full of daydreams of adventure in the wild and untrodden parts of the continent. . . . The East with its comfortable, safe, routine existence was to be no more."[19]

Theodore Roosevelt's *Ranch Life and the Hunting-Trail* became his bible. He devoured it, reading and rereading favorite chapters that told of men "who live in the open, who go armed and ready to guard their lives with their own prowess . . . who call no man master," a world where each man's fate rested in his own hands.[20] As he read of physical exertion, hardship self-imposed and relished for its own sake, in a setting of wild and lonely splendor, Lincoln was filled with a passion for the West.[21] Not realizing he was born a generation too late, he continued to seek this western frontier for the next two decades.

Early in the century, Frederic Remington's Wild West illustrations were very popular. And nearly all of those that show human figures include guns in the picture. In one, four horsemen, guns ablaze, shoot at the sky. Another depicts a barroom brawl, guns smoking. To Lincoln, guns represented virility and they became an obsession, a lifelong passion that reached in many directions. He collected firearms that were of both historic and symbolic significance: a rifle used successively by Nansen, Sverdrup, Johansen, and Amundsen, and a revolver once owned by Wyatt Earp, the gun-slinging frontier marshal after whom Ellsworth would name his antarctic expedition vessel.

For a privately printed publication that recorded his life, Lincoln selected a photograph of himself when a young man, sitting astride a cow pony with a rifle held across his thigh. His most compelling image of Teddy Roosevelt was as a frontier sheriff who once walked into a saloon filled with desperadoes, cowed them with his gun, and herded them all off to jail. In a small Remington painting that later hung in Lincoln's living room, the sheriff whirls to train his six-shooter on an unseen target.

After Lincoln's Wyoming summer, in the fall of 1900, still on academic warning in almost every subject, he entered Yale University's Sheffield Scientific School. His father hoped this would lead to his assuming a responsible role in the Ellsworth mining empire, but Lincoln was on a far different track. When Yale dropped him at the end of the year, he was neither surprised nor particularly distressed.

He then took a job as chainman and lamp carrier in his father's coal mines in Ellsworth, declaring with unconvincing bravado that it was "as much to pass the time as anything else."[22] This assignment consisted of taking the end of a chain to a measuring point and holding a lamp behind the line of the plumb bob so the transitman could make a reading in aligning a tunnel. No skill was required. Noise and dirt were constant. They emanated from moving coal cars and from blasting at the mine headings. When a new wall of coal was dynamited, dust spread throughout the tunnel. It seems likely that Lincoln's motive in taking the job had been to placate his father. At the time, James could hardly have been pleased with his son's college record. At any rate, Lincoln stuck it out through the summer.

Mr. Ellsworth's hope for his son's participation in the business rose again in the fall of 1901, when Lincoln enrolled at Columbia University for courses in mineralogy and mining. Lincoln, however, experienced school as a prison.[23] A listless student, he shuffled half-heartedly through the first year and part of the second. Then, in the early spring of 1903, he read that the Grand Trunk Pacific Railway needed surveyors to build a line from Moncton, New Brunswick, across the entire continent to Prince Rupert, British Columbia. Lincoln was drawn at once to a vision of engineering come to life—hard physical work forging through wilderness, crossing rivers, and tunneling mountains. With spirits soaring as he thought of the adventure, he dropped out of Columbia, before the spring examinations could confirm his own knowledge that he was not cut out for academic life.

The Grand Trunk Pacific put him to work as axman, a job that paid forty dollars a month. By winter's end, he regarded himself no longer as a callow youth, but a "bronzed and toughened man of the open," the stance he assumed for the rest of his life.[24] But there was more to it than that. He spent the summer and fall of 1904 with another crew, extending the survey beyond Winnipeg through the Beaver Hills in Saskatchewan. He was promoted to chainman, and when the work was finished he could run a transit and call himself a surveyor. That job paved the way for his eventual designation as civil engineer, a professional title of which he was fiercely proud. He later took pains for it to be emphasized in his curriculum vitae, and in articles being written by Harold Clark, his father's attorney, who would become his own close friend and advisor.

A Dream to Follow

Lincoln's first expression of interest in polar regions was a diary entry he made in 1905. He was on a steamer, heading to Alaska and a surveyor's job with a gold mining company: "As far as the eye could reach stretched great masses of floating ice. . . . How very lonely and desolate this waste of ice looks and feels. It fascinates me."[25] His journal that summer, written at the mining camp in Kougarok, Alaska, suggests a somewhat self-righteous young man. With obvious approval, he quoted unidentified lines:

Have I claimed one single acre,
Have I marred one single river,
Have I kept one single nugget,
(Barring samples) no not I! (Diary, June 25)

Lincoln was proud of his first independent piece of surveying, although he felt a bit shaky about some of his courses. Camp duties were less satisfying. One evening, after preparing supper and waiting on three different crews, he felt that the only thing he was good for was a job in a restaurant. Another evening he went without dinner to save money. By the end of July, the millionaire's son was thoroughly disheartened by this baptism in hardship, but he recognized the value of his experience, and wrote: "Living this life where there are no flowers to hide the rough places, a man learns what life is like."[26] On many days loneliness welled up, and he wrote longingly of settling down in a cozy home—a dream he never realized and, as events proved, never truly desired.[27]

Lincoln's infatuation with the Plains Indians began that summer with the stories of frontier life he heard from old-timers, who had traded thousands of buffalo hides from the Indians in exchange for rifles. Blind to his own role in the process, he deplored the injustice of Indians being driven from their traditional hunting grounds by railroad and mining companies. His indignation over denial of rights sprang from a basic sense of fairness that prevailed throughout his life. Before he was twelve years old, he had defended women's suffrage,[28] and later was a strong advocate of fair recognition for Matthew Henson, Peary's black assistant.[29] When Russia invaded Finland in 1939, he was among the first to contribute to the Finnish cause.[30]

After five months in Alaska, with the freeze deep and the land-scape chilled by snow, Lincoln contemplated living an easy life, at least for a while. Instead, he surrendered to his father's strong desire that he give up wandering and settle down to a job on the Pennsylvania mine property. For five months he worked in the bleak, smoky mining town of Ellsworth. As resident engineer, he was in charge of layout and construction of 180 byproduct coke ovens.[31] He could barely endure the work, and again yearned for a job outdoors and frontier adventure.

In 1906 the Grand Trunk Pacific Railway presented him with another opportunity for escape. The company was racing against the Canadian Northern Railway to win a monumental competitive advantage—the right of way through Yellowhead Pass near Jasper Lake in British Columbia, which would provide the lowest crossing of the Rockies and the best gradient on the American continent. The railroad that first completed its survey and filed its maps would win the rights to that strategic route. The lure was irresistible. Lincoln quit his job and signed on with the Grand Trunk Pacific.

He departed for Edmonton, Alberta, carrying a strong recommendation from the vice president and general manager of the railroad to his future boss, Henry Van Arsdol. Arriving at the remote frontier town, he was nearly overcome by the same profound loneliness he had experienced in Alaska. Although tempted to give up the whole job, he bolstered his resolve and presented his letter to Van Arsdol. When asked what he could do, Lincoln replied stoutly, "Either transit or level work," although he had done neither on his previous railroad job.[32] The following weeks were a severe test of the young surveyor's seriousness of purpose. He was not good at the work and found it monotonous. Fretfully tied down to a drafting table, he traced alignment and profiles of the country, haunted by the possible failure of his bold gamble. He spent many late nights practicing on imaginary problems.[33] After days of mounting tension, when the order to set out finally arrived, the Grand Trunk crew learned that a Canadian Northern Railway party had already left.[34] It was a long way to the site where their work would begin, some 250 miles, first by wagon trail, then with pack horses. Lincoln was to go as transitman. This was a bit of good fortune, because it meant serving as engineer to the chief, but with no experience, he had qualms about running the survey line. At least he could protect his valuable transit from damage. For weeks, over the rough, tangled course, he carried the thirty-five-pound instrument on his shoulders, sometimes feeling he could not go another step.[35]

When they finally reached the beginning of Yellowhead Pass, the first day of surveying was a daunting challenge. It demanded setting up an instrument amidst rock slides, bare forty-five-degree rock faces, and loose dirt banks that gave way at the slightest touch.[36] After days of this arduous toil, the camp was electrified by a warning from Jones to Englund, the chief engineer: "Look out for the CNR outfit for God sakes!" There is only one route through the pass, Englund told his crew, and the first to get it filed gets the route. You hold the key: don't let it go.[37] They hurried their work even more. The race was so close that on June 28 the CNR surveyors were just below their competitors, not a hundred yards off.[38] Two days later, the Grand Trunk engineers completed their papers for filing, and the race was theirs, wrote Ellsworth proudly.[39]

Now a suitable terminal had to be carved from the West Coast wilderness to handle worldwide shipments. Ellsworth landed the job of resident engineer in charge of making a topographical survey of the terrain and laying out a town site at Prince Rupert, British Columbia.[40] Restless once more, he went to Montreal and hired on as a transitman to work on a Canadian Pacific survey. "Our party," he wrote, "lived in a box which was shunted along to keep pace with the survey."[41] The survey lasted from September 1907 to January 1908.

Once again at loose ends, he enrolled in a railroad engineering course at McGill University, but this led nowhere.[42] His engineering days were over, and his father was not pleased. Nothing could better illustrate the wide gulf between father and son than their respective activities during the next few years. James Ellsworth successfully weathered the economic crisis of 1907 and sold his mines to the Lackawanna Steel Company. Now he could enjoy both leisure and wealth. For his personal pleasure he bought the historic fourteenth-century Villa Palmieri in Florence,[43] looking forward to restoring its gardens to their ancient glory that is so inspiringly described in Boccacio's Decameron. In a display of civic responsibility, if not largesse, he did not forget his home village of Hudson, Ohio. He provided and paid for the town's municipal water works, sewerage, and a lighting plant, after voters agreed to his condition that no intoxicating liquors except beer would be sold. "Town banishes rum for $250,000 gift," announced the *New York World*.[44]

Meanwhile, Lincoln was leading an aimless existence. Using income from a trust created by his father, he engaged in what he called his "interval for adventure." Only the wealthy could spend five years (as he would from 1908 to 1913) with little else to do than seek hardship and challenge in wild, remote regions. One such adventure took him to Yucatan, Mexico, a trip he justified by investigating for a firm of timber dealers the possible use of hardwood for railroad ties.[45]

In January 1909, he and a Yale classmate, Harry Ferguson, set out by cattle boat for Colombia to climb the Central Cordillera of the Andes. Ferguson recalled that their fathers "came down to the boat to see the last of us."[46] As soon as Lincoln returned from the Andes, he went back to Canada. There, while hunting in British Columbia, he met an old prospector. They traveled together from Vancouver, British Columbia, to Edmonton, Alberta, an 1,800-mile trek. Using pack horse, dugout canoe, and a Hudson's Bay Company scow, they reached the headwaters of the Peace River—"river of my dreams," Ellsworth called it. Then they paddled, portaged, and sometimes lined the loaded canoe for two weeks until they reached Edmonton.[47]

Lincoln was in New York on April 21, 1908, when newspapers carried Frederick A. Cook's claim that he had reached the North Pole. Four days later, Robert E. Peary announced that it was he, and not Cook, who had nailed the "Stars and Stripes" to the North Pole.[48] A heated controversy ensued. With increasing venom the two explorers exchanged charges and countercharges, and prestigious organizations took sides, as conflicting stories flooded the newspapers. Lincoln found the furor tawdry and shocking—a great achievement blighted. It led him, however, to read Fridtjof Nansen's *Farthest North*, and he at once identified with Nansen's mystical perceptions, so like his own, when in 1905, he first glimpsed the icebound sea that had lured so many before him. He readily adopted Nansen's belief that there is but one way and that is forward.

At the end of that year, on December 29, Lincoln's sister Clare and Bernon S. Prentice, a New York banker, were married. It was a marriage that would greatly enrich Lincoln's life. Through the years, Bernon proved to be a good friend, and proffered valuable organizational and financial advice. And in time, Lincoln and his niece Clare, born in 1910, developed a relationship of deep devotion.

But for now, Lincoln's unfocused travels continued to cause family problems. His father disapproved, and the two drifted even further apart. Perhaps it would have been much different if Eva had not died. For fourteen years, James had shown her a profound tenderness, and her death seemed to extinguish the light of his life. Although Lincoln had immense respect and admiration for his father, he was never able to break through James Ellsworth's reserve. He gently described his father's iron will and inflexible attitudes as "apt to be intolerant of what he couldn't understand."[49] Others, less generous in their comments, remembered James as a cantankerous survivor of nineteenth-century industrial feudalism, full of such absolutes as *there is no compromise,* or *I won't be beaten.*[50] After a visit at Villa Palmieri, historian James Breasted described his host as "a crotchety, eccentric old gentleman full of inflexible rules for infractions of which his guests were scolded like children."[51] It is easy to imagine that he often humiliated his son.

In the chapel of Western Reserve Academy, in Hudson, hung a cross from an old monastery in southern Spain that was associated with Christopher Columbus. According to the plaque beneath it, James Ellsworth had it placed there as a symbol of Faith in Ideals, "in the hope that it may give assurance and courage to any one struggling to realize a dream."[52] And what of his son's dream?

Untroddden Land

In 1912 Lincoln secured a position that promised experience in the polar regions. Stirred by George Borup, who had been a member of Peary's polar expedition, the American Museum of Natural History was organizing a search for Crocker Land, which was thought to lie northwest of Greenland. Ellsworth was appointed civil engineer in charge of cartographic and topographic work for mapping new lands.[53] His spirits soared. At last he was on his way to becoming a polar explorer; he would join that select band of men whose struggles in unknown regions were rewarded by a public esteem that sometimes bordered on reverence. Then word came that Borup, a leader, had drowned trying to save the life of a friend during a boating accident. The expedition was canceled, and Lincoln was again at loose ends. Later, he said he often felt that this appointment was the greatest honor he had ever received because he was picked on merit alone; in subsequent expeditions, his main role had been to help with financing.[54]

Despite this setback and his father's stubborn disapproval, Lincoln decided to prepare himself further for arctic exploration. He went to London to study geographical surveying under E. S. Reeves, the talented instructor at the Royal Geographical Society and author of numerous technical books and journals.[55] His academic work was soon interrupted by an event so dramatic in personal and international aspects, so understandable to Lincoln, that its memory nourished his spirit ever after. A memorial service in St. Paul's Cathedral was held for Captain Robert Falcon Scott. In spite of his ineptitude, Scott was honored by the British almost as if he were a national saint. It was widely believed that in reaching the South Pole, Scott had upheld British honor in the face of Norwegian trickery. A huge crowd packed the cathedral. The king attended, as well as the prime minister and a multitude of foreign ambassadors and ministers. Many an eye was moist as the great cathedral echoed to the roll of drums introducing the famous "Dead March." At the close, the band played Beethoven's "Funeral March on the Death of a Hero." Outside in the drizzling rain, ten thousand people, unable to squeeze into the cathedral, stood until the ceremony was over.[56]

At the service, Lincoln was one of the multitude swept up in the wave of emotion and hero worship. It is not surprising that he described the fate of the young British leader and his companions as a tale of heroism and self-sacrifice without parallel in the annals of exploration. It was almost as if Lincoln saw himself in that role, his name forever revered. For the rest of his life, seldom did his dwelling lack the famous photograph of Scott and his four companions at the South Pole, Scott's eyes haunted by the specter of death—a reminder that every explorer may face mortal danger.

Here is the story that Lincoln knew in every detail. Amundsen, intent on gaining the North Pole, was crushed when Peary came back from his eighth attempt to reach that goal and announced his success. Amundsen resolved to regain his prestige as an explorer by becoming the first to reach the South Pole. To the British, Amundsen played the part of villain. Aware that Scott was preparing for the same feat,

Amundsen made his preparations in utmost secrecy, lest Scott learn of the competition and get a head start. By carefully worded announcements and conspicuous actions, Amundsen created the impression that he still intended to head for the North Pole because of its scientific potential. Only at the last moment did he send a conscience-saving message to Scott announcing his real goal.[57]

Early in 1911, on the edge of the Ross Sea, and only 500 miles apart, each expedition set up its base. For more than a year nothing was heard from either camp. Then Amundsen's ship, the *Fram,* reached Hobart, Tasmania, on March 7, 1912. The next day, world headlines proclaimed the news: Amundsen had reached the South Pole on December 14, 1911.[58] When Scott's party reached the Pole on January 17, 1912, it was too late. There stood a tent flying a Norwegian flag and the *Fram* pennant. Disheartened by defeat, the British explorers set out for their base at the Ross Sea. Only in 1913 did a search party eventually find Scott's tent. Frozen in their sleeping bags lay the bodies of Scott and two of his companions, Edward Wilson and Henry Bowers. Their last letters and Scott's notebooks told a story of suffering, despair, and selfless gallantry.[59] (It is strange that years later, when Ellsworth chose Roald Amundsen as his leader and hero, he never criticized the ruthless deception Amundsen had employed in 1911. Lincoln had apparently adopted Amundsen's credo that the explorer is a man apart and, because of the unique challenges he must face, is not bound by the same rules as other men.)

Ellsworth's dream for his own arctic expedition now became more focused. Because of past association, it seemed natural to turn to the American Museum of Natural History. He had many talks with Clark Wissler, staff anthropologist and ethnographer, to see what might be developed.[60] The two men already had a common bond. Wissler had just published *North American Indians of the Plains,* a book about a people and culture that fascinated Ellsworth. Wissler's museum colleague, Franz Boas, was eager to extend the museum's research northward, especially since Captain George Comer, a whaler, had brought back to the museum an impressive assortment of material from an ancient Eskimo midden he had discovered on Southhampton Island in Hudson's Bay.

Lincoln saw the advantage of identifying with Wissler. He submitted a proposal to give the museum $15,000 for an expedition to

Baffin Island (Hudson's Bay Territory).[61] His true interest was not in human origins, but in the physical features of land, but he was willing to have the expedition pursue ethnological interests, so long as it did not interfere with his own objective. If he didn't find Crocker Land or that undiscovered continent somewhere in the Polar Sea, he thought he could at least make a significant contribution to geographical knowledge by mapping as much as possible of the unknown west coast of Baffin Island.[62]

By March, plans were falling into place. The president of the American Museum of Natural History, Henry Fairfield Osborn, instructed the assistant secretary, George H. Sherwood, to prepare the expedition letterhead. *Lincoln Ellsworth Expedition / Lincoln Ellsworth, Leader*, it read. Also listed was an advisory committee consisting of a museum trustee and four faculty members.[63] Now all Lincoln's dream lacked for fulfillment was a ship. He scouted for a month but found nothing suitable, and so the expedition was postponed until the following season.[64]

For the next months Lincoln existed in a state of uncertainty. He toyed with the idea of taking up oceanography, but realized that it offered little of the strenuous outdoor activity on which he thrived. He went on expeditions in Death Valley and the Panamint Range in lower California, collecting specimens for the U.S. Biological Survey. Although he dignified his work by characterizing it as hunting for science and specializing in wild sheep, he was not sufficiently knowledgeable to write scientific articles about either the animals or their habitat. He was, however, enthralled by the beauty and majesty of the desert and had no trouble writing eloquently about it.[65]

By autumn of 1914 he was discouraged, wondering after each field trip where he would go next, and he was still no closer to his dream of arctic discovery. He began to talk about using hydro-airplanes to find those elusive land masses that supposedly caused the unusual behavior of the tides north of Alaska. This was a daring aspiration for a man who had no experience, but Lincoln brushed aside such considerations. He had successfully reached beyond the limits of his expertise during his youth. If he could now convert hope into reality, he would be the first to use the airplane for polar exploration.

This would put him in the vanguard of the coming age of air travel, but Ellsworth had a more specific objective. R. A. Harris, of the

United States Coast and Geodetic Survey, was tantalized by the question of the tides. Harris was convinced that a deep Arctic Ocean basin could not extend without interruption from the region of the deep waters (identified by Nansen's *Fram* on its three-year drift, 1893–96, and embracing the Pole itself), to the known waters lying along the arctic coasts of British America, Alaska, and eastern Siberia.[66] Harris' map showed the outline of a land mass, possibly as large as 500,000 square miles. In 1904 he supported his theory with three factors. First, the drift of ships and relics found from vessels lost in early expeditions showed two prevailing surface currents in the Arctic Ocean; one flowing *easterly* along Alaska's northern coast, the other, starting from the Bering Strait, flowing north*westerly* until the two neared one another as they approached the southern coast of Greenland on the far side of the Arctic Basin. Harris concluded that only a large land mass in the vicinity of the North Pole could account for this separate flow. A second piece of evidence was the behavior of tides at Point Barrow: due to the flood coming from the west, high water on the point's western side occurred considerably earlier than on the eastern side (at some locations with a difference of as much as seven hours in its time of occurrence). A third, less scientific consideration was the very old appearance of Beaufort Sea ice; extensive floes of stupendous thickness, as one early explorer wrote, indicated no broad outlet through which the ice could escape as it did north of Siberia.

In 1914 the Canadian explorer Vilhjalmur Stefansson and two companions had made a fruitless search for Harris Land by sledging from Alaska. They thought "it could be an island a good deal larger than Cuba, perhaps the size of Alaska itself, and that it might have Peary's Crocker Land for a northeasterly cape."[67] Now Lincoln Ellsworth declared his intention to find this "untrodden land," as Peary had called it. Inexplicably, when Lincoln poured all this out to his father, James Ellsworth approved![68] Perhaps the daring and scope of his son's ambition for once had so impressed the older Ellsworth that he remembered his own youthful visions. Whatever the reason, Lincoln felt gratified that he could inform Osborn that he had his father's consent—even his "desire to help."[69]

But soon James Ellsworth became troubled. Hoping to divert Lincoln from his plan, he talked with Osborn. Several days later Lincoln received a letter from the museum president. It explained that the head of an expedition must be thoroughly trained in hydro-airplane work and, in the event of breakdown, for arctic travel.[70] The letter did not specifically reject Lincoln's plan, but its meaning was obvious. His future as an explorer now rested in Osborn's hands.

Determined to carry out his dream, Lincoln was oblivious to world events. Germany had declared all-out war and torpedoed the British liner *Lusitania*, killing 128 Americans. Five months later, when President Wilson asked Congress for an increase in military funds, American involvement seemed inevitable, yet Lincoln continued to focus on the Arctic with an intensity close to obsession. In January 1916 he wrote Osborn seeking a guarantee of museum support for a 1918 expedition with airplanes to explore the unknown region north of Point Barrow, Alaska.[71]

Osborn would not make a binding commitment amidst so many uncertainties. During the following weeks, Lincoln persisted, his letters increasingly desperate. This series of exchanges led nowhere, but was, like a musical theme, composed of recognizable motifs in predictable sequence: Lincoln's pleas, Osborn's proffered alternatives, Lincoln's restated request.[72] Osborn suggested oceanography, ethnology, zoology, and photography. Finally, with thinly disguised impatience, he told Lincoln that there was no certainty any undertaking would justify a museum guarantee until Lincoln had the necessary experience.[73]

Perhaps learning to fly would be sufficient qualification, thought Lincoln. Before the United States declared war on April 6, 1917, he was on his way to embattled France with a Red Cross group. Once there he intended to join a Franco-American flying unit for pilot training.[74] Declared too old for flying, he somehow managed to earn the *élevé* insignia of an airplane observer, an embellished silver oak leaf (because of its shape, sometimes called the flying asshole). When he transferred to the American army as a private second class, he was assigned desk work in Paris, where he languished and griped until the summer of 1918.

Proud of his athletic prowess at the age of thirty-eight, he wrestled with husky young cadets, claiming that he won every match and that nobody there could put his shoulders to the ground. It was just as well. Lincoln had little besides physical fitness to bolster his ego. Then the influenza epidemic struck Paris. It was a deadly scourge that killed

20 million people worldwide. Lincoln was hospitalized, and when he came down with a serious case of pneumonia, the army sent him home.

Dream of the Moment

For the next four or five years, despite numerous setbacks, he struggled to regain the strength he had acquired by training and self-discipline. The arduous work of arctic exploration was currently out of the question, and this delay distressed him. Along with being lured by geographical mysteries to be solved, Lincoln was determined to go into the North because of driving psychological needs. He delighted in showing he could handle hardships which men of lesser strength avoided. He needed the satisfaction of proving himself better than the next man. Now, however, dry desert air was necessary to alleviate an acute sinus condition. Hoping to accelerate his recovery, he returned to the deserts of the Southwest.

The ensuing desert years were surprisingly fruitful. Physical inactivity brought out hidden facets of Lincoln's nature, as his intellectual curiosity supplanted the quest for geographical knowledge. During this period, he might have been overwhelmed by his physical frailty and social insecurity had he not kept busy with these new types of exploration. He wrote personal journals that reflect a fine intellect and grandeur of spirit—qualities that to this day have not been recognized by historians and others who are inclined to regard him as a rich idler.

As his writings from the period show, now his wide-ranging interests—geology, fossils, the heavens—seemed to come together and lead to his search for meaning, for eternal verities, for God. He was enraptured by the beauty of the Grand Canyon. Contemplating the calendar of change recorded over millions of years on its stratified walls, his imagination soared. He made frequent visits to the Mt. Wilson Observatory in California. As he peered through the observatory's 100-inch telescope, his curiosity about the galaxies was aroused.

The first tangible result of this intellectual foray was a ninety-seven-page personal journal titled "Astronomy Notes—1920." Here were observations, charts, drawings, and diagrams on many astronomy topics. The notes reflect an understanding of complex phenomena, such as the postulates of Einstein's Theory of Relativity; the relationship between sidereal and solar time; and the newly discovered understanding that "each molecule composing a drop of water constitutes in itself a complete solar system."[75] Meanwhile, wanting to remain a participant in the world of exploration, he besieged Charles D. Walcott, secretary of the Smithsonian Institution, with requests to find some field of scientific work or research he could do for the organization.[76]

In 1921 Lincoln completed a forty-four-page compilation, "News from the Stars."[77] Here, he addressed technical matters such as theories about the spiral nebulae, how the spectroscope tells the secret of light, and life in other worlds. Then, continuing to reflect on man's place in the universe, Lincoln wrote a small work entitled "Nature and Religion." He had it bound in blue cloth with gilt lettering, and inscribed it, "To my father, With the love and affection of his son, Lincoln Ellsworth, Christmas, 1923."[78]

The little book was Lincoln's effort to formulate a personal worldview, or philosophy—an effort to sort out the conflicts between science, philosophy, and religion, and to identify immutable values. "Where science ends, faith begins," he wrote, concluding that "we all live in the constant presence of Deity." Attuned to poetry as well as science, he quoted several lines by Francis Thompson that summarized his philosophy:

All things by immortal power
Near or far,
Hiddenly
To each other linked are,
That thou canst not stir a flower
Without troubling a star.

It is not known how James Ellsworth reacted to Lincoln's present, but one wonders, in particular, how he perceived the message in the opening two sentences: "Dissolve the habitual limits of your vision. Liberate your minds from preconceived notions, and your opinion from its smallest bias."

By February 1925, still with no prospect of going to the Arctic, Lincoln was drawn by an opportunity to use his surveying skills, while at the same time satisfying his interest in rocks and fossils. He and Dr. Joseph T. Singewald, professor of economic geology at Johns Hopkins University, shared leadership of an expedition to Peru to survey three ranges of the Andes Mountains. Although Lincoln contracted malaria and had to return to New York for medical care, this Ellsworth expedition provided Johns Hopkins with important research material.[79]

Soon Lincoln was again writing—this time a small volume of philosophical thoughts under the title "The Wonder of the Universe."[80] It was a rich mixture of poetry and science: observations of man's speculation were enhanced by a Shelley sonnet, which was followed by a discussion of Einstein's query about a limit to the sidereal realm. Pondering infinity and man's insignificance, Lincoln was struck by French astronomer Nicholas Camille Flammarion's comment that in "the eternity of duration, the life of our proud humanity, with all its religious and political history, the whole life of our entire planet, is the dream of a moment."

Exploring the "poetry and beauty that throb through matter everywhere," he cited Niels Bohr, the Danish physicist and leading developer of the quantum theory; astronomer John Frederick William Herschel; Sir Arthur Schuster, the English physicist and expert in terrestrial magnetism; Henry G. J. Moseley, the English physicist; and Daniel Bernoulli, the "learned geometrician of Basil." Ellsworth's theme was unity, harmony, rhythm, and glorious order in both the infinitesimal and the infinite, with constant awareness of the Creator's omnipotence and power to keep alive forever "these celestial fires," as Lincoln called the stars. In this context he noted the tremendous significance of scientific discoveries that would stir the human mind and lead to the development of a few big ideas. He seemed content to sum it all up with Francis Bacon's words, "Knowledge is power."[81]

But for Lincoln, tangible objects were often as meaningful as words. He carried in his pocket a morsel of Vishnu schist he had picked up from the bottom of the Grand Canyon. As a self-proclaimed scientist, he valued it as a piece of the first cooling of the earth, the oldest rock in existence. To his romantic side, however, it was something more. He just liked to put his hand in his pocket and "touch God," his widow Mary Louise recalled.[82]

✦ 2 ✦

The Big Trip

And now started the flight which will take its place amongst the most supreme in flying's history.

—ROALD AMUNDSEN

BY 1924 JAMES ELLSWORTH'S HEALTH was deteriorating rapidly. After suffering a severe shock when his second wife died, he began to vacillate in his judgments.[1] Arranging his affairs, he sold his superb collections of rugs, porcelains, coins, and rare books (a Gutenberg Bible, Caxtons, and other incunabula), adding the proceeds to his endowment of Western Reserve Academy.[2] Another top priority was persuading Lincoln once and for all to abandon his dreams of exploration. During a rare walk with his son, hoping to lure him into a proper Ellsworth world, James offered him a choice of homes and a sizable income. Lincoln replied, "I want nothing but my tent and my gun."[3]

With his desire to explore the Arctic as strong as ever and a father who thought him foolish, Lincoln's spirits sank. He came upon a poem, "The Ship of Fools," that seemed to describe his predicament:

> We are those fools who could not rest
> In the dull earth we left behind,
> But burned with passion for the West
>   And drank strange frenzy from its wind.
> The world where wise men live at ease
>   Fades from our unregretful eyes,
> As blind across uncharted seas
>   We stagger on our enterprise.[4]

Making one more plea for understanding, he wrote that he resolved to devote his life to geographical exploration and discovery in the land of his choice. Despite his father's anxiety, he wanted to accomplish solely through his own efforts something noteworthy for science. Lincoln was ahead of his time in perceiving the North as a promising field for scientific work, and James was a pragmatist. To him, science was a demanding discipline in a specific field, not an endeavor for someone with no special training, poking around somewhere in the great outdoors. Lincoln, unable to convey just why the North had always appealed to him, sought to broaden his father's perspective. He explained his feeling that life would be aimless without some goal to strive for—a dream, and his dream was exploration in the North. He pleaded for moral support, and signed the letter, "Your loving son, Lincoln Ellsworth."[5]

He may have had second thoughts about addressing his father so bluntly, because this letter remained unmailed for ten days. Then one morning Lincoln read a newspaper item that changed his life. Roald Amundsen was in New York to raise funds for a polar flight, but still needed money to pay for the two planes he had ordered.[6] Suddenly hopeful, Lincoln phoned the troubled explorer at his hotel. He described himself as an amateur explorer who might be able to supply some money.[7] Money was the magic word. The two dined together and as they talked throughout the evening, Amundsen's despair changed to optimism. Lincoln offered $20,000 from what he described as a "modest private income."[8] He also expressed hope of gaining his father's support.[9] For both men, the meeting was a turning point. For Ellsworth, life assumed new meaning. For Amundsen, the meeting meant deliverance, or fiscal salvation. The ambition and needs of each man complemented those of the other.

Lincoln wrote a second letter to his father and had it delivered simultaneously with the earlier one.[10] He told of dining with Amundsen, their planned cooperation, and his feeling that fate must have brought them together. Then came a plea for financial assistance, prefaced by a statement that was pathetically untrue: "You have encouraged me in my interest in and preparation of the study of exploration," he wrote. Explaining he wished only to make good in the field of his chosen endeavor, he said he had no desire for worldly possessions that bring comfort and ease. Could he borrow against future income so that he could join Amundsen and help in his plans? Then, in a patronizing tone, seeking to justify spending money for "pure science," Lincoln took a swipe at James' world of commerce. He said pure science concerns what is learned about eternal truths from nature—"things that are solid and real, and upon which life actually rests." This he approved because it "leads onward and upward." Science touched by commercialism, he implied, could not be considered pure, an attitude unlikely to elicit a sympathetic response from his father.

Surprisingly, James Ellsworth ignored the disparaging remark and agreed to provide $50,000 from a fortune made in what his son called the impure field of commercialism and strife. In his letter to his son, he also said, "I ought to have a chance to see you. You don't treat me with quite the consideration you should. However, my best and deepest love to you."[11]

In early November James arranged a meeting with Amundsen to question him about the potential dangers his son might face. Amundsen explained that careful preparation and foresight made the dangers no greater than those confronted by many outdoor workers, such as sailors and fishermen.

"Suppose I don't help you?" asked Mr. Ellsworth. "What will you do?"

"What I have always done," replied Amundsen. "I will get along some way."[12]

Impressed, James met several days later with Lincoln and Amundsen to sign a formal agreement for financing. Pen in hand, unaccustomed to surrender, he paused and turned toward his son. "Lincoln," he said, "if I sign this will you promise me never to touch tobacco again?" Startled, Lincoln agreed, and James, having won at least a shred of victory, signed.

In gratitude, Amundsen pulled from his briefcase his most cherished possession and presented it to his benefactor. Scratched on the worn brass of his Zeiss binoculars were historic dates: the start and completion of his voyages through the Northwest Passage and the Northeast Passage, and of his sledge journey to the South Pole.[13]

With the money now secured, Amundsen directed Hjalmar Riiser-Larsen, a skilled pilot from the Norwegian air force, to revive construction plans for two Dornier flying boats. Because Amundsen had declared personal bankruptcy, arrangements were made for the

Aero Club of Norway to handle finances and business arrangements.[14] Meanwhile, almost immediately after signing the contract, James Ellsworth, having apparently changed his mind, began a desperate campaign to stop Lincoln from going on the expedition. Lincoln said it verged on the unprincipled.[15]

About this time James received a letter from a stranger who insinuated that Amundsen was involved in disreputable but unspecified dealings in connection with an earlier plan to fly from Alaska to Spitsbergen.[16] Mr. Ellsworth summoned his lawyer, Harold Clark, from Cleveland. He instructed Clark to investigate Amundsen's background carefully, with the goal of discouraging Lincoln's involvement. Lincoln endured each day that passed, fearing his father would find some ingenious way to stop him. Clark's detective work hung over him like the sword of Damocles.

During the ensuing weeks, except when Amundsen was on a lecture tour, he and Lincoln were nearly inseparable. They shopped, lunched, and dined together, endlessly discussing plans for the undertaking that would allow Amundsen to finish his career with a burst of glory and would launch Lincoln on the path to fame.[17] The old Viking could hardly believe this miraculous redemption that would save him from loss of hope, home, and possessions. He marveled at the splendor and wealth of the Ellsworth world—the beautiful estate in Hudson, the splendid art in the Park Avenue mansion in New York, the villas in Italy, and the castle in Switzerland. They all underscored how profitable his new relationship might be. He detailed each day's events in his diary in the form of an ongoing letter to a Norwegian woman, Irene, recounting his activities, his hopes, and his disappointments.[18] To her he confided his innermost feelings and expressed deep devotion. When he learned of her involvement with another man, his grief brought him closer to Lincoln, whose feeling of loneliness he now shared.

As trust between the two men grew, Amundsen learned that Lincoln, having suffered many run-ins with his father, had finally left home for good.[19] Amundsen accepted blame for splitting up a family, but concluded that circumstances made it necessary. At forty-four, Lincoln had not yet gained a foothold in polar exploration. He realized it was now or never, and association with Amundsen was the key to his future. Motivated by a sense of camaraderie and sincere fondness for his new-found friend, as well as a strong measure of enlightened self-interest, Lincoln was tireless in his efforts to fund the expedition, and to lavish pleasure on the great explorer. They dined together at fine restaurants, or feasted at his brother-in-law's apartment where Amundsen could meet important and wealthy people. Lincoln also gave his friend a fur coat, and on another occasion, a $400 watch.[20] All this moved Amundsen to express appreciation for Lincoln's great faith in him, and he declared that Lincoln "will always have my loyal friendship."[21]

This feeling was fully reciprocated by Lincoln, and its intensity led his brother-in-law, Bernon Prentice, to make himself always available for counsel on the logistics or financing of Lincoln's exploration or planning.

In late December 1924, James tried a new delaying tactic: a third plane, he argued, should be provided to improve safety.[22] Riiser-Larsen pointed out that the Dornier company was unable to manufacture a plane soon enough, and that a third plane would not necessarily increase safety.[23] At this time Amundsen and Ellsworth assured the Aero Club that even though a crossing from Spitsbergen to Alaska was their ultimate goal, they would agree now to a reconnaissance flight just to the North Pole. When they signed this unqualified commitment, they had already privately agreed to ignore its provisions. They shared a secret understanding that if everything went well, they would abandon one plane at the Pole and fly on to Alaska in the other.[24]

The following weeks involved a series of calculated deceptions for which Lincoln cavalierly offered the explanation that no man more than the explorer was tempted by the doctrine of ends justifying means.[25] An equally cynical but more explicit explanation can be found in J. R. L. Anderson's provocative book *The Ulysses Factor*. It lists cunning and unscrupulousness among traits of explorers,[26] characteristics that had once before led Amundsen to risk honor for the sake of achievement in his deception of Scott about his South Pole objective. The Norwegian Storting (Parliament) voted support for the Amundsen-Ellsworth Expedition to the North Pole,[27] and on January 23, 1925, Haakon VII, the king of Norway, approved the Aero Club request, submitted through the War Office, for use of the naval transport vessel *Fram*, which was actually the king's yacht.[28]

By February, Harold Clark had completed a detailed memorandum about Amundsen, finding nothing against him beyond expressions of petty annoyance. He found that the letter writer who had prompted the investigation owned a gold mine in Alaska and apparently hoped James Ellsworth would feel sufficiently obligated to purchase the mine! Amundsen's financial trouble rested on loss of anticipated revenue from certain motion picture rights, Clark explained. Owing £14,000 for two Dornier planes, and saddled with other debts besides, he had filed for voluntary bankruptcy.[29]

Before reporting to Mr. Ellsworth, Clark talked with Lincoln's sister Clare, knowing that Lincoln had confided in her and that she was in sympathy with her brother's aspirations. They frankly discussed the trip's dangers and he said to her, "But suppose Lincoln doesn't come back?" to which she replied, "I think he should go anyway." Sensitive to Lincoln's past frustrations and the passion that drove his present ambition, she felt he would be forever crushed in spirit if he didn't go.[30]

Before the month was out, Lincoln complied with his father's request that he confirm in writing the promise that he would take part *only* in the first flight to the North Pole and back to Spitsbergen and would have nothing whatever to do with the second expedition from Spitsbergen to Alaska—financially, morally, or otherwise.[31] Dissatisfied with this iron-clad promise, James again summoned Clark to New York and instructed him to block Lincoln's participation. In view of Mr. Ellsworth's unsettled state of mind and his determination to have his own way, it took courage for Clark to proceed as he did. He pointed out to James that he had been in his forties when he achieved his great success, and that Lincoln, now in his forties, was motivated by the same spirit that had moved his father to strike out for great things.[32]

Lincoln's father seemed to soften—but only briefly. Soon he was in touch with highly placed public figures, including his cousin, U.S. Vice President Charles Dawes, in an unsuccessful attempt to have Lincoln's passport cancelled.[33] When Lincoln drew a draft of $10,000 on his own bank account in Cleveland, James tried to use his financial clout to prevent the bank from honoring it.[34] Only upon hearing that the money was to buy parachutes did he withdraw his opposition.

In February 1925, Amundsen, about to sail for England, announced his plans: he would make a flight from Spitsbergen in June, and "after a few hours at the Pole to make observations," he expected to fly to Alaska.[35] The announcement gave no indication of what Lincoln would do after reaching the Pole. Their departure date neared, and in early March, Lincoln was still in a quandary about going on the *big trip* he had promised not to make. Going all the way to Alaska would break the agreement with the Aero Club, but this seemed less serious to him than violating the carefully drawn covenant with his father, to which he'd agreed after weeks of tortured negotiations. By this time Harold Clark had sized up Lincoln pretty well and suspected that both the explorers would attempt the big trip. He asked Lincoln to give to someone he trusted the most definite possible word about his intended course of flight, so that in case of emergency, search efforts would be more effective.[36]

Clark's usually acute perception failed miserably when he now told Lincoln his father was fairly well reconciled to the expedition. Three days later James wrote his son a letter of suffering and petulant criticism that at the time crushed Lincoln's spirit and burdened him with a lifelong sense of guilt. The letter opened by deploring their present relationship. A more unnatural condition could not exist between father and son, James declared. He accused Lincoln of absolute disregard for his parent's life, of filling his days and nights with apprehension and agony, and of twice bringing him close to death's door. Amundsen, he wrote, had betrayed him and flagrantly broken his promises, while taking his money. James would be compelled to give up his son entirely until Lincoln realized the error of his way.[37]

Possibly the cruelest blow to the son, who struggled for acceptance and respect, was the father's contemptuous dismissal of Lincoln's belief that the expedition would promote science. Only a year earlier, in an obvious effort to please, Lincoln had dedicated his "Nature and Religion" to his father. In his recent letters, Lincoln had expressed his longing for the opportunity to accomplish something noteworthy for the sake of science, to make good and satisfy his inward self. How could a father fail to recognize the urgency of such an appeal? But James, completely self-absorbed and long accustomed to having his own way, continued for two more querulous pages. He made one final appeal, which opened with the startling assertion that he had tried faithfully to meet his son's every wish. "But the more independence I give you," he said, "the more independent you are against me, your father."[38]

Undeterred by this letter, Lincoln proceeded with his plan. "So far as I know, only once in his life did [my father] meet failure in any major exercise of his will. Unhappily, I was the one to defeat him then, though there was nothing else I could do," he later noted ruefully.[39]

While Lincoln made last-minute preparations for departure, he found time to celebrate the accomplishments of Paavo Nurmi, the great athlete known as the "Flying Finn" and the "Phantom Finn." Nurmi had become a world celebrity by breaking most of the world's records for running, a sport that Lincoln knew from his participation in track at school. Lincoln was a hero worshipper. He commissioned a bronze cameo of the great runner and presented it to Nurmi in person, with a tribute that spoke of "the beauty, the grace and the rhythm of his wonderful running."[40]

Off at Last

On March 24, the day of sailing, Lincoln went to bid his father good-bye. He described the meeting in four words: "a most dismal experience."[41] Later, when Lincoln went aboard the SS *Oscar II*, he found that James had not come to see him off. Clare, realizing the extreme danger of the trip and fearing that she would never see her beloved brother again, broke down and wept. Around his neck, beneath his shirt, he wore a silver cross she had given him, inscribed with Swinburne's words: "Where Faith abides / Though Hope be put to flight."

On the ship was a beautiful twenty-four-year-old Danish woman, Helene Larsen, who was returning to Copenhagen after spending two years in America. Lincoln sat next to her at the table, and it was love at first sight. "We were both 'kaput' immediately," she wrote to her sister.[42] To Lincoln, this emotion was surprising and unfamiliar, and his response, at first, was cautious. He started by sitting out on the bow reading Kipling's poems aloud to her and then gave her the book. They exchanged gifts—her ruby ring for him, his French observer's medal for her. She described the last night out, when, as they fell into one another's arms, she didn't even feign resisting his kiss. Helene promised to wait for him. In turn, he sent her five letters and three telegrams during the first six days after she disembarked in Copenhagen.

Lincoln stayed with Amundsen at his home in Bundefjord, near Oslo, amidst a veritable museum of polar souvenirs. They spent several memorable days there, socializing and quaffing Aqua Vit liberally.[43] Lincoln had never before spent time with such relaxed and hospitable people. He felt utterly carefree, perhaps for the first time in his adult life, and his enjoyment showed. "Ellsworth is so sympathetic, so moving," wrote Amundsen.[44] After this brief visit, they left to join their expedition in Tromsö, where Amundsen's pilot, Hjalmar Riiser-Larsen, and Lincoln's pilot, Lief Dietrichson, had assembled equipment and personnel on the *Fram* and the chartered motor ship *Hobby*.

From Tromsö, Lincoln wrote Clare a farewell letter expressing appreciation for her help in starting the expedition. He told her in strict confidence that the *big trip* was the only one that would be undertaken, and not to worry if she did not hear from him for a year. "I hope you will tell father about the girl I care for in Copenhagen," Lincoln continued. "When I get back I shall marry."[45]

On April 8 the expedition ships left Tromsö for the first leg of the great adventure. Amundsen said the *Hobby*, weighed down with gear, with crated flying boats stowed on deck, "looked like a mass of gigantic cases wandering along over the sea."[46] After a rough voyage—everyone seasick but indignantly denying such frailty—the ships were immobilized by a mass of hard ice in the harbor of Kings Bay, Spitsbergen. It took three days of skilled maneuvering and dynamiting to penetrate the massive barrier and reach the coal company quay, where they finally tied up and started unloading. Photographers and journalists immediately burst into action, ensuring worldwide publicity.

Lincoln lost no time in preparing himself for possible emergency. The next day he went skiing for the first time in his life. Amundsen was relieved to see how accomplished he was, and every day thereafter they kept in trim by making ski trips together across the fjord.[47]

The only certainty in this undertaking was the distance from takeoff in Kings Bay to arrival at the North Pole—600 nautical miles each way. Uncertainties were numerous—performance of engines, conditions of ocean surface for landing either on ice or leads of open water, strength and capacity of the flying boats' hulls to withstand damage from jagged ice, and the crafts' relative efficiency when taking off from ice or snow rather than water.

Ellsworth must have thought long and hard after revealing to Clare that he would take the big trip. And Amundsen noted in his diary on April 18 that they had definitely given up flying to Alaska because Ellsworth's father had made Lincoln promise not to get involved in such a flight.[48] This calm statement, unaccompanied by any expression of dismay or disappointment, was inconsistent with Amundsen's character. A few days later, his alternate plan for the big trip emerged.

On April 28 Amundsen had a meeting with Riiser-Larsen, Dietrichson, and Ellsworth to tell them that he now planned to continue with one of the planes from the Pole to Alaska, while the other would go back. Riiser-Larsen, the more experienced of the two pilots, met the proposal with total resistance, and Dietrichson, though less emphatic, was also opposed. Furious, Amundsen grumbled about lack of guts and vowed to bring up the proposal again when they got back from the Pole.[49] For the pilots, it was not a question of courage, but of judgment. This was a pioneer venture. No long flights had ever been made over the polar ice and little was known about weather conditions or possible landing opportunities. For example, flying boats of that size had never been tried on snow. The pilots worried lest there be insufficient fuel to ensure both planes completing the round trip to the Pole. They felt that in case of irreparable trouble with one plane, the expedition could continue in the other.[50] However, in the event that both planes were to become useless, each plane would stow a sledge and canvas boat for possible use in a long march toward land. No cost was spared: the total came to approximately $130,000, of which Lincoln and his father provided about $95,000.[51]

Their Dornier-Wal planes were outfitted with the best equipment: two Rolls-Royce Eagle VIII 360-horsepower engines mounted in tandem, the forward one pulling, and the aft one turning contrariwise, pushing. Two mechanics, Feucht and Zinsmayer from the Rolls-Royce factory, were brought along to ensure proper installation and servicing. To prevent subzero freezing, ingenious procedures had been developed to drain water from the radiators after flight, and to keep the engines usable for starting at a moment's notice should an emergency require moving a plane away from sudden danger.[52]

Careful thought had been given to selecting the best type of undercarriage—skis, floats, or flying boats—for getting airborne in a machine that weighed an average of six tons when fully loaded with fuel and equipment. Several factors had led to the choice of the flat-bottomed Dornier-Wal flying boat. Its duraluminium hull proved resistant to punctures and serious dents. It had no floats or other projections that might catch on ice obstacles. Its flat bottom would stay atop loose snow, rather than pushing it aside and thereby causing a drastic reduction in speed as it strained for takeoff. Recognizing the significance of this undertaking to the future of aviation, Herr Schulte-Frohlinde, technical director of the Dornier-Wal factory (S.A.I. di Construzioni Mecchanice i Marina di Pisa), accompanied the expedition to Spitsbergen to make sure that all plane-related mechanical and functional components were properly tended.[53]

The crucial key to success was the capability of making a reliable forecast of weather conditions over the projected flight path to the North Pole and back, and this was the responsibility of the expedition meteorologist, Dr. Jakob Bjerknes. He would try to determine conditions likely to be encountered, using stations throughout Europe and America for reports of barometric pressure, temperature, wind direction and velocity, humidity, and fog and cloud conditions.

The planes had to be assembled in the open, since there were no hangars. Only severe cold interrupted the work. Two journalists sent reams of copy to the outside world, while the fliers awaited favorable conditions. And as the days wore on, Ellsworth moved out of the room he had been sharing with Amundsen because of the latter's thunderous snoring![54] During the weeks of preparation, Lincoln experienced feelings of tremendous exhilaration. He felt they were "the cynosure of the world's eyes."[55]

With crew and all equipment aboard, each plane would carry a thousand pounds more than it was designed to lift, and the engineer from the Dornier-Wal factory advised the pilots to make trial flights. They had taxied with full loads, but they had not attempted takeoff. Riiser-Larsen and Dietrichson refused. Rated capacity meant capacity to lift out of water. Since they were to lift off from a surface of hard ice, where drag on the hull would be much less, they had no doubts about getting airborne and did not wish to risk a possible accident or damage.[56]

For two weeks the fliers awaited favorable weather conditions, their hopes alternately raised and dashed, as reports came in from stations around the world. At last meteorologist Bjerknes announced they should be ready to start on short notice.[57] On May 18 Amundsen wrote in his diary: "My own dearest little wife! It is possible that tomorrow about this time I will be close to the Pole. . . . If things happen so that this is my farewell to you . . . you know that I love you. God protect you forever, my own dear lovely wife. Au revoir!"[58] (This message remains a puzzle, as there is some question as to whether Amundsen ever married.) Two days of tension followed as bad weather closed in.

But on May 21 the sky was clear. Spirits stirred with jubilation. This was the day. By then two particularly significant announcements had been made: the return of the flying machines might be expected within fourteen days of departure.[59] Amundsen had been authorized by Prime Minister Mowinckel of Norway to take possession, in the name of His Majesty the King, of any land discovered, and similar instructions were given to Dietrichson in case the planes became separated.[60]

There was minute inspection of every detail of the planes, including attentive listening to the rhythm of both engines as they were run up one at a time. Then came the looking into flying gear: layer after layer of clothing, so that whether they were sitting in the open cockpit or were forced into strenuous physical activity, the six men could quickly adjust the quantity of covering and thus avoid falling victim to that enemy of warmth—sweating followed by clamminess. Riiser-Larsen described his clothing: against the skin, a thin woolen vest and pants; next, heavy pants and vest; then long trousers and a jumper with woolen helmet to pull over the head. That was the rig for working and skiing. For flying, the whole outfit was covered by a leather suit with camel hair on the outside, and, finally, a sealskin anorak and a leather-lined flying helmet. Gloves of double pigskin were sheathed with wool both inside and out, and over these went windproof gloves, elbow high.[61] Feet were protected by woolen socks, boots, and enormous canvas shoes lined with senna grass, which Amundsen had found from long experience provided superb insulation.[62]

The men pulled on parachutes and climbed into the planes. Amundsen took the nose seat of plane *N-25*, as Ellsworth did in the *N-24*, each functioning as both navigator and observer. Behind sat the pilots, Riiser-Larsen for Amundsen and Dietrichson for Ellsworth, and further behind, the engineers, Karl Feucht and Oscar Omdal. (Neither plane carried a radio. Ellsworth believed they were left behind to lighten the planes and thus increase their fuel-carrying capacity.)

As Ellsworth settled in his seat, fifteen years of frustration vanished. It seemed at last that nothing could mar success. Elated, his ambition accomplished, he watched the *N-25* a few yards away. Lightly frozen to the surface, it tugged at the ice, pulled free, and then roared off in a flurry of snow. Lincoln's plane was more severely frozen and had to be rocked by many hands before it could pull free and follow. As her metal belly dragged along the packed takeoff run, Dietrichson heard the sound of ripping on the bottom of the hull and realized that some of the rivets had been wrenched loose.[63] The overloaded plane managed to gain the air. Ground objects grew smaller below, engines were synchronized, and the *N-24* joined her sister ship.

Had the planes carried radios, Dietrichson undoubtedly would have reported the suspected damage. Then Amundsen would have had to face three harrowing choices—to proceed alone, turn back and await repair of the *N-24*, or ignore the damage and continue as they were. Under different circumstances, Dietrichson, a veteran pilot, probably would have turned back for repairs. However, he thought it was better to put life at risk than to stop the trip, a decision Amundsen later applauded with ringing words: "Courage—splendid, brilliant, indomitable Courage."[64]

When a blanket of fog came rolling in shortly after takeoff, Amundsen likened the feeling to jumping blindfolded into the universe. They climbed above the fog and flew on, and when the fog lifted they looked down on an endless expanse of ice. Speeding along at seventy-five miles an hour, they had "crossed the threshold into the Unknown!" exclaimed Ellsworth.[65]

On they flew for six more monotonous hours. This should have put them at the North Pole, but Riiser-Larsen suspected that wind had caused them to drift westward. He thought they should land in order to accurately determine their position. With no intercom, hand signals were the only means of communication. He saw a small bit of open water and, having caught Amundsen's attention, pointed to it while pantomiming the sign of taking a sun shot. Amundsen clapped his hands together, indicating that the ice would close in and squeeze them, so Riiser-Larsen looked for an ice floe big enough for landing.[66]

Then, without warning, the rear motor of Riiser-Larsen's plane conked out. Since the plane was too heavy to stay airborne with one engine, they looked for a stretch of water for landing. Riiser-Larsen headed for a small basin filled with pieces of old ice. Banking the plane first to one side and then to the other to avoid the surrounding hummocks, he landed "squat in the slush." Sitting in the nose of his plane only a few feet from each approaching obstacle, Amundsen would not forget the vivid impression made by the emergency landing: "When I say we cleared the iceberg by two millimeters it is no exaggeration."[67]

From his plane, Ellsworth saw the *N-25* lose altitude and finally disappear among the cluster of ice hummocks. Dietrichson immediately looked for a landing spot. The water was filled with ice hummocks and pressure ridges of ice blocks standing on edge or piled high atop one another. It was like trying to land in the Grand Canyon, said Lincoln, describing how they finally settled onto a little lagoon among the ice floes.[68] Then, as the plane taxied, Ellsworth heard a bell ringing madly. It was the bell used for communicating between the pilot's seat and the rear of the plane. Dietrichson was shouting, "Omdal, Omdal, the plane's leaking like hell." They anchored the plane to a huge ice cake and stumbled out, wobbly and cramped.[69]

Oscar Omdal pumped to keep the water from rising in the hull. Ellsworth and Dietrichson climbed a high hummock nearby, looking about in vain for the sister aircraft, which was nowhere in sight. It would be just like him to have taken off and gone to the Pole without us, remarked Dietrichson, only half jokingly.[70] Observations showed their position at latitude 87°44′ N, longitude 10°20′ W. A westerly wind had caused them to drift nearly a full degree from their intended flight course meridian.[71] The resulting fuel consumption might become a critical factor in their ability to reach the Pole, or indeed to fly to safety, but this was not the only bad news. Omdal reported that the forward engine, jarred when they struck an ice cake after landing, was disabled. Water in the hull had risen almost to the bottom of the fuel tanks, despite his vigorous pumping.[72] It was now clear that the sound of ripping metal heard on takeoff had been rivets tearing away from the hull. Their only hope was to find Amundsen's plane.

FIGURE 2. Child-hood pictures of Lincoln and his sister, Clare

FIGURE 3. James W. Ellsworth, Lincoln's father

FIGURE 4. Lincoln Ellsworth shown with the Hill School track team (1900), front row, second from left; Number 2 on the Columbia University freshman crew (1905); and at age 40, as a wrestler.

FIGURE 5. Photo of Robert Scott and his companions on their ill-fated
South Pole expedition.

FIGURE 6. Lincoln sits astride a mule while working for the U.S. Biological
Survey, studying mountain sheep in lower California.

FIGURE 7. The abandoned *N-24*, after its crash on the ice.

FIGURE 8. On the ice 130 miles from the North Pole, crews of the *N-24* and the *N-25*, shown here, labored to build a runway.

FIGURE 9. The device Amundsen and Ellsworth brought on board to cancel mail when they reached the North Pole; an inveterate collector, Lincoln kept it as a memento of their harrowing journey.

FIGURE 10. Amundsen, third from left, and Ellsworth, far right, with crew members of the *N-24* and *N-25* after their rescue.

3

On the Ice

May 22, 1925, Day One

Right after landing the *N-25*, Amundsen's crew tried to turn the plane to an open lane in the ice where they could get airborne and continue the flight as soon as they determined their position. But the plane was already frozen tight in the slush and without the help of the other crew, the three men were not strong enough to wrench it free. All day they wondered what had become of the *N-24*. Unbeknownst to them, from a high hummock of ice three miles away, Ellsworth's group had spotted the *N-25*. Hoping to attract attention, they had released several small weather balloons, only to see the wind instantly carry them in the wrong direction. Meanwhile, the immediate concern of Amundsen's group was that the plane, which contained all of their survival equipment, might be crushed where it lay, surrounded by hummocks of moving ice.[1]

Now Amundsen drew upon his great leadership qualities, a blend of personal magnetism and domination that brought out the best in others and kept morale high. He made the seemingly hopeless appear possible. The nearest land was 400 miles away, and there was no way of knowing what ice conditions they might encounter. Refusing to contemplate failure, Amundsen and his two companions prepared to find refuge, and removed the canoe, a gun, and a month's provisions from the downed plane. They lashed them to a sled and planned an escape from their icebound peril. If they could not get clear of the slush within two days, they intended to set out for Cape Richardson in Grant Land and then continue to Fort Conger, where a food depot had been laid down in 1919 on the Third Thule Expedition. "It will be a difficult task but we'll no doubt make it," Amundsen wrote in his diary.

May 23, Day Two

In the afternoon, Amundsen climbed onto one of the wings to reconnoiter. From this position, he suddenly spied a flag through his binoculars. Then he spotted Ellsworth's plane, and a tent. The two crews were soon in contact, but the process was painfully slow. Thanks to their navy training, Riiser-Larsen and Dietrichson were practiced flag signalers who used Morse code to exchange messages. Because the planes were three miles apart, they had to use field glasses to read the signals, stopping constantly to clear lenses that misted over in the extreme cold. Two messages at last became clear: The *N-25*'s engines were okay, but she was frozen tight twenty meters from the water lane. The *N-24*'s hull was leaking badly.

May 24, Day Three

The temperature was minus 11.5°C, water in the *N-24* was rising, and the pump was now frozen. Ellsworth, Dietrichson, and Omdal decided to make for the other camp. They lashed the canoe to the sled and started across the mountains of hummocks. When exhaustion set in after only a few hundred yards, they realized their task was impossible. Abandoning the sled and canoe and continuing on skis, they each carried eighty-pound packs. Two hours later, their way was barred by a risky channel of thin ice. Despondently, they returned to their wounded plane, set up camp, and cooked pemmican soup. Dietrichson introduced brief cheer by producing a little tin of George Washington coffee, to which they added some of the pure alcohol carried as fuel for the Primus stove.[2]

May 25, Day Four

Their luck was improving. Shifting ice, which could have spelled fatal disaster, was gradually bringing the planes closer together. Signals snapped from *N-24* to *N-25*, "We are coming!" With their feet thrust only loosely in their skis, which they had to be ready to cast off if they got in trouble, the trio set out, each carrying eighty pounds. Omdal was in the lead, followed by Ellsworth, then Dietrichson. Cautiously, they pushed their way out over the thin ice that covered a newly frozen channel—their only route to the other camp.[3]

Suddenly Dietrichson dropped through the ice and was submerged up to his neck. He screamed and Ellsworth scuttled sideways as the surface sagged beneath him. By a miracle of good fortune, Ellsworth landed on a thick block frozen into the new surface, but just then, Omdal fell through.[4] Ellsworth was already crawling toward Dietrichson, pushing his skis ahead of him. Dietrichson grabbed a ski and Ellsworth, seizing him by his pack, dragged him to firmer ice. Then he rushed to Omdal, who shouted in terror, "I'm gone! I'm gone!" as he clawed frantically at the slippery edge of the hole to avoid being dragged under by the strong current. Ellsworth gripped the helpless man's pack, and held on with all his strength as the current tugged against him. At the final moment, Dietrichson managed to crawl over and the two men combined their strength to haul the third to safety, back from certain death. Omdal's skis were gone, but he managed to put on Ellsworth's, and the three men crept from cake to cake across the rest of the treacherous passage.

From the moment the three started this perilous trek across the ice, Amundsen had been watching their progress. Seeing them disappear and hearing their shrieks, he was sure their end had come. And then, there they were! Dripping, shuddering, staggering, but alive! A good drop of spirit along with a change of clothes and a cup of hot chocolate revived them.

Ellsworth was shocked by the look of strain on Amundsen's face—a noticeable change in only five days.[5] Yet the old explorer remained calm and clear-headed. This was not the first time he had faced the grim realities of sharing a battle for survival, and his camp was already following an orderly routine—systematic hours for everything—work, sleep, food, smoke, talk.[6] Routine created confidence, Amundsen maintained, a sense that tomorrow would see the same progress as today. But progress awaited Day Six.

May 27, Day Six

With the temperature at minus 9.5°C, the *N-25* was locked down by new ice that had formed overnight. One upward movement of ice could fracture the hull and destroy their means of escape. Even if the plane could be pried loose from the frozen surface, three huge hummocks of piled-up ice blocked its move to a safe location. The six men set about the formidable task of carving the plane's release, hacking with knives, a small ice anchor, and a tiny ax. After hours of work they had managed to chop the hummocks into small pieces. Then they shoveled masses of snow that would prevent jagged fragments from tearing holes in the hull when the time came to maneuver the plane across them. By day's end they had formed a passable escape route. They chopped ice and shook the hull loose from its frozen embrace and, with a brief assist from the engines, pushed the plane onto a secure ice cake.

"It was a wonderful moment," Amundsen said. "One upward movement of the ice would have condemned us to death." They were living on half rations (pemmican, 200 grams; chocolate, 125 grams; oat cakes, 60 grams; dried milk, 50 grams; malted milk, 60 grams—a trifle more than a pound in all), but to celebrate their triumph over the day's ordeals, they drank hot chocolate that evening.

Feeling somewhat safer with the plane's new location, all six men took up quarters inside. Amundsen and Ellsworth covered the cockpit with canvas and slept under the pilot's seat, surrounded by so many uprights, struts, and pipes that their bedroom resembled a bird cage.[7] Riiser-Larsen crawled through a narrow passage leading to the tail compartment, where he slept squeezed between tightly converging ribs. The other three men occupied the main compartment, which served as kitchen, dining room, and dormitory. Their makeshift beds were skis, laid on the floor as insulation from the cold metal. While this spartan setup was less than comfortable, it was warmer than tenting on the ice.

Despite stress and constant discomfort, the group did not lose sight of scientific possibilities. Ellsworth recorded the findings of their echo sounding apparatus—3,750 meters water depth,[8] which all but eliminated the possibility of land existing in that part of the Polar Sea. Yet there was little time to contemplate geographic hypotheses. During the days that followed, their plight was a continuous race against death. Their food supply was insufficient. The *N-24* was useless, with one engine beyond repair. The *N-25* was designed for landing and takeoff on water. But unless they could get her into the air from a surface of ice, they would remain stranded, a daunting thought as they looked out at the jumble of hummocks around them. They were located on a cake, secure, but far too limited for takeoff.[9] In order to relocate, they had to build a ramp from the six-foot elevation of this site, which entailed hacking apart heavy ice blocks using only a two-pound ax. On reduced rations, they all felt the lack of adequate nourishment. "[I] . . . feel a bit weak under any heavy pull," Ellsworth revealed, for him a rare confession.[10]

May 31, Day Ten

"I don't believe six men ever found themselves in a more hopeless position," Lincoln wrote on their tenth day of struggle.[11] Recognizing that the *N-25* might not get airborne, they discussed whether they could reach Greenland, some 400 miles away, on foot and by canoe. Although hardened by a lifetime of physical training, Ellsworth questioned whether he could go even a hundred miles over the ice without collapsing.[12] Amundsen admitted that getting to Greenland would be a hard journey, but declared that "it *can* be done."[13] He immediately bolstered this optimism with practical action, ordering daily rations cut to just one half pound—a quarter of the original provision for each man.

Amundsen set June 15 as the date on which each man would have to decide if he would start on foot for Greenland or stay by the plane in the hope of somehow getting back to Spitsbergen by air. Meanwhile, every effort would be made to get the *N-25* into the air. A straw vote showed divided opinion.[14] Amundsen favored staying by the plane, as did Dietrichson. Riiser-Larsen would walk, rather than "stay and die." Ellsworth chose to hold any decision in abeyance. Omdal said he would follow the majority. Feucht, the German mechanic, suffering from despondency and a sense of defeat, muttered that he would not walk a step, even if everyone else went.

June 1–2, Days Eleven–Twelve

Stretched to their limits, they completed a rough ramp to the hoped-for takeoff stretch. Would they, tomorrow, be on their way? Early the next morning, belongings packed and motors warmed, they climbed on board. Ellsworth's diary told the story. "With lots of hope started motors. Plane plunged into ice and wouldn't rise. So many disappointments!!"[15]

June 3, Day Thirteen

On the thirteenth day, superstition and scientific quest seemed to col-
lide, and they experienced luck that was undeniably bad. The ice had
shattered beneath the plane and jagged floes were edging up out of the
water. Feucht, who was on night watch, called Riiser-Larsen. One
look was enough. "Everyone out," he bellowed to his companions,
who were asleep. Flinging their provisions onto solid ice, they rocked
the hull up and down, up and down, to permit the fast-closing ice to
pass underneath. Pressure dented the hull and tore joints, but they still
had a possible means of escape beyond the hell of walking.[16] Riiser-
Larsen took it all in stride. "It's another chapter to add to the book,"
he said with seeming nonchalance.[17]

Despite gloom caused by the repeated breakup of laboriously constructed takeoff courses, Ellsworth remained curious about the possible existence of a large body of land that might explain the behavior
of the polar currents. This was a possibility that had long intrigued
Nansen, Harris, and other explorers, and had drawn Ellsworth to the
Borup expedition, the one he had signed up for in 1912. Now he noted
that "We have drifted on this ice just 20 miles S.E. This is a most
interesting observation, showing the location of current? [sic] from
Pacific across Pole into Atlantic."[18]

Concentrating on their immediate concerns, Ellsworth and his
comrades were willing by now to try anything that offered hope for
takeoff. They took a chance the following day on a newly frozen lane
that looked as if it might be a feasible runway, despite a curve at the
far end. They climbed in, raced ahead, but were forced to reduce speed
at the curve. The plane broke through the ice, stopped, and lifted her
tail into the air.[19] "Once more fate is against us," Ellsworth said. "We
are pocketed in like rats in a trap."[20] Amundsen merely noted that the
plane was leaking a lot and they were uncomfortable—although later
he admitted that he often had regarded their predicament as "hopeless
and impossible."[21] Defying the odds against them, and fighting
exhaustion, the six men immediately set to work to lengthen their
takeoff course for another effort. "If we don't succeed in getting airborne," Amundsen wrote in his diary that day, June 4, "we will set off
(across the ice) for Fort Conger on June 15 with provisions for forty
days. It will be a strenuous trip but it can be done."[22]

They started work on a new runway, but the following morning their leveled track was a jumbled mass of upturned ice. For the fourth time their takeoff course had been destroyed, and Ellsworth now referred to their position as "desperate."[23] Day after day, each man called forth courage and determination, forcing a weary and under-nourished body to accomplish seemingly impossible tasks. Each night, alone with their thoughts, they wondered whether they could prevail against yet another defeat, the destruction of a day's work. In the morning, hunched over meager rations, each man masked his anxiety. Minds and senses were dulled by the very monotony of failure. They all were developing polar nerves, and trivialities became obsessions. Amundsen's refusal to drink water was a source of annoyance and confusion to his crew. And Ellsworth's heavy sighing in his sleep was a source of irritation to Amundsen, who complained that it kept him awake.[24]

June 5, Day Fifteen

Only ten days remained before the June 15 decision deadline. Riiser-Larsen's declaration that he would rather walk than slowly starve to death was troubling to everyone. Dietrichson might make a similar decision, thus leaving them with no pilot. Furthermore, if any two were to leave, the combined strength of only four men would be insufficient to move the plane. And how would they divide up the limited supply of food?

These thoughts were interrupted by the grinding sound of ice that piled up during the night. Again and again, they broke it up with their assortment of miserable tools, each time barely succeeding in saving the plane.[25]

By now it was clear that they were not likely to find an expanse of water broad enough to allow the wings to clear the adjacent ice, and repeated experience with temporary channels had shown them that such a takeoff surface was never adequate. Riiser-Larsen and Omdal disappeared into the smother of fog, grimly determined to find a solid floe large enough for a runway. The others remained with the plane, pumping out water that leaked through the torn joints of the hull, and keeping a watchful eye on walls of ice that moved closer, inch by inch. One gigantic block towered above, malignant and menacing. They dubbed it the Sphinx.[26]

Toward evening, Riiser-Larsen and Omdal emerged from the fog. Half a mile away they had located a large, solid floe, but in between its location and the plane were two other floes, separated by a wide crevasse. There was even further obstruction. The route was barred by a fifteen-foot pressure ridge of hard ice. Even if they could get the plane onto the far floe, they would then have to level 300 meters of potential runway. While they considered these grim obstacles, the Sphinx loomed closer. They warmed the engines to taxi, and in the nick of time turned the plane around and moved her to the spot where they were building a new ramp. By late evening, in great excitement and a near coma of exhaustion, they completed the ramp and maneuvered the plane up on thick ice—to safety.[27] It was a close call. Behind them, the Sphinx lay on the exact spot where the *N-25* had so recently rested.

June 7, Day Seventeen

In fog and rain, they spent the whole day on their knees, chopping with pocket ax, ice anchor, and sheath knives lashed to ski poles, their hands raw and swollen, until at last they had hacked from the fifteen-foot-thick wall of ice a gap sixty feet wide—just enough to allow wing clearance. Maneuvering the plane across two laboriously filled-in trenches and through the gap, they reached the big floe where a possible runway awaited them.[28] Everything set! Takeoff in the morning!

June 8, Day Eighteen

Morning. The big floe offered 300 meters of runway, only enough if they could gain quick lift by leveling a course that headed into the wind. Once again they hacked throughout the day, cutting, smoothing, leveling, trying to complete their fifth starting course. Now for takeoff. The wind had dropped. They bumped over the ice but could gain no speed and had to stop before sliding into an open lead of water.[29] Riiser-Larsen set about developing a new runway that he said would provide 300 feet more for their takeoff run.[30]

June 10, Day Twenty

On June 10 they shoveled, but the situation seemed so hopeless that Ellsworth wondered if they would have to "make the great sacrifice" for their adventure.[31] The work required more than simply throwing each shovelful to one side. The shoveler had to walk to one edge and hurl dense, heavy wet snow far beyond, leaving clearance of twenty feet on each side—enough to accommodate the wing spread if the plane were to swerve during the takeoff run. Equipped with only three shovels, they had to take turns, and the short rest was a boon to aching bodies.[32] For a few moments, their fatigue was replaced with excitement when two geese flew toward their site from the north, and Ellsworth speculated that there "must be land out there."[33] Amundsen, perhaps recalling instructions from his king to claim for Norway any land he found, wondered whether perhaps the legendary Crocker Land might be nearby.[34]

At day's end they had cleared only 100 feet, and at that rate it would take about ten more days to complete this runway. Hopeless. As they stood discussing their plight, they watched Omdal walking up and down in the snow. Suddenly he shouted, "See. This is what we can do instead of shoveling," and he pointed to the hard surface he had tramped down.[35] Omdal's innovative substitute for shoveling was the ingenious method that would save them. For two days they stamped, each man taking a square area as his responsibility.

June 14, Day Twenty-Four
This day they made takeoff attempts six and seven, but the plane sank down into the snow and failed to accelerate for takeoff.[36] Preparing for their next try, they dumped emergency equipment, half the remaining food, both sledges, one canoe, rifles, ammunition, parkas, ski boots, cameras, field glasses—even the little device brought along to cancel mail at the North Pole. An inveterate collector of trophies, Ellsworth could not resist pocketing it at the last moment.[37]

June 15, Day Twenty-Five
Amundsen's diary for June 15 opens with the light-hearted approach he often adopted in moments of extreme crisis: "The weather provided such visibility as one can expect in this region, that is, one couldn't see anything." Because the track was so obscure, they marked the middle of the runway with small dark objects to increase visibility. At half past ten, all six men climbed into the plane—Riiser-Larsen in the pilot's seat, Amundsen and Dietrichson on the floor in the same cabin, Omdal and Feucht by the motor, Ellsworth in the tail. Once

again, they braced themselves and awaited their fate. Riiser-Larsen let out the throttle. The plane trembled and began to move—scratching and grating at first, then advancing in a series of mighty bumps, with each lunge forward taking them a little farther. The rough ride made them feel as if the plane's undercarriage were about to be pushed in beneath their feet. After a final jerk forward, they were in the air. "At last—at last," wrote Amundsen. "I believe I have asked God for help a thousand times during these weeks, and . . . I firmly and surely am of the opinion that He reached out His hand to us."[38]

In ecstatic terms, his diary describes the details of the ensuing hours of a flight where sometimes, to remain below the fog, they could not fly an inch lower. It was a flight that would always seem to him to be "one of the greatest feats in the history of aviation."

After two hours, sunlight appeared, and they obtained a position fix that showed they were on course. Then fog again. They tried to stay below it, but could not fly low for very long. It became unbearable to skim just above the tips of hummocks. Gasoline was giving out fast. But as they climbed, the fog vanished. They sighted land! Spitsbergen? Could they reach it?

Just beyond the edge of the polar pack, Riiser-Larsen coaxed the flying boat down onto the rough sea, reaching the coast after thirty-five minutes of taxiing. The sight of solid land made them ecstatic. Suddenly someone shouted, "A ship!"

The ship continued out to sea, chasing a wounded walrus. They taxied frantically in pursuit until at last the crew caught sight of them and abandoned the chase. It was a small sealing vessel, the *Sjöliv*. The following day, at Spitsbergen's Lady Franklin Bay, they brought the plane up on land to be fetched later, and the *Sjöliv* headed for Kings Bay.[39]

Aside from Amundsen's "warm thanks to God who guided everything so well," there is little in the diaries that conveys the wonder of their breakthrough from hopeless plight into safe return. Their urgent concerns were sleep, sleep, food, more sleep, and then—since they could send no radio message from the ship—an anxious desire to reach Kings Bay and let news of their safety end the widespread search. The search party included their own ships, the *Heimdal* and the *Hobby*, which had been joined by Russian icebreakers and Norwegian government planes as well, according to the *Sjöliv*'s captain, Nils Vollan.

June 18, Expedition Base, Kings Bay

Norwegian correspondent Fredrik Ramm, journalist for the expedition, described their arrival: ". . . the people noticed how a little sea-boat came in through the evening haze . . . they all thought it was one of the many vessels which . . . call to get coal and water." Then they saw heavily fur-clad men standing near the bow and waving. "It's Amundsen!" a voice shouted.[40] A few minutes later the quay is black with people . . . in a second *Sjöliv's* deck is filled with people who go mad with joy.

Lt. Bernt Balchen, a member of the search party, said the expedition was one of the most stirring tales ever to come out of the Arctic, "a shining example of arctic survival." Ellsworth was ". . . almost unrecognizable by dirt and grime [and] all much thinner from their ordeal . . . but ready to get going again." Then Balchen identified the key to Amundsen's capacity to beat seemingly impossible odds. There was one statement that Amundsen refused to accept and that was taboo under his command: "It cannot be done." No matter how impossible a task might seem, a solution had to be found.[41]

Throughout those days of struggle, Amundsen's diary of setbacks and challenges was infused with such consistent optimism that it must have been reflected in his bearing. And surely his invincible spirit must have fortified the spirits of his companions. For example, in his diary, one can read:

> the open lane in the ice, about to close but I have no doubt it will soon open up again. (May 27)
>
> The runway is the worst but it will get better with time. (May 29)
>
> If we can close the gaps we will have an excellent runway. (May 30)
>
> When things are darkest they usually get brighter. (June 2)
>
> As soon as the weather allows we will be off. (June 7)

Welcomed Home

Telegrams poured in from all over the world, swamping the service between Spitsbergen and the Norwegian mainland. The *N-25* was fetched from North Cape and loaded on the steamer *Selmer* which, with all members of the expedition on board, set out for Horten, the naval base near Oslo. The voyage lasted a week, and whenever the steamer passed a settlement, she was greeted with boats festooned with flags, and big ovations as the crowds paid homage to the hero-explorers.

"If we had toiled hard, we were now being rewarded for it," Amundsen noted.[42] At the Norwegian naval base five days later: "Colossal reception. People going completely wild."[43] But that was modest compared to their reception in Oslo, when the six survivors, escorted by Norwegian navy and army planes, flew in on the *N-25* for the official welcome. Dropping down into the harbor, she taxied past thirteen British warships with crews lined at attention on deck. The horns and whistles of naval vessels and other craft shrieked a spectacular welcome, airplanes circled overhead, and quays and wharves were jammed with a throng of thousands.[44] (In his diary entry of July 5, Amundsen estimates 50,000.)

As the men stepped ashore they were greeted by a committee of dignitaries in frock coats and uniforms. In open carriages they rode through streets lined with crowds of cheering spectators, on their way to the palace for an audience with the king. Lincoln's life was changed. That evening, like the shining jewel in the crown, came their majesties' dinner at the castle. "It was an intoxicating draught for one who had never known celebrity or the feeling of being treated as an important personage," he wrote. "It created an appetite that could never be once and for all appeased."[45]

But Lincoln's feelings were profound, not merely on the level of ego gratification over public acclaim. Before the expedition ship left Tromsö, he had written his sister, "These people have won my heart. I have been treated as I never knew it was possible to be treated before, and I have lost my heart to them."[46] And Norwegian hearts belonged to him. The Norwegians perceived him as a native son. "You brave, stalwart, American Viking," wrote one.[47] Another said, "You overcame nearly superhuman hindrances! . . . The old Vikings have come back!"[48] The Norwegian National League wrote, "Your name will never be forgotten by us Norwegians."[49] A Norwegian ship owner asked and was granted permission to name one of his vessels the *Lincoln Ellsworth*.[50]

The Norwegian Storting awarded him the Medal for Bravery for saving the whole expedition, and Amundsen declared that "no one who wears it has earned it more bravely."[51] Perhaps more precious, though, was a simple gift from Dietrichson's wife, an ashtray inscribed: "Lincoln Ellsworth with hearty thanks for everything from Gunvor Dietrichson, July 1925." Accompanying it was a letter overflowing with gratitude. "I wanted also to try to thank you specially for what you did for my husband and for me there up in the north—so many thousand thanks . . . only a little remembrance." And a postscript: "The English in this letter is awful, I think! But you must be kind, try to understand the meaning."[52]

Amundsen and Ellsworth had lunch with the king at the royal estate on July 21 and the following day Lincoln sailed for home, ready to begin work on plans for an airship flight across the Polar Sea the following summer. But a shadow clouded the celebratory atmosphere. "If you persist it will cause my death," James Ellsworth had warned his son. Now, almost as he stepped ashore in Norway, Lincoln learned that his father had died without knowing that his son was safe.

"Father and son stand with a world between them—one living in the past and one living passionately in the future," wrote Morris Markey in the *New York Evening World* at the time of James Ellsworth's last illness.[53] Their parting had been a most dismal experience, and now Lincoln suffered pangs of regret because his father had not lived to hear of his triumph.

From Clare came a letter overflowing with devotion and pride, written on the black-bordered note paper used in those days to denote mourning. "Dearest Link, I am so happy and thrilled about you that I can think of nothing else. Your safe return was miraculous, but I knew you would do it somehow. . . . I am known only as Lincoln Ellsworth's sister. And when father died the notice read, 'Lincoln Ellsworth's father is Dead.' So you see what a marvelous name you have made for yourself to pass down in history." Attempting to reassure her brother, she told him she'd learned that just before their father died, he suddenly sat up in bed and said, 'Lincoln is alright [*sic*], he will come back safely.' He did not worry about you at all, which I know will be a comfort to you. And let's hope he knows you are safe and such a hero."[54] Perhaps Clare's message conveys more devotion than fact. Historian J. F. Waring said of

James: "The only name he spoke was that of his youngest brother Frank."[55]

Clare mentioned to Lincoln his letters about Helene. She hoped that from now on his life would be overflowing with happiness to make up for everything he had missed. Tenderly supportive, she closed, "Goodbye beloved boy. And if you really love your girl, we will meet you in Norway for the wedding!"[56] But there was no wedding. Lincoln's attention was already focused on his next polar expedition, and there is no record of his having seen Helene again.

Although it failed in its specific objective, a continent-to-continent flight, the Amundsen-Ellsworth Expedition made important contributions to knowledge of the Arctic. Requests poured in for information about the instruments and other equipment they had used.[57] By taking soundings of ocean depth of 3,750 meters and by flying over some 120,000 square miles, Ellsworth and Amundsen all but ended speculation that a land mass might exist on the European side of the North Pole. But the direction of the flood tides reaching the Alaska coast gave reason to believe, they wrote, that there was land between the Pole and Alaska.[58] That phenomenon, left unexplained for two more decades,[59] held Ellsworth's attention for several years when he corresponded with the National Geographic Society about a contemplated search in the region of Peary's Crocker Land.[60] The 1925 experience also produced a more immediate and practical result. During their three weeks on the ice, Ellsworth had kept a record of barometric readings, wind direction and force, dry bulb temperatures, clouds, and precipitation.[61] Thus, among other "Results of the Expedition" was the finding that prevailing meteorological conditions over the Polar Basin presented no hindrance to its successful exploration by means of suitable aircraft.[62]

After enduring years of frustration, Ellsworth was now a success. He had earned world renown. He had shared in making a contribution to scientific knowledge. He had won Amundsen's unqualified praise for saving the lives of two men, and in so doing, the lives of all, because, explained Amundsen, the plane could not have been moved to safety without the power of six men. From this turning point, Ellsworth was ready to go forward. Before they left Kings Bay on their way south, he agreed to Amundsen's proposal that they undertake a flight by a lighter-than-air ship the following year "to attack the Arctic unknown."[63] Understandably, Amundsen's sense of relief was immense when Ellsworth pledged $100,000 for the venture. It would be the veteran explorer's seventh preparation (his first was in 1909) for a flight across the Arctic Ocean. At last, it seemed certain that he would complete his career with a crowning success.[64]

It was agreed that a semirigid dirigible would be safer in gales than a rigid one like the navy's *Shenandoah*. Since the only such airship in existence was the Italian government's *N-1*, Amundsen invited Colonel Umberto Nobile, its designer as well as pilot, to come to Oslo for a conference. Nobile arrived well prepared, with the specific proposal that the Italian government would make a gift of the *N-1*, on the condition that the expedition fly under the Italian flag.[65] Amundsen was emphatic in his rejection of this idea. He had carried the Norwegian flag through the Northwest Passage and to the South Pole, and his dream of seventeen years now was to be fulfilled under the Norwegian flag. Amundsen's dream! Amundsen's expedition! Amundsen's flag! Nothing, he declared, could induce him to make the first Arctic Ocean crossing under any other. In light of later developments, it appears that Nobile's proposal was a deliberate effort to gain for the Italian political regime, and for the Italian people, a worldwide visibility that would allow them to claim the plan as their own. While relying on Amundsen's skills for guidance, they would keep the credit and glory for themselves.[66]

Attempting to solve the problem, Amundsen offered to purchase the *N-1* outright, and the Italian government agreed to sell the airship for £15,000. In August it was announced that Norsk Luftseiladsforening A/S Polflyvning (commonly referred to as the Aero Club) had assumed the role of administering future polar expeditions under the leadership of Roald Amundsen and with the help of Lincoln Ellsworth.[67] Little did Ellsworth realize the disappointments this all-Norwegian emphasis would cause him. Nor did he recognize another cloud about to loom over his future, this time in the person of Richard E. Byrd.

4

Undeclared Race

THE WAVE OF INTENSE PATRIOTISM that swept across the land during and after World War I was exploited by both the U.S. Army and Navy as they sought to arouse congressional pride and national feeling to support their aims. On January 20, 1924, banner headlines in the *New York Times* announced the proposed flight to the North Pole by the navy's first rigid dirigible, the *Shenandoah*. Secretary of the Navy Edwin Denby explained and glorified the project's objectives in the *Times* article.[1]

Although a number of zeppelins had exploded, burned, or been lost since the end of World War I, the navy's confidence in its own airship, the first using helium for lift, remained unshaken. Seven years of planning and effort had produced the airship, originally known as *ZR-1*. Denby had expressed unqualified satisfaction with her performance after her test flight in 1923, emphasizing it as an American success.[2] During these years, army fliers were much in the public eye. They performed the first one-day, coast-to-coast flight in 1922, flew nonstop from New York to San Diego in 1923, and were planning around-the-world flights. Now the navy was determined to earn similar prestige through a spectacular flight of its own, promoted by Rear Admiral William A. Moffett, Chief, Bureau of Aeronautics, U.S. Navy.

Moffett, commander of the proposed flight, explained its purpose: to explore the unknown area of the north polar region and establish the practicability of a transpolar air route. Two vessels with mooring masts, six planes, and one dirigible would be involved in a flight from

Nome, Alaska, to Spitsbergen, a distance of some 2,200 nautical miles. Almost as an afterthought, the *Times* mentioned scientific investigation and possible commercial development.[3] At a congressional hearing, Secretary Denby said the real purpose of the North Pole flight was to annex land in that area to the United States. "If it is not photographed and mapped by us it will be by another power within a year," he said.[4] The other power Denby had in mind was Norway. Amundsen, with Riiser-Larsen, had prepared for such a flight, but it was canceled at the last moment due to lack of funds. He reportedly intended to claim for his country any lands he discovered, and an official note to that effect had been presented to the U.S. Department of State by Norwegian Minister Bryn.[5]

To stimulate action, Moffett evoked past naval heroes such as Charles Wilkes, who had discovered part of the Antarctic continent in 1840, and Robert Peary, who had claimed the North Pole. The spirit of American patriotism so loudly voiced by Moffett was not lost on Lieutenant Richard E. Byrd. It was a theme he would echo time and again as he forged his way up the ladder of fame, always intent on staying ahead of any competition.

This was the start of an era in which polar exploration would resemble a game of musical chairs. The main players were known: Amundsen, Ellsworth, Wilkins, and Byrd. The number of chairs—major geographical targets—was limited. One goal was to find and claim any land mass that might exist in the unknown area between Alaska and the North Pole. Another target was the North Pole itself, where arriving first by air was the coveted prize. A third major breakthrough would be to find land in the Arctic Ocean between Greenland and Spitsbergen, especially Crocker Land (supposedly seen by Peary). Each explorer kept a wary ear cocked for what others might be planning. An outward semblance of cordiality often masked feelings of animosity, which were exacerbated by the need to remain in the public eye. This was the political landscape which awaited Ellsworth, who entered the competitive arena with romantic idealism about polar exploration.

On February 8, 1924, Byrd was assigned temporary duty with Moffett and attached to the Arctic expedition for the *Shenandoah* flight from Point Barrow across the Pole to Spitsbergen. Four days later, the navy announced the ship would be ready for the trip on May 1. However, Washington's approval was still needed. Hopes suddenly collapsed when President Coolidge ordered the Navy Department on February 14 to cease preparations for the North Pole flight.[6] Coolidge was jittery about scandals involving high Republican office holders and party officials. The festering sore of the Teapot Dome oil scandal was about to burst.

Frederick S. Dellenbaugh of the Explorers Club predicted the chance of successfully returning from the Pole as fifty-fifty; an "eminent" but unnamed geographer set the chances at one in a thousand. Secretary Denby resigned, and Coolidge ordered the *Shenandoah* journey suspended, pending clarification of the attitude of Congress.[7]

Byrd found himself once more "in my usual position, out on the end of a limb," but he had gained momentum.[8] With the prospect of America being first to reach the Pole by air, he continued planning, and his cause received a boost when a special act of Congress promoted him to lieutenant commander. He said this was simple recognition of his loyalty and energetic work in plugging for the service to which he was devoted and that might have been a consideration. General Billy Mitchell, who exercised tremendous political influence at the time, was not kindly disposed toward the navy; Byrd, as a naval liaison officer with Congress, had to do what he could to offset Mitchell's unfriendliness. However, the timeliness of the promotion, which would enable him to accelerate his race to the Pole, suggests that he commanded behind-the-scenes clout that could smooth his way. Indeed, this was so.[9] After years of lobbying, he had many cronies on Capitol Hill. Moreover, he had been friends with Franklin Delano Roosevelt since boyhood, and Roosevelt had served as assistant secretary of the navy for seven years (1913–20).

Byrd lost no time in starting to organize his own North Pole expedition. The two things he needed quickly were money and someone committed to the importance of airplanes. Edsel Ford filled both requirements. Byrd told Ford he planned a North Pole flight the coming summer, pointing out that the navy would assist because its plans for the *Shenandoah* flight had collapsed. Ford was impressed. He wired John D. Rockefeller Jr., saying, "I have taken the liberty of suggesting that [Byrd] call upon you for the purpose of laying before you his plans for a North Pole flight this summer by aircraft . . . have agreed to give him assistance."[10] Leaving nothing to chance, Byrd also outlined his plans to Charles D. Walcott, secretary of the Smithsonian Institution, who wrote Rockefeller's advisor, Raymond Fosdick, strongly recommending the project as worthy of support.[11] Before even talking with Byrd, Rockefeller agreed to match Edsel Ford's contribution of $15,000.[12]

Ford made clear to Rockefeller the intentions expressed to him by Byrd. First, Byrd promoted the possibility of making the United States the first nation to fly to the North Pole. But he also had stressed the point that in the vast area west of the Pole, unpenetrated by previous expeditions, there might be another large continent that could be taken in the name of the United States.[13] He cited Peary's conviction that land existed westward of his course, and voiced the same patriotic theme expressed by Secretary Denby in connection with the *Shenandoah* project.

When Byrd was unable to obtain the Goodyear blimp he had counted on for his own trip to the Pole, he joined an expedition sponsored by the National Geographic Society under the leadership of Donald MacMillan. He did so with the approval of the navy and the president, and with the assignment of three navy planes. MacMillan, Byrd confided to Ford, was not "as likely as I was to make a dash for the Pole." He hoped Ford would keep open his offer in case in the next year there would remain something important to do for science. (This presumably reflected Byrd's concern about the impending Amundsen-Ellsworth Expedition. If it reached the Pole, there would be no purpose in Byrd duplicating that aeronautical feat; and unless a landing was planned for the purpose of taking observations, no scientific interest would be served.)

In the same letter, apparently fearful of losing his benefactor's approval, he urged Ford three times to let him know if there was any feeling that he was not doing the ethical thing. Then, reminding Ford of the navy's close identification with his personal plans, Byrd concluded on a note of flattery: "Everyone down here is much pleased at your generosity and patriotic spirit in offering to contribute to my expedition."[14] Ford released Byrd from the tentative arrangement, expressed hope that the National Geographic Society venture would enable Byrd to fly to the North Pole and return, and indicated his interest in financing a trip the following year.[15] Strangely, this correspondence contained no specific reference to the Amundsen-Ellsworth Expedition or to the famous German, Hugo Eckener, and his intended polar flight and stopover at the Pole. Perhaps Byrd feared those plans might diminish the allure of his own proposal to Ford.

Byrd spent the summer of 1925 in Greenland, exploring the ice-cap[16] while, back from his expedition, Lincoln Ellsworth was still basking in the heady novelty of worldwide fame. He anticipated even greater acclaim the next year, when he and Amundsen would be the first to reach the North Pole by air and the first to cross the Polar Sea. They would be the explorers to determine, once and for all, what lay in the huge unknown expanse between the Pole and Alaska—some one million square miles. Any rewards resulting from this great venture would depend entirely on the worldwide attention generated by being first to the Pole. That's what the public wanted to read about, to hear about in lectures, to see in photographs. The *first*.

Little did Ellsworth realize how much Byrd's activity throughout that fateful summer would affect his own future. Experienced leaders, he and Amundsen were confident. They had their airship. And they saw no immediate competitors on the horizon. Said the *New York Times*: "The last hope of discovering new land in the Arctic by airplane vanished so far as the MacMillan expedition was concerned, when Secretary of the Interior Ray Lymen Wilbur ordered Commander Byrd to make no further attempts to fly over the Polar region and to withdraw with MacMillan. . . . The field seems to be left to Captain Amundsen for the present," concluded the *Times*.[17] How wrong this was! Admiral Moffett and the secretary of the navy remained interested in Byrd's plans, and several months later Edsel Ford sent a $20,000 check for Byrd's expedition.[18]

Captain Amundsen, with Ellsworth's financial support, was ready for the challenge. Little did these two happy collaborators foresee the devastating conflicts that were to mar their coming achievement. Each of the three major participants in the undertaking held a trump card: Ellsworth, the money; Amundsen, the prestige; Nobile, the airship. None could succeed without the cooperation of the others. But from the very beginning, national pride, personal ambitions, and conflicting expectations created an atmosphere of rancor. No longer was the polar explorer assured of heroic stature, prestige earned through braving the earth's harshest climate and enduring unimaginable hardship. The collaborators were to become sparring partners, with bickering often escalating into barbed words, and finally, public recriminations.

Ellsworth returned to the United States to sell the story and photo rights in the western hemisphere, while Amundsen and Riiser-Larsen planned to go to Rome in late August to sign a contract for purchasing an airship. Financing had to be assured and Ellsworth had not committed a specific sum. He intended to help substantially, but only after he received detailed plans and satisfied certain doubts.[19] One of these related to a telegram from the Aero Club—already anxious about meeting expenses—asking him to inquire whether Coney Island might be interested in purchasing or renting the N-25 for exhibition. Ellsworth was disgusted. This was the plane that had saved their lives, and in his mind it was sacred—a symbol of the high ideals and spirit of their adventure. He refused to have it connected with what he regarded as cheap commercialism. The proposal was dropped.

Yet 500,000 kroner, made available from the proceeds of their 1925 expedition, was far short of their need. There was no time to mince words. Amundsen wired Ellsworth: "Please state whether you deem it possible raise above-mentioned $130,000 as contribution."[20] Lincoln, still uncertain what his position would be in the expedition, responded with a request for more information—"very definite," he stipulated—about his own standing.[21] Amundsen replied that his position should be leader of scientific work and navigator.[22] Somewhat reassured, Ellsworth undertook personally to contribute $100,000, subject to certain conditions he would discuss when Amundsen arrived in New York. Lincoln was not happy with an undertaking that was seen as entirely Norwegian, and one of his conditions was the addition of an American newspaper to cover the expedition.[23]

In Rome, Amundsen and Mussolini signed an agreement for delivery of the dirigible N-1 to the Amundsen-Ellsworth Expedition 1926, with the object of making a passage "from Spitsbergen to Alaska, across the North Pole." The Italian government agreed to provide an officer to command for the expedition's duration; there was no mention of Nobile by name. The price was $75,000. The Italians agreed to repurchase the *N-1* for $46,000 if she came back in good condition.[24]

"Now there are 1001 things to do," wrote Amundsen. He told Ellsworth about the agreement, about plans for flying the airship from Rome to England and thence to Kings Bay, and about the possible need to build a hangar there, all of which they would discuss when Amundsen reached New York. The letter closed on a note of grim humor. Two days earlier, the *Shenandoah,* almost twice as big as the *N-1* and designed to be 30 percent stronger than contemporary vessels of the same size, had been ripped apart and destroyed in a line squall. "But of course the air is not quite safe yet," he wrote. "What do you think?"[25]

Still uneasy about his role and sniffing trouble ahead, Ellsworth telegraphed the Aero Club that his contribution depended on an immediate statement to the foreign and American press that the expedition would officially be known as the Amundsen-Ellsworth Transpolar Flight, that he would be the only American, and that the final published record would be written exclusively by Amundsen and himself. He stipulated that his official connection and responsibility be definitely stated.[26] The Aero Club had no objections to these conditions, and advised him that his part and responsibility in the expedition had been announced to the press.

This resolution was short-lived. By this time Amundsen was in New York on a lecture tour. Rolf Thommessen, president of the Aero Club and the wealthy owner and editor of Norway's well-known daily newspaper *Tidens Tigen,* cabled him about a press statement announcing that Ellsworth would serve as navigator, together with Dietrichson. Dietrichson had responded that he would not accompany the expedition if Ellsworth was navigator. In his opinion, Ellsworth was unable to navigate and the arrangement would be "humbug."[27]

Amundsen was stunned. This great man's destiny seemed to be ever subject to the whims of others, and his future lay in Ellsworth's hands. So close was Amundsen to financial ruin that he had taken an advance payment of $2,700 from his lecture booking agent to pay one of his old debts. "I had a court decision go against me," he explained in a letter to Thommessen, "and would have been arrested if they hadn't been paid." He added, "Discipline . . . is everything. Both Ellsworth and I are sad to lose him [Dietrichson], but it *will have to* happen, if he sticks to his opinion."[28]

Thommessen and his Aero Club colleague Arnold Raestad must have then done some serious soul searching, for on October 20 Amundsen received an extraordinary telegram. In an effort to redeem Dietrichson's tarnished image, Raestad told Amundsen he had misinterpreted Dietrichson's sentiments and that he took full blame for the misunderstanding. Dietrichson had never used the offending word *humbug*. It was Raestad who had used it in summarizing the gist of a telephone conversation. Dietrichson was worried that he would be blamed if navigation went wrong, but that he would not be honored if it was successful. Raestad cautioned that if a breach with Dietrichson became public, Ellsworth would be the object of unmerited ridicule and Amundsen would be diminished in the mind of the public, who regarded him as a hero. Dietrichson's great services and unflinching loyalty entitled him to reassurance, he continued, asking Amundsen to advise promptly what he could tell Dietrichson.[29]

This was no time to offend Ellsworth, who had just been tapped for $100,000, and Amundsen promptly wrote Raestad. The letter was blunt: Dietrichson's behavior was beyond understanding. Ellsworth's position could not be taken away from him; the expedition could do without Dietrichson but not without Ellsworth, whose sole interest was in the expedition's success and who was willing to withdraw from the navigator position if he sensed he was not ready for the job. They should feel indebted to Ellsworth for making the last expedition possible, and must realize they could still end up in a tough situation where Ellsworth's help would be the only thing that could save them. The letter ended by cautioning Thommessen to do nothing. Amundsen calmly declared that it would be resolved naturally to everyone's satisfaction.[30]

It is difficult to understand Dietrichson's ultimatum, unless one concludes that Ellsworth was indeed inept in navigation. In light of later events, it appears that Dietrichson got this idea when he and Ellsworth were together on the ice for days, using sextant and computation to establish their position after the *N-24* and *N-25* had landed on their flight toward the Pole. There is a big difference between academic learning, such as Ellsworth had acquired, and

Dietrichson's understanding of principles, sharpened by years of practical application in actual flight. Dietrichson wrote that he himself made two good observations, but in the same sentence he noted that the spirit level which Ellsworth had brought with him was too small and of very unsuitable construction.[31] Amundsen's diary noted that "Dietrichson made 3 excellent observations" which placed them at 87°34′N and longitude 12° west of Greenwich.[32] There is no mention of Ellsworth's observations.

Ellsworth, himself uneasy about his navigational skills, announced his intention to go to Norway to study navigation at the Oslo Sjømannsskole (Sailors' School). But instead, he went to the Grand Canyon, hoping that the dry desert air would bring relief from a sinus condition so acute that it eventually required surgery. Amundsen, unaware of any health problem and suspecting Lincoln of being self-indulgent, wrote that he was glad to hear Lincoln was enjoying life and wished he could say the same for himself. He contrasted his own never-ending discomfort, sleeplessness, and indigestible fare on a lecture tour with the pleasures of Lincoln's days in the Grand Canyon, one of the most beautiful spots on earth. In a tone of reproof he told Lincoln that he ought to be in New York where they could talk over their plans for "the biggest Polar expedition which ever took place."[33]

By mid-December, anxiety about Dietrichson's connection with the expedition had been allayed. He announced that he would not take part in the coming flight. During five years of marriage, he had been absent 80 percent of the time, and in justice toward his family, he said, he could not take on this big new challenge.[34] The Aero Club closed the year with its assurance to Ellsworth that all statements to the news media would make clear that he was leader with rights and standing equal to those of Captain Amundsen, and that the record of the expedition would be written cooperatively by the two leaders.[35]

Nobile, however, was not to be shunted aside, and it was soon apparent that trouble lay ahead in that quarter. Responding to pressure from Nobile, the Aero Club implored Ellsworth to accept Nobile as a collaborator in writing the technical part of the book.[36] Failing to foresee the possibility of disagreement about such limited authority, Ellsworth consented.[37] Almost immediately he had second thoughts, and sought advice from his friend Herman Gade, Norwegian minister to the United States. Quite correctly, as it turned out, Gade perceived Nobile's request as a source of potential conflict. He counseled Ellsworth to withdraw his consent and to exclude Nobile as an expedition author. Following his advice, Ellsworth cabled the Aero Club, but it was too late. The club had signed a contract with Nobile immediately after Ellsworth's consent, on January 16, 1926.[38] Nobile contended that under its terms he was now authorized to write about the preparation, maneuvering, and navigation of the airship and to send communications to the Italian government signed by himself.[39]

Amundsen was outraged. His redemption from bankruptcy depended on earning substantial fees for lectures and writing, and his only hope was to keep that field for himself. Furthermore, having initiated the project, obtained financing, and arranged outright purchase of the airship, he had no intention of allowing a hired employee to assume equal status with the leaders. He minced no words in expressing personal animosity. How could Thommessen "knuckle under to this piece of brazen effrontery," he sputtered, and fail to think of the pride of Norway and of his and Ellsworth's interests?[40]

Three times in as many weeks, the Aero Club cabled Ellsworth to come to Oslo as soon as possible for consultation on several important points, one of which was the Italian government's request that the expedition be renamed to reflect Italian participation.[41] By the time Ellsworth arrived in Oslo, positions had solidified, governed by chauvinism and personal ambition. Nobile persisted in demanding that his name be included in the expedition title. Ellsworth was firm in withholding the balance of his financial commitment until assured of recognition on a par with Amundsen. They argued about which flags would be dropped, and how, and in what order.

The Aero Club suggested adopting the name "Amundsen-Ellsworth Norwegian-American-Italian Transpolar Flight," and identifying Nobile as the airship commander. This pleased no one. Negotiations continued. At one point in the endless bickering over leadership, name, and publicity, Amundsen and Ellsworth became so disgusted they considered abandoning the entire expedition. They were deterred from this drastic step only by the fear that someone else would accomplish the transpolar flight before they could organize another one.[42] The fear was well founded. Aero Club administrator Alf

Bryn reminded his colleagues that Wilkins was waiting at Point Barrow to take off for Spitsbergen as soon as weather permitted—a threat to their efforts if he got off first.[43]

But a more serious problem was festering. Nobile was becoming anxious not to go all the way to Alaska and wanted the right to turn back, even after passing the North Pole.[44] A month later he repeated this demand in stronger language and even proposed that the entire crew swear loyalty to him so that no one could question such a decision. A confidential message from the Norwegian legation in Rome said that if these demands were not met, the Italian government would not allow its people to participate.[45]

Riiser-Larsen made no effort to conceal his disgust and outrage. He was fighting to preserve the Norwegian character of the expedition and was determined to block attempts to squeeze out Norwegian participation. The more Italy gained, the harder it would be to resist further damaging demands, he said hotly. No concessions were necessary. The Norwegians could go without the Italians and with the same degree of success. If Nobile's demands were met, Riiser-Larsen would withdraw and demand his money back.[46] Half a dozen of his colleagues signed a message to Thommessen deploring the notion of relinquishing the Norwegian character of the expedition. It affirmed their support of Riiser-Larsen's position, and they asked about their right to withdraw entirely.[47]

Thommessen was aghast. Obliged to produce funds to meet towering unpaid bills for preparation of the base at Spitsbergen, he again faced the project's possible collapse. He wired Riiser-Larsen: "I urgently appeal to you as friend and Norwegian not to make difficulties," pointing out that the matter of names was only a tribute to Italy and that the expedition legally and financially still remained Norwegian.[48]

Ellsworth saved the day. He came to Thommessen and said he did not want to be an obstacle to the resolution of expedition problems and would be willing to agree to change the name to Amundsen-Ellsworth-Nobile Transpolar Flight.[49] Thommessen instructed Bryn at the Aero Club office to use the new name and print new stationery.[50]

A document formalized compromises reached on four major points: the new expedition title; a maximum crew of sixteen, six of whom would be Italian; an expedition goal "to cross the Arctic region from Spitsbergen over the North Pole to Alaska"; the two leaders were identified as Amundsen and Ellsworth, with Colonel Nobile as commander of the airship and Riiser-Larsen as vice-leader.[51] When Ellsworth read the agreement he conceded readily to having Colonel Nobile's name connected with the expedition. The Aero Club thanked him warmly for what they saw as a personal sacrifice.

However, Ellsworth's sacrifice failed to accommodate differences peacefully in nationality, temperament, experience, and, last but not least, personal objectives. With the expedition organization seemingly resolved, Amundsen, Ellsworth, and Thommessen remained in Rome to take possession of the airship the following day. Tension between the Norwegians and Nobile was at the breaking point, but all seemed in order to proceed with the dedication ceremonies. Then word was received that the airship would not be delivered until $15,000 was paid to the Italian owners to provide insurance for the Rome to Spitsbergen flight. The Aero Club had no funds to meet the request.[52]

Amundsen, having gone through bankruptcy, had no money to help. The New York Times had already paid the first installment of $19,000 on its $55,000 contract, dated October 2, 1925, for exclusive news rights. The next payment of $18,000 would not be due until the airship reached Spitsbergen.[53] Meanwhile, the cost of preparations for its arrival had to be met.

In October 1925, First Lieutenant John Höver, an engineer on leave from the Norwegian navy, had gone to Aalesund, Svalbard (as the Norwegians called Spitsbergen), to plan and supervise the erection of a hangar and mast. The magnitude of the undertaking staggered him.[54] Before the job was completed, nearly 2,000 tons of cargo were conveyed to Svalbard in connection with the expedition. On October 23, the steamer Alekto arrived at Kings Bay, bringing 600 cubic meters of timber, fifty tons of iron for the hangar, and tools and equipment. The ship also carried twenty-one workmen and winter provisions for thirty-two people. An extension was built for connection with the mining company's railway line almost a quarter mile away. Two hundred cubic meters of concrete casting were made to provide anchoring blocks for the mast and hangar. As winter closed in, working conditions became difficult. Temperatures fell below zero degrees Fahrenheit and the materials were sometimes buried under snow. But on

February 15, 1926, the skeleton of the hangar was raised, 110 x 34 x 30 meters high. Twenty-seven kilometers of beams were used. Workmen attached 10,000 square meters (2½ acres) of French hangar cloth to the sides and gables of the hangar. On March 24 the *Hobby* arrived carrying the three sections of mooring mast, as well as 900 hydrogen cylinders that weighed 140 tons. The *Knut Skaaluren* later brought 3,900 more hydrogen cylinders, weighing 635 tons.

The cost of all this material and labor had greatly exceeded estimates, and the sudden demand for insurance money posed a serious obstacle to delivery of the airship. Ellsworth suggested that public contributions might be sought, but his brother-in-law Bernon Prentice counseled against it. "This [is] your big life effort," he said, and you should "not share honor, credit and reputation with anybody."[55] Thanks to Lincoln's "opportune financial position," as Prentice phrased it, he arranged for $30,000 to be forwarded from James Ellsworth's estate (to be repaid as Lincoln's income accumulated) to cover the insurance and help defray Spitsbergen expenses.

The dedication ceremonies took place March 29, 1926, in Rome. Mussolini made an impressive speech. Thommessen, as president of the Aero Club, replied in acceptance. Mrs. Riiser-Larsen broke a bottle of champagne over the airship's bow. To rolling drums, the Italian flag came down and the Norwegian flag went up.[56] Leaving Rome together, Ellsworth and Amundsen would not see their airship again until rendezvous in Kings Bay, Spitsbergen.

Soon after they left, the agreement of January 16, 1926, was replaced by a revised contract dated April 6. It was signed by Umberto Nobile, and by Rolf Thommessen for Amundsen and Ellsworth. Its intended purpose, along with providing life insurance and specifying payments in gold lire to Nobile at each stage of progress, was to clarify lines of responsibility among the three named leaders and to emphasize the limitations governing Nobile's privilege to send radio or telegraphic communications and publish articles. Like every previous effort to get things squared away, this document also failed to bring accord.

While in Oslo en route to Spitsbergen, Ellsworth attended a ceremony on April 10 to receive from U.S. Minister Swenson an American flag to be dropped at the North Pole. Ellsworth felt he was representing his country in a significant role, and the importance he attached to his part in the upcoming expedition was reflected in his words as he accepted the flag at the United States embassy. "I am deeply conscious of the significance of this occasion . . . because I have been entrusted by my President to carry the flag of my country to the North Pole," he said.[57] As he sailed from Oslo, ever mindful of his sister's support, he cabled Clare: "My thoughts are of you and only of you as I start on our great adventure. Love without measure. Lincoln."[58]

A Sporting Feat

In early March 1926, under the headline "Across the Pole by Dirigible," the New York Times announced the Amundsen-Ellsworth Expedition. A long article in the same edition (by Fitzhugh Green, one of Byrd's navy colleagues) was headed "Massed Attack On Polar Region Begins Soon." It referred to "races"—a harbinger of the press hysteria to come.[59]

Edsel Ford increased his pledge to Byrd from $20,000 to $30,000 and Rockefeller did the same.[60] In mid-March, Byrd wrote Isaiah Bowman asking for charts of northern Greenland.[61] At the end of the month, a full-page article in the Times heralded Byrd's imminent departure for Spitsbergen. "Byrd Outlines Plan To Reach The Pole," the headline read. But the objective of this first flight would not be to reach the Pole but to find a landing field on Peary Land, at the northern tip of Greenland. There the expedition would deposit supplies and gasoline. Then it would fly back to Kings Bay to load up and return to its Peary Land air base.

Only after the second flight to Peary Land would they be ready "to fly to and around the North Pole," Byrd told the Times reporter. Their objective would be to explore the unknown stretch of about 400 miles from Peary Land to the Pole ". . . and possibly to accomplish the sporting feat of reaching the Pole from the air."[62] Byrd's conspicuously casual reference to his life's ambition as merely a sporting feat was obviously calculated to mask his true intent. In the same way Amundsen had deliberately and successfully misled Scott before his race to the South Pole, Byrd was laying a false trail about his own determination to become the first man to fly to the North Pole. Roald Amundsen would have a dose of his own medicine!

On April 5, at a send-off luncheon at the Brooklyn Navy Yard aboard Vincent Astor's yacht *Nourmahal,* Commander Byrd handed Rockefeller a copy of his statement to the press. It continued in the high-spirited vein of his previous remarks. "The clean sport and adventurous side of this expedition appeals to every man going on it," the statement began. It spoke of impetus to commercial aviation, development of air commerce, hopes to accomplish something useful for progress and add scientific knowledge of the world. In terms that would appeal to Rockefeller's high sense of idealism, Byrd concluded: "The men, all great fellows, are going from a spirit of adventure and patriotism. . . . We are trying to keep the expedition on a sporting and high plane."[63]

Amundsen and Ellsworth, aboard the coal company's supply steamer *Knut Skaaluren,* left Tromsö, Norway, on April 17. Three days out, in terms reminiscent of the rapturous descriptions in his youthful journals, Ellsworth recorded seeing Spitsbergen, "no more than a golden cloud on the horizon . . . a fairy dream indeed."[64] Once ashore, the fairy dream changed to days of impatient waiting for the weather to give promise. "We would be lost in a storm such as today," he said a week after their arrival.[65] That day they sent a telegram to Riiser-Larsen, who was staying with the *Norge* in Leningrad, saying that because of sudden storms, it would be advisable not to start the flight until after June 1.[66]

This early composure vanished the next day when the *Chantier* steamed into Kings Bay carrying Commander Byrd and a crew of fifty men. "The prospect don't [*sic*] look rosy for him," wrote Ellsworth wryly, looking out at the fjord choked with floating ice.[67] Byrd was undeterred. His men, most of them connected in one way or another with the U.S. Navy, had been cranked up to a high degree of patriotism and Byrd was confident he could rely on "the eager young American spirit" of his crew to perform wonders.[68]

Byrd had counted on using the dock at the coaling station to unload his plane, but it was occupied by the *Heimdahl,* a vessel connected with the *Norge* expedition. Byrd asked that she be moved to allow the *Chantier* to unload. He was told that besides taking on coal and water, the *Heimdahl* boiler was being repaired. She could not immediately be moved away from the quay to make room for the *Chantier*. There were some suggestions, indignantly denied by Amundsen and Ellsworth, that this refusal was a deliberate effort to hamper Byrd so he would not get to the Pole first.[69]

"While I was not actually racing to be the first man to fly across the Pole," Byrd later wrote, "I knew the public construed our relative expeditions this way."[70] Unwilling to wait, he decided to take a tremendous chance. He ordered a raft to be constructed by laying heavy planks across the gunwales of four whaleboats. Then he lowered his plane, the *Josephine Ford,* onto this platform, and managed to push through the floating ice to shore.[71] "It was a very risky business," Amundsen wrote admiringly, "but its success was as brilliant as its conception."[72]

Practical considerations prompted Byrd's sense of urgency. "It was either get our personnel and equipment ashore this way or come back to the States ignominious failures," he explained.[73] And he voiced the trenchant fear that Amundsen knew all too well—that he would become bankrupt, unable to pay his debts from newspaper stories alone.[74]

Once ashore, Byrd's men dragged the plane and equipment up a long incline to a spot near the *Norge's* empty hangar. They erected a field kitchen, commenced work on the plane, and ate as they worked, with no thought of sitting down for a meal.[75] By the evening of May 1 the *Josephine Ford* was almost assembled. Ellsworth's diary confirmed, without comment, what he must have known but had not allowed himself to believe: "We intercepted a telegram sent by [Byrd] today saying he will start for the Pole as soon as possible."[76]

Amundsen, believing in the likelihood of finding a land mass in the unexplored area beyond the Pole, had consistently declared that the purpose of the *Norge* expedition was to cross the Arctic Ocean.[77] "We are not interested in the Pole," he had told Byrd six weeks earlier.[78] The evening after intercepting Byrd's telegram, he and Ellsworth invited Byrd and his reserve pilot to dinner. It was a cordial occasion. They gave Byrd and Bennett a sled, boots with senna grass (Amundsen's proven insulation against cold), and straps for their snowshoes.[79]

On May 3 Byrd and his pilot, Floyd Bennett, attempted takeoff for their first trial flight. The plane plunged into a snowdrift, breaking a ski. "Strange to see all our Norwegians running about to help him, saying what fine fellows they are!" observed Ellsworth.[80] Amundsen grumbled that it was all right to give Byrd's men help, but not to push them off.[81] He and Amundsen abandoned their former decision to wait until June. Why wait? They thought perhaps they might become the first to reach the Pole. They sent a message that everything was ready for the *Norge* to come at once.[82]

The following day tension increased when Byrd admitted that he was going direct to the Pole. Amundsen and Ellsworth sent Riiser-Larsen a message: "For heaven's sake hurry here. Getting awfully sick of this place and all the tension."

Byrd had the broken ski replaced immediately, and the *Josephine Ford* attempted a trial flight the next day; but for a second time, the skis broke. "It really began to look doubtful if they would succeed in getting up at all," wrote Amundsen.[83] Fortunately for Byrd, Bernt Balchen was in Spitsbergen with the *Norge* expedition in case a crew member gave out. He was an experienced pilot and resourceful mechanic. This could have been the moment of triumph for Byrd's competitor, but instead of withholding help from his rival, Amundsen sent Balchen over to the Byrd camp to see what he could do.[84]

Amundsen's willingness to help Byrd seems astonishing. Their rivalry was intense, and with good reason—the first to reach the Pole by air would reap significant financial rewards from publicity, photographs, and lectures, not to mention permanent historic enshrinement. Balchen had an explanation: "Practical as ever, [Amundsen] admitted to having more than one reason to wish them safely back: should something happen to them, he would have to call off his own expedition and go out searching."[85] But there was another, deeper reason. The Amundsen-Ellsworth Expedition was to be Amundsen's swan song, his farewell claim to glory. No public acrimony should tarnish his name—above all, never again would he suffer the personal guilt that had eroded his South Pole victory over Scott. When Amundsen learned of Scott's fate he told reporters that he would gladly have relinquished any honor or money if that would have saved Scott from his terrible death. But it was too late. Scott had become the hero, Amundsen the villain. Amundsen had been haunted by the memory. This was not going to be another race. If anything happened to Byrd as a result of hurrying off unprepared, once again Amundsen might be accused by the world of heartlessly allowing a competitor to die needlessly.

There was to be no race this time, but nevertheless, Balchen recognized the tension between the two camps. "All Byrd's men were imbued with one thing," he observed, "to see that Byrd got off as soon as possible. . . ." He said everyone realized that "extra honors would inevitably go to the persons reaching the Pole first."[86]

On the opposite side of the Polar Sea, Wilkins and his pilot, Ben Eielson, were still waiting in Point Barrow, Alaska, for favorable weather to attempt to take off in a single-engine Fokker on a flight to Kings Bay "for the first transpolar flight."[87] When the Kings Bay radio operator picked up a message from Wilkins asking for a weather report, it stirred up quite a bit of interest.[88]

Until the *Norge* arrived, there was little to occupy Ellsworth other than to stay in good physical condition, and this he did by snowshoeing for four hours every day, carrying a pack containing twenty pounds of canned sardines. Daily ritual required a return to camp at 4:00 P.M., "for Aqua Vit has come to be the most important and serious thing in our lives here (we have supper at 5:00 P.M.). We take our schnapps like school-boys eating forbidden fruit."[89]

On May 5 the *Josephine Ford* made a trial flight of more than two hours and showed unexpectedly low gas consumption. This resulted in a complete and sudden reversal of their plans, explained Byrd long after.[90] Instead of landing at Cape Morris Jessup, as intended, it now appeared that they would have enough fuel to go direct to the Pole and return via Cape Morris Jessup.

Deception

In light of Byrd's activities during the previous few months, his explanation for plan reversal seems all too frail. The year 1926 had opened with Byrd trying to fund his own North Pole expedition and being invited to join the Detroit Arctic Expedition as second in command under Captain Wilkins. By January 6 he had assurances of $20,000 each from John D. Rockefeller Jr. and Edsel Ford.[91] That was not enough, but two days later Byrd wired Ford, whom he likened to his commanding officer: "Vincent Astor has subscribed to my expedition and I am now in a position to start preparation."[92] Yet he asked Ford's approval of his decision to remain committed to the Detroit expedition, at least for the moment. Incredibly, Byrd assured Ford that this would not interfere with "our own expedition" because Wilkins would make his flight before April and Byrd could return to complete the work of "our own expedition," adding that Mr. Rockefeller's representative did not object.[93]

The next day, Byrd wired his acceptance to Wilkins and the Board of Control of the Detroit Arctic Expedition, care of Dr. Isaiah Bowman, who was president of the American Geographical Society. "The subscribers to my proposed expedition approve of my accompanying Detroit Arctic Expedition and I will be delighted and honored to serve as second-in-command. I do this unconditionally as I do not hesitate to follow the leadership and judgment of Captain Wilkins."[94] Before two weeks had passed, however, Byrd withdrew from the commitment. He told Bowman he was going ahead with his own expedition after all. He had received additional pledges of support and the Navy Department was anxious to have him go on his own.[95] He then wrote Ford a long appreciative letter explaining his change of mind. He thought it advisable, and it seemed more ethical too, he said, to decline the Detroit Arctic Expedition's invitation; to not expend funds on his own preparations and then chance getting lost in the Arctic first, on another venture. He emphasized the support he had from his navy friends and the tremendous interest in his expedition expressed by Admiral Moffett, Admiral Eberlé, and the secretary of the navy.[96]

Despite avowals of seeking greater fairness for subscribers and attempting to please Mr. Ford, Byrd's letters of explanation and apology to Bowman and Wilkins betrayed a sense of unease. He told Bowman he had done his best to play the game with him frankly and squarely and ethically, and asked him to set straight any of the Board of Control who felt he had been inconsiderate.[97] To Captain Wilkins went a letter of profuse apology for holding up a decision so long.[98]

All of this reveals a major reason that Byrd exhibited such frantic haste to become airborne when he arrived in Spitsbergen and found the Amundsen-Ellsworth-Nobile Expedition, which awaited only the arrival of its airship before taking off for the Pole on a flight to Alaska. There would be no glory for Byrd—or for his country, the U.S. Navy, or Edsel Ford, John D. Rockefeller Jr., Vincent Astor, and his other supporters—if he reached the Pole after Ellsworth and Amundsen. Coming in second was not what Byrd had in mind.

The 1925 and 1926 correspondence between Byrd (written on Bureau of Aeronautics letterhead that lent the prestige of official support), Ford, and Rockefeller and his representatives referred repeatedly to reaching the Pole, and it is clear that the major financial backers had been lured by that prospect. Moreover, as Byrd's preparations gained momentum, he had personally committed himself to financial obligations that could have bankrupted him had the expedition failed.

In a February 4 memorandum to the secretary of the navy, Byrd had asked for navy backing for an expedition that exploited the theme of "America first."[99] Obviously thinking of Ellsworth's coleadership of the *Norge* expedition, Byrd pointed out that his own undertaking was the only thorough-going American expedition under way; the United States should not remain entirely idle while foreigners locate and take over land that probably is in the Polar Sea and could be of value to the United States within twenty-five years as a landing place for transpolar flights of a commercial or military nature.[100] Although Byrd proposed to proceed to Kings Bay, Spitsbergen, a number of paragraphs in his memo alluded to Greenland. The Chief of the Bureau of Aeronautics approved the request for the temporary loan of navy equipment, the assignment of two experienced machinist mates, and Byrd's assignment to the expedition, with the understanding that the navy assumed no responsibility for its outcome.[101]

A few days earlier, Byrd had issued a statement announcing his plans. Apparently feeling twinges of guilt, he wrote Bowman that he specially avoided saying anything about his expedition being an all-American one, because "such a statement would be highly unethical and unfair."[102] Byrd's statement also took pains to emphasize that his plans did not put him in competition with the Detroit expedition he had just abandoned. This was not the only time Byrd sought to endow questionable tactics with a mantle of righteousness, but Bowman, wise statesman that he was, responded with encouragement. "There is abundant room in exploration for a number of enterprises," he wrote, "even if they are rivals for a given goal. . . . There is no reason why we should not all 'play the game.' "[103] Diplomatically, he mentioned Shackleton's great asset of generosity toward the other fellow.[104]

Byrd realized it was important to remain on good terms with Amundsen, who could be useful to him in future plans for Antarctica. In late February 1926 he had written Amundsen to tell him about some plans he was making "for some flights this coming spring in the Arctic." He said he hoped to fly from Spitsbergen to Cape Morris Jessup, in northern Greenland, and if he could put a base there, then toward the Pole and maybe out a little distance into the unexplored region west of the line from Cape Columbia to the Pole. He was not in competition, he wrote in an offhand yet cunning manner. For his project was "too insignificant as compared to [Amundsen's] to count for anything."[105] Amundsen was indeed being treated to a taste of his own medicine.

A Dream Shattered

On May 7, Nobile and Riiser-Larsen radioed that the *Norge* was close to Svalbard. In the Norwegian camp, excitement ran high. Perhaps Byrd would not win the race! Ground personnel assembled in their assigned positions in a V formation, prepared to grab mooring lines. A small dot appeared on the horizon, growing bigger and bigger as the ship came in. A cannon boomed a welcome. The air was calm. The *Norge* circled and threw out mooring lines. Orders to the ground crew were shouted by megaphone, some in Italian, some in Norwegian. Carefully, the ground crew led her into the protection of the hangar.

The atmosphere grew more tense. "Byrd's only thought the Pole," wired correspondent Odd Arnesen to the *Aftenposten*.[106] The plan for Greenland had apparently been abandoned. Riiser-Larsen and Nobile were of course eager to beat Byrd, and Nobile assured Amundsen that the *Norge* could be ready in three days, in spite of the need to replace the port engine and repair the torn rudder, the stabilizing surfaces, and damage to the lower level.[107] Amundsen demurred. He explained once more that the purpose of the *Norge* expedition was to explore the vast unknown area beyond the Pole—which was merely a station on the way—whereas Byrd's objective was "the Pole only." Consequently, he said, preparations would proceed in a careful and orderly manner.

Amundsen sought to crown his career by adopting the new technique of exploration by air. This, his last hurrah, must not be tarnished either by defeat or by the stigma of bad sportsmanship, so he hedged his bets. By denying he was competing with Byrd, Amundsen could preserve his options. If the *Norge* reached the Pole before Byrd, it would be another first for Amundsen. If Byrd got there first, it wouldn't appear to matter. Either way, Amundsen's reputation as an explorer would remain undimmed. "We are not running a race with Byrd to the North Pole," he declared.[108] Despite the stout assertion, it is unlikely he really felt this way. It certainly did not reflect Ellsworth's feelings. He was forty-six years old, and his position in polar exploration had not been established. This flight, as his brother-in-law had reminded him, was to be his big life effort. Being first to the Pole would add immeasurably to the distinction he sought.

"I would be less than honest if I maintained that Byrd's North Pole flight was not an annoyance," he admitted later. ". . . We had reason to be disgruntled. In the first place, Byrd's flight divided the publicity from Spitsbergen. The *Norge* expedition was costing a fortune. We needed to cash in every penny we could get as a result. We wanted the complete attention of the public, so that afterwards it would buy our book, see our picture, and attend our lectures."[109] If these considerations were so important to Ellsworth, with his large fortune, Byrd was understandably even more determined to reap the rewards of being first.

Explorers have frequently displayed a similar sense of proprietary claim. Peary, when he had his eye on the North Pole, resented Sverdrup being in the same area. Robert Scott could not believe that Amundsen would come into his own region of operation in Antarctica.[110] Byrd became indignant when Ellsworth announced his intention to go to Antarctica "to do exactly what [Byrd] proposed to do."[111] Now Ellsworth was taking just such a position. "Our expedition," he argued, "was conceived ahead of Byrd's, to which indeed we were extending the hospitality of Kings Bay, and we felt that we deserved the first chance."[112]

> May 9, 1926
> Wakened up at 2:00 A.M. by the roar of motors and cheers. It was Byrd starting for the Pole. Returns at 5:30 (16 hour flight).[113]

So read the stark entry in Ellsworth's diary record of an event that shook the world of polar exploration. For Ellsworth, it was a dream shattered.

"Among the first to meet us," wrote Byrd of his return to Kings Bay, were "Captain Amundsen and Lincoln Ellsworth, two good sports."[114] Amundsen's welcome of the victorious fliers was so emotional that he grabbed Byrd and Bennett by their arms and kissed them on both cheeks, "a thing I never believed Amundsen could do," wrote Balchen.[115]

"Byrd Flies To The North Pole, Circles It Several Times," announced headlines the next morning.[116] At the time, neither Amundsen nor Ellsworth nor any of their group questioned the validity of the flight or the performance of the aircraft.[117]

Byrd was extolled as a national hero. Two years later he still voiced satisfaction that "the dream of a lifetime at last had been realized."[118] But he was living with a dark secret.

Such record breaking is unimportant to science, of course. But if Byrd's contemporary notebook with navigation figures had been discovered in 1926 instead of 1996, or even in Ellsworth's lifetime, the story of polar exploration would have read very differently. Lincoln Ellsworth, not Richard Byrd, would have been the first American to fly over the Pole.

But overnight Byrd had become a legendary figure to millions of Americans. Finn Ronne hit the nail on the head when he said that people would not have believed any suggestion that Byrd failed to reach the Pole.[119] Furthermore, Byrd's personal magnetism and his network of political power had provided a shield that deflected well-founded doubts—even those of such authorities as Finn Ronne, Isaiah Bowman, and his own pilot, Floyd Bennett, to say nothing of the renowned meteorologist Gösta Liljequist.[120]

Not long after Byrd's flight in 1926, Bowman, at the American Geographical Society, told Ronne of his doubts that Byrd ever flew over the Pole, and that requests to examine Byrd's compilations and navigational aids were always met with evasive answers.[121] Finally, in 1930, on a long, nearly four-hour walk with Bowman, Byrd confessed that he had not reached the Pole, but "missed it by about 150 miles."[122] (Byrd and Bowman were accompanied by another man on this walk. Although in Ronne's statement the man was purposely cited as an anonymous party to Byrd's admission, he was subsequently surmised to be W. L. G. Joerg.)

Two years prior to this reported confession, Byrd had, in his own words, submitted "everything" to the National Geographic Society, including two charts with his "original records" of his observations, calculations, and plotting of positions. Based on its examination of these "original records," the society concluded that Lieutenant Commander Richard Evelyn Byrd was at the North Pole, as claimed.[123] The committee had no reason to suspect that "everything" failed to include Byrd's doctored log book—discovered among his papers some seventy years later.[124]

Floyd Bennett, Byrd's pilot, told Balchen that the truth about the North Pole flight, if known, "would shake you to your heels." Bennett's story confirmed Balchen's opinion—based on their performance tests of the plane—that Byrd never reached the North Pole, and consequently Amundsen, Ellsworth, and Nobile were the first to reach the North Pole by air.[125]

✼ 5 ✼

First Crossing of the Polar Sea

TO NORWEGIANS PICKING UP their newspaper on May 11, 1926, it seemed as if nothing mattered more than the flight of the dirigible bearing their country's name. The headline "'*Norge*' Startet" ran across the top of page one of the nation's leading newspaper, *Aftenposten*. Columns of detail filled pages one, two, and three with information about personnel, plans, photographs, and a map of the projected route.[1]

The day had dawned with a favorable weather forecast for takeoff. Natale Cecioni and the Italian mechanics ran the motors briefly to heat them for instant use. The ground crew pulled the *Norge* slowly from the hangar, being careful to avoid damage to her rubberized plastic envelope. Good-bye handshakes were exchanged, and the two leaders climbed into the crowded cabin. Sacks of sand ballast were thrown out. At 8:55 A.M. Nobile gave the order to let the ropes go, and the great 348-foot airship rose slowly, at an almost vertical angle. She was finally on her way to the unknown, carrying sixteen men, six and a half tons of gasoline, and ten and a half tons of useful load—flying suits, tents, sleeping bags, skis, snowshoes, rifles, shotguns, ammunition, a big canvas boat, and food for two months in case of emergency.

Ten men were crowded into the narrow, thirty-foot-long gondola: Amundsen and Ellsworth; Nobile, with his small dog Titina (clad in a woolen jersey); designated navigator Riiser-Larsen; meteorologist Finn Malmgren, a graduate of Upsala University who had been with the 1922–25 Maud Expedition; helmsman Emil Horgen, a first lieutenant on leave from the Norwegian navy, at the side wheel; helmsman Oscar

Wisting, who had been with Amundsen to the South Pole, at the elevator wheel; wireless men Birger Gottwaldt, a captain in the Norwegian navy, and Fridtjof Storm-Johnsen; and journalist Fredrik Ramm. At stations throughout the ship were motor expert Oscar Omdal, the flying lieutenant on leave from the Norwegian naval air force, and five riggers and mechanics, all Italians.[2]

From Kings Bay to the Pole, Ellsworth recorded successions of pressure ridges and narrow leads. He summed up his impressions as a "feeling of nothingness."[3] The main event on May 12 was festivity occasioned by his forty-sixth birthday, which they celebrated with toasts of tea, "I using Amundsen's South Pole cup," he said. Absent from Ellsworth's log is any sense of elation upon reaching the North Pole. The American flag, to which he had attached such significance in his ebullient acceptance speech at the American embassy in Oslo, no longer symbolized what he had expected—an American explorer representing his country on the first expedition to reach the North Pole by air. Byrd had already claimed that honor. Dropping the flag was now an empty gesture. His diary flatly reports: "THE NORTH POLE 90° 1:28 A.M. G.M.T. Fog cleared & the sun came out. Came down to 130 m. & with hats off dropped our flags. Both the Norwegian & American struck standing. We circle once around."[4] He makes no mention of the Italian flag.

As they moved into the unknown reaches of the Polar Sea, the real purpose of their expedition began. After four hours looking down at the sameness, a region like the one where they had landed the previous year, a note of excitement sounds in Ellsworth's notes, as imagination replaces apathy. "It's wonderful to think that with every revolution of our propellers we are wiping out unexplored territory—area never before seen by man."[5] At 7:00 A.M. on May 12, the *Norge* reached the so-called Pole of Inaccessibility (Ellsworth's diary records "LAT. 86° N"), almost halfway to Point Barrow.

There were two hours of good visibility, then fog. The *Norge* rose higher, but a ceiling of clouds pressed steadily lower. Anxiety mounted. Already flying at 1,100 meters, the *Norge* crew dared not take any action that would require releasing gas, since they had to preserve every possible degree of buoyancy to offset the increased weight anticipated from ice formation on the ship. A coating of only one millimeter over her whole surface would add several tons to her weight, meteorologist Malmgren explained.[6]

Seeking safer conditions, they flew lower—and ran into snow. Ice began to form, settling thickly on the forward section of the bow, which upset the ship's balance by making her nose-heavy. Through an open porthole, Malmgren constantly took temperature and vapor measurements, trying to determine the altitude least likely to produce this dangerous condition. Up they went again. "We thought the situation rather serious," Riiser-Larsen acknowledged.[7] Worse conditions would follow.

Pieces of ice broke off from the guys near the engines and hit the propellers, which slung the icy shards with such velocity that they hit the airship's flanks like projectiles from a machine gun. Mechanics scrambled to patch the holes torn through the canvas.[8] The motors were stopped by turns to enable the engineer and riggers to chip ice off the propeller blades.[9] Ice built up on the trailing radio antenna until it looked like white porcelain. When it encased the windmill of the wireless generator, they became cut off from the outside world and were blanketed in dense fog. Weather reports no longer came through. Just as they could expect to sight land and their need for radio contact was crucial, they could obtain no radio bearings, and their calls went unanswered.[10]

Then Riiser-Larsen thought he spotted some faint dark points sticking up above the snow. But after forty hours of virtually sleepless duty, he did not trust his eyes. A quarter hour later, he was certain that his vision was not an illusion.

"Land ahead and on the port bow!" he shouted.[11] They had realized the purpose of their expedition: first to cross the Polar Sea in the search for the great body of land believed to be the only possible explanation for the behavior of the polar tides and currents. But where were they? Because of heavy fog and thickening black clouds, they dared not head south over the mountains. So they followed the coastline west, waiting to come to a settlement where they might get assistance in hauling the ship down.

Rime began to accumulate on the bow. Malmgren monitored the air temperature continuously, seeking the altitude that would provide the warmest temperature to avoid further buildup. He alerted the vertical helmsman, who would then put the ship into a climb or descent. But even this maneuvering toward safety would bring them close to calamity. Above the clouds, the sun was high and unusually warm, generating enough heat to expand the hydrogen cells to a bursting point. Immediate cooling was essential, which demanded descent into the cloud cover. But the ship failed to respond to the vertical helm. The crew, dragging whatever heavy items lay within reach, hurried forward on the keel into the nose. The weight added to full helm and engine power was enough to force the nose downward. Then, barely in time to prevent a fatal crash, the crew scrambled aft to restore level flight. Winds and eddies were so violent at one point that the ship was thrown several hundred feet up and then down, so that a man in the stern could see its whole skeleton move in waves.[12]

When the storm abated, Riiser-Larsen took advantage of a rare moment of sunlight and climbed up onto the top of the balloon. There, he took a sun shot that enabled him to compute their position.[13] A furious storm had driven them so far off course that now, an observation showed, they were not far from Cape Serdze Kamen on the coast of Siberia.[14] They struggled back to the Alaska coast but, exhausted, abandoned the original plan to land in Nome, where they would have enjoyed a splendid welcome celebration. A settlement appeared below, with a crowd of villagers rushing out and gazing up at this apparition from the clouds. The expedition team had now been in the air, virtually without sleep, for seventy hours, and Riiser-Larsen was so weary he was hallucinating. An excellent place for landing, he announced, because "there is plenty of help; I see a whole lot of cavalry down on the shore."[15]

No one had ever landed a dirigible of this size without a trained ground crew to handle the ropes. The *Norge* circled for an hour, while riggers prepared a device to prevent the anchors from dragging when dropped. They constructed a bag 15 inches in diameter and some 60 feet in length, and stuffed it with 600 pounds of tools, spare engine parts, and pipes. Then they used steel wire to attach two ice anchors to the bag they had created for ballast.[16] Meanwhile, Amundsen, Ellsworth, Riiser-Larsen, and Nobile debated the surest method of evacuating the men. Nobile favored breaking out the canvas sides of the gondola; when they were close enough to the ground, everyone would jump simultaneously and let the ship rise and float away. Riiser-Larsen, with a financial stake in the expedition fixed at 15 percent of any profits, was reluctant to scrap a ship which they expected to sell to the Italian government for $46,000, pursuant to the original purchase agreement. Amundsen and Ellsworth agreed that the ship should be saved.[17]

Nobile brought the airship lower and stopped the engines. The crew dropped the improvised contraption to which they had attached the anchors. Gas was blown out and landing ropes were thrown to the waiting villagers, who seized them. More gas was released, and the gondola, cushioned by an enormous air fender, bumped on the ice and settled, enabling the men to leave the cabin.[18] As the last hydrogen was dispelled, the airship's great form began to sway, and then she dropped on her side, her work completed.

In the midst of his triumph, Nobile grieved to see his ship, the child of his own design and engineering skill, lying limp and lifeless on the white snowfield. "She had brought us safe and sound, for thousands of miles, to our goal, always obedient to commands. . . . She had withstood wind, snow, frost, rain and fog. Now she was lying on her side, mortally wounded—and it was I who had dealt her the deathblow!"[19]

After a seventy-hour flight, they were in Teller, Alaska, ninety miles from their intended destination. Ellsworth and Amundsen, with Wisting and Omdal, took off for Nome, leaving Riiser-Larsen and the others to dismantle the dirigible and pack her for shipment to Italy.

Tarnished Triumph

There now followed an exchange of angry charges and countercharges over reporting their story. Did the agreement with Nobile give him the right to sign press articles about the flight? Before the *Norge* left Kings Bay, Nobile had written an article that appeared in the news, and Ellsworth had expressed bitterness to the Aero Club for failing to make clear that Roald Amundsen and Lincoln Ellsworth were the expedition's exclusive leaders.[20] He was further exasperated by Nobile's insistence that for their official story, Ellsworth consent to Nobile writing "all the part concerning the flight."[21] Ellsworth sent Thommessen a stern directive: "I will not permit you to include any story by Nobile to newspapers. He is not a leader of this expedition."[22]

Thommessen's response was blunt. Nobile had the right to supply an independent supplementary story; according to contract the Aero Club was sole administrative and economic leader, and the club insisted that the parties adhere to this agreement.[23]

Ellsworth, not involved with the business side of the expedition, had no idea of the financial crisis that Thommessen was attempting to solve. There was no money to pay 200,000 kroner (almost $100,000), due in a week, to the men who had struggled through the hardships of building the hangar in Spitsbergen. The Kredittkassen (a large Norwegian bank) had recently refused a loan, but finally advanced money when Thommessen agreed to guarantee the sum personally. Furthermore, the *New York Times* was refusing payment on its contract until it received the full 25,000 words called for.[24]

Amundsen and Ellsworth booked a hotel room and, with Riiser-Larsen, Malmgren, and news correspondent Ramm, buckled down to the job, puzzled by what they could say about a 2,000-mile flight where there was nothing to see except continuous expanses of jumbled ice, yet where this very fact was in itself a historic and vital contribution to geographical knowledge. Their hope of finding new land, at least in that vast area of the Polar Sea, was unfulfilled. But for Ellsworth, their search was not conclusive and the mysterious action of the Arctic Ocean currents and tides remained unexplained. Until he was drawn by the lure of Antarctica four years later, he would continue seeking the means for further exploration in the Arctic.

Now, funds were still needed to pay for their completed expedition. Alf Bryn addressed a private plea to Riiser-Larsen: "Ongoing disagreements ... can be utterly disastrous for financial situation. ... Do something to calm the tempers. Things are very difficult here now and if there is an official break the whole thing may fall apart."[25] As the Aero Club administration saw it, Amundsen's vindictive and petty behavior, and sometimes "puerile anger," were at the root of the trouble. Amundsen confessed that he was irritated with Nobile,[26] and he was so angry with Bryn that he demanded, to no avail, that Bryn be fired.[27]

Nationalist pride fanned the flames, and by June 9, all hope of hiding the conflict vanished. The editor of the New York daily newspaper *Progresso Italo-Americano,* writing about Nobile's contribution to the expedition, expressed pride in Latin nationality, "superior en todo momento a sus detractores" ("superior in every respect to its disparagers").[28] Another press release on the same day referred to Nobile as chief organizer and as commander bearing responsibility for presenting the results to the world.

Two days later Thommessen received a telegram from Riiser-Larsen expressing indignation, anger, and despond. Nobile had no right, he said, to cosign the lead article about the expedition; the Aero Club had corresponded with Nobile behind the leaders' backs; Nobile's chicaneries had led to lies in press coverage. "All happy feelings completion expedition totally ruined for all and we all wish to creep home and forget," his message ended.[29]

Meanwhile, the Italian government kept the upper hand and refused to purchase the airship until its conditions were met. Thommessen was so uncertain of closing the sale that he started talking with representatives of the Russian government about their possibly purchasing the airship. Thommessen tried bravely to soothe Riiser-Larsen with assurances that local enthusiasm was strong, little was known of controversies, there was no need to creep home.[30] Nevertheless, venomous sentiments eroded any satisfaction that might have remained.

Ellsworth was especially unhappy over the embittered atmosphere. He remembered Nobile's cordiality immediately after the flight, and he wondered if he could draw upon the amicable feeling to help clear up misunderstandings. With high hopes, he arranged a meeting with Nobile and Amundsen to talk things out. It was a disaster. Nobile grandiloquently shouted that he had the entire responsibility of the flight.[31] Enraged, Amundsen delivered a stinging rebuke to this "strutting dreamer." What a piteous spectacle he would have presented on the polar ice if the *Norge* had been forced down, he reminded the self-important aviator, and how ridiculous his claims to effective leadership would have appeared under those circumstances.[32] After such an outburst, reconciliation was impossible.

The issue escalated to the diplomatic level. A three-page letter to Nobile from Ambassador de Martino referred to various conferences; traced and interpreted communications between Ellsworth and the

Aero Club and others; stressed the significance of the club's refusal to accept Ellsworth's position; and reported that "His Excellency the Honorable Mussolini" was distressed by Ellsworth's role in diminishing the importance of Nobile's participation and denying that he was one of the heads of the expedition.[33] The Honorable Mussolini, the letter concluded, wanted to know if—assuming that a certain article were to be published under the auspices of the Aero Club, reestablishing recognition of Italian participation—there were any other reasons for action by the Italian government to protect its interests.

Dr. Gertrude Nobile, Umberto Nobile's wife, later considered this letter especially important, because it placed blame on Ellsworth for instigating Amundsen's hostility toward her husband.[34] In light of Nobile's admission that his relations with Amundsen had been unhappy from the start, the Italian effort to place major blame on Ellsworth is unjustified.[35] In his memoir *La Tenda Rossa,* Nobile theorized that Amundsen's vindictive behavior stemmed from his awareness that the preparation and conduct of the expedition depended entirely on aeronautical considerations to which he was an outsider.[36] While Nobile may have been partly right, a more likely explanation, in view of Amundsen's many excoriating utterances, would be the old Viking's violent repugnance for a personality so different from his own. Thereafter, Ellsworth took pains to separate himself as far as possible from what developed into a lengthy, acrimonious quarrel between Nobile and Amundsen.

After their intensive stint of writing, Amundsen and Ellsworth departed for Seattle on the SS *Victoria,* the same ship that had carried Lincoln to Nome twenty years earlier. Nobile also was aboard, but the three were not on speaking terms.

"We expected to create a little stir in Seattle," wrote Ellsworth, "but were not prepared for the vociferous welcome we received."[37] The harbor was jammed with launches overflowing with cheering admirers. But when Amundsen and Ellsworth stepped to the rail to acknowledge the welcome, nobody noticed them. Nobile stood alone on the bridge, clad in the uniform of an Italian colonel, his arm raised high in the Fascist salute. Seattle's whole Italian community had turned out to greet its hero.[38] This was only the first of a long sequence of ovations for the *Norge* aviator. In late July, Ellsworth—impatient over the glorified role the media ascribed to Nobile—issued a statement to the press that Riiser-Larsen had navigated the entire flight across the Polar Sea and Nobile's only part in navigation had been to relieve the wheelman for three short periods.[39]

Possible Results

What had been proven by this $300,000 expedition? Congressman Roy O. Woodruff of Michigan, in a speech delivered to the House of Representatives on February 25, 1927, cut to the heart of the matter: the *Norge* crossing of the Polar Sea had opened the north passage from the Atlantic Ocean to the Pacific Ocean, and was a geographic achievement equal to that of Christopher Columbus. The *Norge's* flight, blazing the way for navigating and utilizing "the Arctic air ocean," would result in benefits comparable to those realized through the Panama Canal and the Suez Canal, he declared, since each provided a geographic shortcut between centers of commerce then far apart.[40] As his fancy soared, Woodruff quoted Ovid: "Let them close all passages of earth and sea; / The heavens are open and it will be / Through there that we shall pass." For Amundsen, more explorer than scientist, it was enough that they had crossed the Arctic Ocean from continent to continent. His abiding dream had come true, and he could enjoy it as the crowning achievement of his career.

Ellsworth was less satisfied. The expedition was a far cry from his youthful vision of polar exploration, of "the painfully established bases, the bitter journeys with sledges and dogs, the heroic battle against the elements."[41] It was the physical challenge that enthralled him. He seemed almost to regret the absence of some misadventure that would have called for his survival skills on the ice, that would have tested his leadership. Tepidly, he expressed gratification that he, as much as any other man, had "opened up the Arctic."[42]

In their official narrative of the expedition, Amundsen and Ellsworth asserted that no land mass existed between the North Pole and Point Barrow, but they did not postulate an explanation for patterns of the tides, which seemed to belie this assumption.[43] Anticipating future airship travel, they believed the expedition proved that meteorological conditions over the Polar Basin would not prevent a modern airship from flying across the entire expanse of the Pole.[44] The *Norge* flight had reinforced awareness of the global interrelationship of weather conditions, and when radio failure suddenly cut off their reception of meteorological reports at a critical time, the need for further scientific research in meteorology became dramatically apparent.

At the American Geographical Society, Isaiah Bowman was conscious of the need for research relating to opportunities and limitations in the use of airplanes for polar exploration, map making, and development of transpolar routes, and the society was about to publish a volume that Bowman was convinced would set a standard for years to come. He urged Byrd and Ellsworth each to contribute an article. Hoping to make his request irresistible, he wrote Byrd a seemingly innocent yet targeted appeal. Byrd's authorship, he said, would result in his name being associated with serious scholars who were interested in actual scientific problems.

At the same time, Ellsworth's scientific expertise was being contested. In his description of the voyage, Amundsen asserted that Ellsworth was occupied a good part of the time taking observations to measure the atmospheric electricity of the regions through which they passed. Further, Amundsen said that these observations were made by means of a special machine lent them for the purpose, and they were conducted at the request of the Curie Institute of Paris.[45] As if to emphasize the unfairness of Nobile's accusation that Ellsworth was only a passenger, Amundsen again declared that Ellsworth had had enough to do with his electrical observations.[46] For these observations, Amundsen had intended to take a specialist on the flight—François Behounek, a Czechoslovakian scientist "attached to the University and the Radium Institute of Prague," who had studied in Mme. Curie's laboratory.[47] Behounek had traveled to Spitsbergen on one of the expedition vessels and had placed the equipment on board the *Norge*. At the last moment, he was told he must relinquish his place on board in order to reduce weight and increase the plane's fuel-carrying capacity. He arranged with Malmgren to take measurements, and after the flight he and Malmgren jointly published the results.[48] Yet, neither of the early accounts of the expedition written by Amundsen and Ellsworth refers to Ellsworth participating in these observations, and Mme. Monique Bordry, director of the Curie Museum and Archives, assured the author that the laboratory records do not refer to Lincoln Ellsworth.[49] If Ellsworth actually made any observations to aid Malmgren, it seems they were too minimal to warrant recognition or even mention.

Why, then, was Amundsen embellishing Ellsworth's contribution, bolstering it beyond the truth? Since Amundsen was not above telling a white fib now and then, "if it made someone happier or if it extricated him from some trivial embarrassment," it seems likely that he believed this story might make his friend happier, even though it was largely a fabrication.[50]

The American Geographical Society refused to accept the unqualified statement that no land existed between the North Pole and Point Barrow. "It is probable that no land exists along the line of the *Norge*'s flight; but a final statement on this point cannot yet be made," declared a notice in the October 1926 issue of the society's *Geographical Review*. "A shallow submarine terrace might exist with every possibility of land outside the range of visibility."[51]

The unusual behavior of the polar tides remained unexplained for another decade, while geographers and oceanographers continued to speculate that it must be caused by the existence of unknown land somewhere in the Polar Sea. The search went on. The American Geographical Society suggested that the most probable areas to explore for new land were "the reported position of Crocker Land southwest to Alaska" and along the Siberian coast from Nicholas II Land eastward, "where Nansen reported sighting new islands."[52] Bowman, in frequent touch with Wilkins and Ellsworth, invited Byrd's suggestions as to the best combination of ships, planes, and dogs to accomplish such a search.[53]

Aftermath

It was fortunate for Amundsen and Ellsworth to feel personal pride in their own achievement, for it did not arouse public enthusiasm. The reason was clear. The publicity attendant on being the winner had already been exhausted by Byrd. This is similar to the situation in 1969, when the public bestowed its admiration on Neil Armstrong, the first man to set foot on the moon. Though Armstrong was lauded as a hero, there was little attention directed toward subsequent moon walkers. Also, as Riiser-Larsen explained, compared to the dramatic situation of 1925, when all six crewmen reappeared after being missing for twenty-four days, this expedition was uneventful, despite some narrow escapes. "The public were not anxious about their safety, and the interest in the expedition was consequently not particularly great."[54] Moreover, the American public had little sustained interest in an expedition that flew the Norwegian flag and, except for Lincoln Ellsworth, was made up entirely of foreigners.

On June 26, 1926, escorted by warships, Byrd arrived in New York to be greeted by an ovation "greater surely than any ever extended to a Caesar."[55] Guns boomed, whistles shrieked, airplane formations roared overhead. Between throngs of cheering people, under a deluge of ticker tape and confetti, Byrd and Bennett rode triumphantly up Broadway to City Hall, where the mayor gave them the keys to the city.[56]

Ellsworth and Amundsen had received similar adulation in Oslo a year earlier, but their arrival in New York on July 3 was a stark contrast. They were greeted at Grand Central Station by a small procession, unimpressive in itself but headed, to their astonishment, by Commander Byrd.[57] What motivated the charismatic hero? Guilt? Respect? A desire to be observed on the scene? Nobile, now promoted to general, was not present. Two weeks later, at a spectacular welcome in New York's Lewisohn Stadium, attended by twelve thousand of his admirers, Nobile was acclaimed as "the Columbus of 1926."[58] This was too much for Ellsworth. "Pole Flight Chiefs Clash On Navigation," the New York American trumpeted the following day. "General Had No Responsibility For Course Of Dirigible, American Officer Declares."[59] Ellsworth conceded that Nobile played an important part and was respected by crew and officers, but denied that he had any responsibility for directing the vessel's course.[60] After making these factual remarks, Ellsworth indulged in a vicious jab: "In fact, I doubt if he understands navigation."[61]

Nobile was outraged. "This is the first time I have ever heard the captain of a ship criticized by one who was merely a passenger," he retorted.[62] "Tart Reply By Gen. Nobile!" crowed the New York Times. "Mr. Ellsworth on our expedition was just a passenger whom I took on board at Spitsbergen and left at Teller," Nobile indignantly declared. Nobile admitted that the wealthy American had given $120,000 for the expedition—but acknowledged no other contribution.[63]

Just a passenger. Thus Nobile dismissed the man who had unforgettably demonstrated his survival ability on the ice and whose quick action had saved the entire 1925 expedition and the lives of its six members; the hero who had received the Norwegian Medal for Bravery. Nobile's words were an insult. Moreover, his intemperate attack lost sight of reality: Without Ellsworth's $120,000, there would have been no flight, no fame.

Amundsen scornfully rejected Nobile's comments as irrelevant. Nansen, Peary, Nordenskjöld, and many other leaders of earlier polar expeditions were not seamen, he pointed out; they relied on technical assistance for transportation, just as he and Ellsworth, unfamiliar with flying, relied on a specialist with aerial expertise. With aviation still in its infancy, though, the explorer had to reckon on a forced landing, and that was when leadership and experience would make the difference between life and death. What could a man inexperienced in work in ice and snow do in such an event? "Nothing, absolutely nothing. He is doomed from the start."[64] To be sure, neither Amundsen nor Ellsworth had played an operational role aboard the *Norge*. They had made the flight to find out whether land lay in the unexplored area between the North Pole and Alaska. Having provided the means of reaching the area, their function during the flight, except in an emergency, was merely to observe.[65]

Hoping to head off further confrontation, Ellsworth now said he had the greatest respect for Nobile's contribution toward the expedition's success, but felt it was unfair not to give credit to Riiser-Larsen for navigating the whole flight across the Polar Sea.[66] This statement fell on deaf ears. A cablegram to the Aero Club, signed "General Nobile," complained that Ellsworth had made some very disobliging remarks about him and his work. Consequently, the angry general said, "I have been compelled to declare that he was on the *Norge* only a passenger."[67] In a further attempt to bring peace, Ellsworth offered to issue any statement Nobile requested to emphasize that there were no differences between any of them relative to the flight, and that Italy was entitled to as much credit as any other nation, or more.[68] He emphatically repudiated a newspaper report about dissension during the flight, and assured Nobile that he would under no circumstances issue any further statement.[69]

In response, Nobile disavowed responsibility for any misunderstanding and suggested that Ellsworth could straighten things out with a public explanation.[70] Despite Lincoln's resolve to issue no further statements, he offered conciliatory comments in the press regarding Nobile's participation. He conceded that at times he might have spoken too freely, denied holding any grievance toward anyone, and expressed belief that the whole affair would be settled to the satisfaction of all concerned.[71]

How wrong he was! Nobile was in a difficult position. In correspondence with the author long after, Gertrude Nobile pointed out that Mussolini, seeking glory for Italy, instigated the dispute over leadership and name, and had insisted on the lecture tour in America, which had annoyed Amundsen.[72] Granted that Nobile was under great pressure from Mussolini, he was also strongly motivated by personal ambition, since leadership status would advance his career.

At this time Amundsen was behaving so badly[73] that Thommessen apologized to Nobile and asked him to be tolerant.[74] But the situation grew worse. The Norwegian legation in Rome reported new confrontations.[75] "Stick to your statement," Amundsen told Ellsworth. "You know as well as I that Nobile was no leader."[76] Lincoln needed no prompting. The *Aftenposten* reported that his latest words on the fracas were: "I repeat, Nobile was nothing but captain on board the airship."[77] A few days later Amundsen cabled Ellsworth that he had broken with the Aero Club completely.[78]

Despite all this, Ellsworth continued to seek further arctic involvement. He was determined to search for new land—that will-o'-the-wisp that had lured Fridtjof Nansen, Vilhjalmur Stefansson, Hubert Wilkins, and others. He hoped the Norwegian government might be interested in cooperating. He also wrote Byrd, suggesting that a combined operation could once and for all settle the problem of the Arctic by having one plane cruise down the Greenland side of the ocean looking for land, while the other plane bisected the course of the *Norge* at right angles. Since he and Byrd looked at things in about the same way, concluded Ellsworth, disagreements such as they had with Nobile would never arise.[79] At the time, Byrd was hatching a plan for a flight across the Atlantic Ocean. He sent Ellsworth a cordial but noncommittal response, addressing him as Lincoln and urging him to come for a visit. Keeping his options open, he expressed interest in combining forces with Ellsworth. "Do let me know what the Norwegian government says," he wrote.[80]

Ellsworth soon had his answer: Norway was not interested. Lincoln then suggested to Amundsen that they make one more trip together.[81] Amundsen was agreeable to another trip, but not by air. He told Ellsworth he would join in exploring Czar Nicolai Land in an ordinary ship.[82]

This was not what Lincoln wanted. He was set on a flight looking for new land. More immediately, he wanted Norway to commemorate the transpolar flight.[83] It was "rottenly unappreciative," he said, that none of the governments directly interested in transpolar flight were doing so.[84]

To those unaware of Ellsworth's lifelong loneliness and insecurity, his repeated expressions of self-pity and his impetuous criticisms were hard to understand. On occasion he was even perceived as being a rich spoiled brat. From another perspective, he found himself at middle age with vast amounts of money and noble aspirations, yet with every dream seemingly thwarted or somehow turned into disappointment. After an unhappy childhood and a disastrous relationship with his father, he yearned to gain inward solace through accomplishment, as well as public recognition for some significant achievement entirely his own. That was his constant focus, and for the rest of his life he resisted any commitment that, by tying him down to a permanent home or obligation, might interfere with this aim.

Amundsen's financial plight overshadowed every aspect of that summer and autumn, as the bankrupt explorer struggled to free himself of debts. The secretary of the Aero Club, Per Skjoldberg, met with Amundsen and his lawyer in mid-August. Skjoldberg found it impossible to deal rationally with Amundsen, who wanted to decide everything himself. Angry at everybody one moment, the great Viking was suddenly friendlier in the next, his mood changing faster than the weather. Skjoldberg concluded that it was wiser and easier just to pretend agreement and give credit to Amundsen for all decisions.[85]

Unfortunately, Ellsworth repeatedly embroiled himself in the *Norge* controversy. Thommessen was vacationing when an urgent summons reached him. Confirming requests from the Norwegian legation, the message read, "You absolutely have to come to Rome and talk to Nobile . . . as soon as possible."[86] A few days later the Norwegian newspaper *Aftenposten* received word from Weyer Internews that the Ellsworth-Nobile conflict had reopened, with Amundsen preparing to go to the United States and take Ellsworth's side.[87] Ellsworth attempted to forestall another public quarrel by immediately cabling the Aero Club: "Any statement attributed to me in criticism of Aero Club of Norway absolutely without truth. Have given no statement to press and have no criticisms whatever to make."[88] He sent a similar disavowal to the editor of *Aftenposten*.[89] But the fat was in the fire.

The following day's European edition of the *New York Herald Tribune* carried a front-page headline, "Oslo Aero Club And Nobile Plot, Ellsworth Charges." Ellsworth was "most bitter," reported the paper, and had charged the Aero Club with bad faith and collusion with Nobile by permitting him to write, in violation of their contract, on subjects other than purely technical matters. The newspaper quoted Ellsworth as saying, "They have handed me a rotten deal."[90] Lincoln sent out another denial, but now the Italian government refused to close the sale of the *Norge* until Nobile's critics issued a formal declaration acknowledging the great contribution of the Italians. There was no doubt that the government, fortified by Mussolini's specific expression of interest, held the trump card. Ellsworth had fleetingly been cast in the role of a modern Don Quixote. A detailed statement was worked out providing contractual recognition for the Italian government, and Thommessen finally sent a message that the *Norge* was happily and well sold.[91]

In the States, Bernon Prentice was serving as chairman of the American Advisory Committee to raise funds for the *Norge* expedition. As Lincoln's brother-in-law, friend, and advisor, he now sought to end the smoldering vestiges of misunderstanding, or at least to distance Lincoln from further conflict. In September, he sent identical telegrams to Henry Prather Fletcher, American ambassador in Rome;

to Salvatore Cortesi, with Associated Press in Rome; and to Commander Felice Cacciapuoti, a member of the Italian military in Florence. The telegram asked each of them, at Ellsworth's specific request, to widely publicize a message saying that the newspapers had grossly misquoted Ellsworth: he had no quarrel whatsoever, except for that regarding leadership in the expedition conceived and started the previous year by Amundsen and himself.[92] In lavish terms, the message emphasized his high respect for the Italian people, praised the splendid efficiency and loyalty of the Italian crew, and gave unreserved credit to Nobile for construction and command of the airship. With startling distortion of fact, the message ended by lauding "the splendid spirit of cooperation" of the three participating nations.

In contrast to this overture, Amundsen remained embittered and embattled, acting in such unruly fashion that the Norwegian legation in Rome wired Thommessen that someone with authority should appeal to Roald Amundsen's feeling for his mother country in order to avoid a demeaning scandal.[93] Amundsen was not to be pacified. He characterized the Aero Club as "those crooks," and expressed indignation that neither he nor Ellsworth had received any recognition, although "everybody else was decorated."[94]

Lincoln's loneliness at this time was reflected in a cable to Amundsen. "Will never forgive you if you don't spend the month of November at Grand Canyon [I] paying all expenses."[95] A second cable the next day mentioned the possibility of joining Byrd in the spring.[96]

Ellsworth also was feeling uneasy about his navigational skills, and he told Byrd he was willing to give up everything in order to become a proficient navigator.[97] Recognizing this as genuine anxiety, Byrd came directly to the point: he would be delighted to undertake teaching Lincoln what he knew about navigation. Byrd realized that if his other plans did not work out, it would be much to his financial advantage to combine an operation with Ellsworth. He said he would soon begin planning for "a trip up North together" and promised to do everything possible to help—find a suitable ship, pick out the planes, and look for a good pilot, who was also a capable mechanic.[98] In late September, Byrd told Isaiah Bowman, head of the American Geographical Society, that Ellsworth anticipated making a flight across the North Pole from Greenland and they might go up together, although nothing was definitely settled.[99] Two days later Byrd wrote Lincoln that he intended to try the transatlantic flight in the spring.[100]

The continuing indifference of the American people wounded Ellsworth deeply. "I have been entrusted by my President to carry the flag of my country to the North Pole," he had said proudly before the *Norge* flight, adding the hope that the significance of the coming event would remain through the ages "a symbol of devotion to a common ideal." Until Byrd's arrival in Spitsbergen, Ellsworth had felt assured of gaining his place in history as the first American to fly to the Pole. But that dream had been shattered by Byrd, who was now once again seeking his own flight for glory.

Depressed and floundering, Lincoln prepared to depart for his annual stay in the Grand Canyon, which he called a pilgrimage ". . . because like the sojourners to Mecca, I come from afar to worship and meditate at this 'Shrine of Nature,' and in its silent depths to find peace and relaxation from the din and strife and superficiality of modern civilization."[101]

Before going west in 1926, Ellsworth sought Bowman's advice about a possible expedition to the Patagonian Andes, and he asked what the American Geographical Society thought of his work. Bowman seized the opening. He knew Lincoln well and recognized his feelings of letdown. Here was an opportunity to motivate him to contribute serious scientific insights to the society. In an exercise of tact that nevertheless made clear his disappointment, Bowman wrote Lincoln, who was by then at the Grand Canyon:

> There are some people who wish to do a job and stop there, neither writing nor speaking upon the subject, that is, they are not interested in recording their results. This always makes a difficult situation in the scientific world. . . . We have been terribly keen about having you appear on our platform. We want to hear you. We are interested in you as an American rather than Amundsen, whom we have already honored and whose reputation is secure. . . . But you decline to speak![102]

Again concerned about the society's new book on problems of polar research, Bowman wanted Lincoln to prepare an article on the scientific results of his two polar flights—a scientific article, he stressed, not a popular one. Bowman expressed interest in Lincoln's future and encouraged him to do the thing he wanted to do, offering to help with advice, maps, instruments, and the formulation of plans addressing the critical spots where future work could be done. "But if we are to help you," he continued, in a persuasive tone, "we must have communication with you and above all, we want to have you set down your geographical results in writing."[103] He suggested that as soon as Lincoln returned from the Grand Canyon, they should sit down for several hours and talk things over in detail.

In July 1926, Lincoln satisfied his craving for exercise by hiking each day to the bottom of the Canyon and back, a distance of fourteen miles, he liked to point out, if you include the 5,000-foot vertical drop. During recuperation from influenza and pneumonia after World War I, Lincoln had pondered and written about the wonder of the heavens, after gazing through the Mt. Wilson telescope. Now he had become engrossed in the wonder of the earth as he gazed through the shimmering air at "the sublimity and grandeur of this titanic gash" in the flat plateau.[104] His restless mind probed beyond the visual splendor. Although reluctant to write the article requested by Bowman, when drawing on his extensive knowledge of geology, he did not hesitate to write about the forces that created the wonder that ". . . holds the record of the whole of earth's past life history. On the granite floor exposed in the lower gorge, life had its beginning, and its progress up through the ages can be traced from the fossils to be found in the deposits of limestone, sandstone, slates and shales, that rise thousands of feet to form the great plateau surface into which the Colorado River has chiseled the Grand Canyon."[105]

In those eons of change he perceived nature's two greatest forces—creation and destruction—forever shifting in cycles that established a balance. This was not the result of chance, he reasoned, but was the story, told by the rocks, of orderly progress—a principle running through all creation. "I had learned enough," he concluded, "to be led to believe in a God who is love, and that . . . beneath all our troubles and sorrows, the Universe is really friendly."[106] It seems that Lincoln had experienced the healing he sought, at least for the moment.

In December the Nobile conflict flared up again, like a chronic infection. Amundsen was about to set out on a lecture tour of the United States when he learned that Nobile, under instructions from Mussolini and with the consent of the Aero Club, was already lecturing to American audiences. Especially irritating was Nobile's repeated declaration that Mussolini had originated the idea of the *Norge* flight. Amundsen and Ellsworth cabled the Aero Club, withdrawing from honorary membership and expressing indignant protest against Nobile's U.S. lectures and "gross misstatements" about the *Norge* expedition.[107]

Riiser-Larsen, Norwegian navy first lieutenant and next in command of the *Norge* under Nobile, also was disillusioned and angry. He wrote Ellsworth, thanking him for the medals he provided for members of the 1925 expedition. "It will allways [*sic*] recall to me our first flight when I learned to know and appreciate your personality—a flight which I will never forget while I am trying to forget the last one as quickly as possible." Riiser-Larsen said he planned to return to his old job and settle down. "It may help me to forget Nobile, who keeps me awake night after night as he has done all this year. I am so sorry for all the troubles."[108] In the appendix to Amundsen's book *My Life as an Explorer,* Riiser-Larsen disputes Nobile's misstatements point by point.[109]

Something had to be done to counter Nobile's bombast and put him in his place. Before Christmas 1926, Ellsworth, Amundsen, and Byrd met for dinner in New York to create the Polar Legion. Qualification for membership required leadership of an expedition that had reached either the geographical North Pole or the South Pole. To give added distinction, the three explorers elected Scott and Peary posthumous members. "The Club is not likely ever to be crowded," remarked Amundsen whimsically.[110] Whatever its other purposes, if any, the Polar Legion certainly made it clear that Nobile was not recognized as a leader of the *Norge* expedition. "E stata creata apposta per escludere Nobile," complained the Italian-American press.[111]

By January 1927, Ellsworth still had not answered Bowman's letter about an article for the American Geographical Society (Byrd had replied enthusiastically to Bowman's request). Bowman asked again. "Because of your achievements up to this time and of the work that I am sure you will do independently in the future," he said, "it would seem to me a great pity if our book on Polar Research were published without a contribution from you." Anticipating Ellsworth's reluctance, he tried to make the job as simple as possible, suggesting the single idea of visibility. Expedition records would provide the data. He urged Lincoln to make a draft, then come up and have lunch and go over the whole thing at leisure. "And also over a lot of other things that we still have to discuss."[112]

One of the other things was the fact that Hubert Wilkins, an Australian, planned a flight from Point Barrow. In 1926, after he had sighted the *Norge*, fog never cleared sufficiently to permit Wilkins to make a takeoff. Now, in the spring of 1927, he was again at Point Barrow awaiting favorable weather. His project, if successful, might answer the same question that Ellsworth intended to explore on his own, or perhaps in collaboration with Byrd—did Crocker Land exist? With Wilkins positioned for a flight from Point Barrow and Byrd still uncertain about joining Ellsworth for a future expedition, Lincoln waited anxiously for developments.

By late April, Wilkins and his pilot, Carl Ben Eielson, had made a 550-mile flight over the ice. They took a sonic depth sounding that indicated 5,000 meters, which suggested the approximate limit of the continental shelf north of Siberia. After a forced landing to repair the engine—"nippy work on the fingers at 38 below"—they had taken off again, and run out of fuel. Downed again, for five days they scrambled across moving ice, each night building a house of snow, before finally reaching land and shelter.[113] It was Wilkins' exceptional mechanical ability, navigational skill, long experience in arctic survival, and imaginative handling of emergencies that kept them alive. This was the man who would later organize and manage Ellsworth's antarctic expeditions, but for the moment they were in competition. Wilkins was planning to search in 1928 for precisely the Crocker Land area that both Byrd and Ellsworth hoped to cover.[114]

Nothing came of Bowman's plea for an article on the limits of visibility. Ellsworth's contribution to the American Geographical Society book consisted of short accounts of the 1925 and 1926 flights, noting their scientific significance. In 1925, ocean soundings showed a depth of 3,750 meters, which precluded the likelihood of any land between the Pole and Spitsbergen; prevailing meteorological conditions (observed for twenty-five days) offered an encouraging prospect for aerial transportation in arctic conditions. When it crossed from Spitsbergen to Alaska, the 1926 flight became the precursor of modern transpolar flights. It passed over an unexplored area two-thirds the size of the United States, between the North Pole and Alaska, sighting nothing but icy surface where geographers and oceanographers had predicted the existence of a large body of land.

In late July 1927, Ellsworth wrote Dr. Gilbert H. Grosvenor, president of the National Geographic Society, that he had been laid up with tick fever, but was now ready to make another journey into the Arctic. He was still convinced that a body of land awaited discovery and that a flight from Etah (Greenland) to Alaska would more or less settle the question.[115] He offered to provide $85,000 if the news rights could be sold for $20,000.

By summer's end, Bowman had a fair idea of what each man was planning for next season, and what needed to be done. He expressed to Wilkins his great satisfaction in the results of his recent flight, saying that the sounding Wilkins took made it pointless to look for land anywhere near the line of his flight. However, he cautioned, geographers would never be satisfied that land did not exist between the line of the Norge's flight and Ellesmere Land until someone had covered the possible site of Crocker Land by airplane.[116] Bowman explained that Ellsworth could not complete his plans for this search until the following year, and Byrd had definitely decided to direct his attention to the Antarctic, so the field was clear. Anticipating possible sighting of new land, Bowman advised Wilkins to take someone with him as a witness.

If a significant discovery was in the making, and if Wilkins' flight did not work out, there was no reason why the National Geographic Society should not sponsor Ellsworth. Consequently, the society asked him to explain in writing his proposed expedition. He told Grosvenor that he wanted to find out if land existed in the unknown area of the Polar Sea lying north of the American archipelago, in the region of Peary's Crocker Land. Besides suitable officers and crew for a vessel, he intended to take a pilot and a good air navigator and fly from a base in northern Greenland. He said he could contribute $80,000 toward the expedition if he left in 1928 and could increase that sum to

$100,000 if he left in 1929. Unwilling to become involved in the unromantic details of preparation, he imposed a condition: the National Geographic Society should assume responsibility for the venture's business management and financial details until sailing, at which point he would assume leadership.[117]

Ellsworth then departed for his near-annual pilgrimage to the Grand Canyon, but his peace was soon shattered. Amundsen had published an article, "The *Rows* Aboard the *Norge*." "The Explorer Complains That Nobile Nearly Wrecked The Airship Over The Arctic, But Tried To Seize The Honors," a subheading ran. In several episodes in his career, Amundsen had displayed an unforgiving spirit. Now, resurrecting his quarrel with Nobile, he indulged in a malicious attack. Undoubtedly, he received a large payment for this flamboyant piece of writing, which was filled with anti-Nobile invective: erratic nature, brazen effrontery, insolent suggestion, brutal lack of consideration, imperious manner, illusions of greatness.[118]

Nobile was incensed. The article, "containing the most incredible accusations, insults, trivial and impertinent complaints," was brought to his attention by King Victor Emmanuel, who requested that he answer it at once.[119] This he did, and eventually devoted many pages of *My Polar Flights* to refuting Amundsen's charges, point by point. He also wrote a polite letter asking Ellsworth, "gentleman as you are," to confirm his own contradictions of Amundsen's allegations.[120] The letter finally caught up with Ellsworth in Grand Canyon National Park. Lincoln was not happy with the request. Two scribbled drafts testify to his apprehension about tactfully handling this hot potato.[121] Previous statements had exploded in the press and he was determined not to get caught again. He finally responded with a letter denying controversy, grievance, or prejudices of any kind so far as he himself was concerned. He assured Nobile that the glorious memories of their flight had enabled him to banish from his mind everything disagreeable.[122]

Twenty-four hours later, Ellsworth poured out his heart to Amundsen in five longhand pages, starting, "I am sorry you had to return home for I miss you, as I always do, when you are away. I guess I will never have two such wonderful years again and [*sic*] we had together." He summarized Nobile's letter and his own reply, concluding: "Don't you ever be afraid I'm going to give him any chance to use me as a prop, I'm with you 100% as I always have been, and you know it. Your troubles are mine too as far as Nobile is concerned and I'm always right there when it comes to fighting for our just rights. If anybody ever says anything against you they have got to answer to me." He added, "Nobile's letter was most polite though, he showed no enmity whatever."[123]

"You gave him the right answers," Amundsen replied, "and I know you always will be 100% with me." But he was not mollified. He characterized Nobile's recent request to Lincoln as "a little unbalanced," and wondered whether Nobile was mentally all right. He also complained indignantly that Thommessen had given Nobile "free use of our hangar and mooring mast in Spitsbergen for three years!" He told Ellsworth he would get his best lawyer to fight Thommessen to a finish, promising to keep Ellsworth entirely out of the fight.[124]

Either Amundsen had failed to learn the facts, or he deliberately chose to disregard them. Rather than allow the masts and hangar in Spitsbergen to deteriorate, the Aero Club, with authority to handle the business affairs of the expedition, had prudently arranged for the Italian government to pay the expense for conserving and maintaining them, since it was planning a new polar flight under Nobile's command.

Breaking his promise to keep Ellsworth out of the fray, Amundsen asked for his support in refuting Nobile's claim of coleader status, his public lectures, and his writing about the *Norge* expedition, all of which violated contractual restrictions. In a long memorandum, Amundsen's attorney Michael Puntervold traced the episodes leading to confrontation: the March 28 agreement expressly named Amundsen and Ellsworth as the two leaders, Riiser-Larsen as vice leader, and Nobile only as airship commander. Amundsen insisted this original agreement had been illegally canceled when Thommessen signed an entirely new agreement with Nobile without consulting the others. Seeking Lincoln's confirmation, Amundsen closed his letter, "I am—as you will understand—left alone but I am a good fighter."[125] That was the time for Lincoln to honor his ringing affirmation, "Your troubles are mine too as far as Nobile is concerned." He assured Amundsen that he had not agreed to any alterations in the March 28 document signed in Rome and that Puntervold's statement was correct.

With Byrd heading for the Antarctic and Wilkins planning the arctic flight that had been Ellsworth's longtime objective, Lincoln was in a quandary. The National Geographic Society seemed favorably disposed to make a moderate grant to support his search for new land, but postponed commitment until the results of current expeditions would become known. Restless over the uncertainty, Ellsworth told his trusted advisor Harold Clark that if it wasn't for his desire to find that new land in the Arctic, he would spend the rest of his life in Africa studying and collecting for the American Museum.

On April 22, 1928, Wilkins and Eielson completed a flight of 2,200 miles from Point Barrow to Spitsbergen, of which 1,300 miles was over the unknown area between Point Barrow and Greenland. This was the region that had consistently held Ellsworth's interest since his involvement with Borup in 1912. At the time, no one imagined that further search for land would be futile, or that the answer to Harris' puzzle lay hidden beneath the ice floes of the Polar Sea. More than thirty years passed before the mystery was solved. On April 27, 1938, Russian scientists discovered a submerged mountain chain, the Lomonosov Range. Sometimes reaching a height of 2,000 meters above the ocean floor, it stretched 2,000 kilometers, from north of the New Siberian Islands toward Ellesmere Island.

Lincoln recognized that Wilkins had pulled off a great flight, but he wrote to Amundsen: "If Wilkins hasn't really penetrated the Crocker Land area I'm going there next summer." His feelings rushed from his pen: "Wish there was some way we could be together again because I am forever missing you." The letter concluded, "With kindest regards . . . I am, Always your loyal friend, Lincoln Ellsworth."[126]

There was no reply. A few weeks later, Amundsen, on a rescue mission to save a man he scorned, vanished in the Arctic.

FIGURE 11. The dirigible *Norge* arrived at Kings Bay, Svalbard, on May 7, 1926.

FIGURE 12. A special hangar was constructed to house the huge airship *Norge*.

FIGURE 13. Ceremony in which Italy turned over the *Norge,* which had been purchased by the Amundsen-Ellsworth Expedition; in the front row are General Umberto Nobile (third from left), Roald Amundsen (center), and Lincoln Ellsworth (right).

FIGURE 14. Having made the world's first transpolar flight, the *Norge* crew posed with its leaders: (seated in front) Amundsen, Ellsworth, and Nobile, holding his dog Titina, who also made the trip.

FIGURE 15. General Umberto Nobile, 1885–1978.

FIGURE 16. Roald Amundsen, Richard E. Byrd, and Lincoln Ellsworth, celebrating their formation of the exclusive Polar Legion, whose membership comprised only those who had reached one of the Poles. While Scott and Peary were named members posthumously, Nobile was not invited to join this club.

FIGURE 17. Schloss Lenzburg, the castle in Switzerland that Lincoln inherited from his father and visited for the first time in June 1929.

FIGURE 18. Lincoln Ellsworth standing alongside the Lenzburg castle gate in 1929.

~*~ 6 ~*~

This Hero Business

"ALL SMOKE AND NO FIRE," Lincoln wrote in 1928, looking back at his two-year struggle for a medal to honor his polar work.[1] Because he believed that great events should be celebrated with tangible objects, following the 1925 flight, he ordered medals for each member of the expedition and asked Amundsen to present them, calling them "but a feeble reminder of friendship and service rendered."[2] He regretted that his government had given him no reminder of service rendered on the 1926 *Norge* flight, where he represented America on the first crossing of the Polar Sea. He told Amundsen it was "rottenly unappreciative."[3]

Pondering the long struggle, he wrote to Commander Richard E. Byrd: "I only want *some* recognition from my country so I can go on in the Arctic."[4] Those six words, "can go on in the Arctic," were a driving theme behind Ellsworth's determination. He remained convinced that undiscovered land lay somewhere in the Arctic and he wished to find it. But he lacked sufficient recognition, and his leadership credentials, in particular, were underappreciated. His part in the 1925 and 1926 expeditions had been overshadowed by the illustrious name of Roald Amundsen. Prestige, gratifying as it might be for personal reasons, was equally important as a practical matter; it provided leverage.

In January 1927, George Kunz, president of the American Scenic and Historic Preservation Society, arranged a joint meeting with the American Museum of Natural History, at which Ellsworth and Amundsen were awarded gold medals. At the recipients' request, sixteen similar medals were cast in bronze to honor those who had signally contributed to the success of the expedition.[5] On one side the medals showed the route of the *Norge;* the reverse side bore the words "First Crossing of the Polar Sea—under Leadership of Roald Amundsen and Lincoln Ellsworth." Determined to see Ellsworth further honored, Kunz wrote to Senator Hiram M. Bingham of Connecticut, urging that Ellsworth be awarded the Congressional Medal of Honor.[6]

One of the museum medals was sent to the Reale Societa Geografica, but the acrimony beclouding the entire *Norge* expedition was as severe as ever. The full weight of the Italian government was behind the effort to obtain recognition for Nobile as one of the leaders. Following instructions of his government, N. G. de Martino, the royal Italian ambassador, returned the medal. "This medal cannot be accepted by an Italian Scientific Institution," he wrote, "until in it be paid homage to the historical truth which cannot but recognize the important part taken by General Nobile in the construction of the Airship and in the piloting of it during the memorable Polar Trip flight."[7]

Lincoln's plans were at a standstill until October, when he hoped to hear from the National Geographic Society about support for a flight to search for new land in the Arctic.[8] By midsummer he was losing heart. In the midst of his ongoing self-doubt, it was not encouraging to recall that Italian recognition had been extended even to Nobile's little dog Titina, awarded a gold medal as the only domestic animal that had ever crossed the North Pole![9] He was further stunned to learn from his cousin General Charles E. Dawes, who as vice president of the United States presided over the Senate, that Senator Bingham was not going to back up Kunz's request because the expedition was supposedly an Italian one.

"How could anyone think such a thing?" Lincoln asked Byrd, in view of Amundsen's article in the *World's Work* for August. "It is the truth as I know it, everything he says," Ellsworth continued.[10] He went over the facts, point by point. The airship did not fly any Italian flag, and clearly the expedition was not an Italian one. Proudly patriotic, Ellsworth pointed out that President Coolidge had given him a flag to drop at the North Pole, and that he had carried a duplicate across to give the president so the American people would have a symbol to commemorate the crossing of the Polar Sea. His desire for recognition was not entirely personal, he declared; it also reflected his wish for Americans to recognize the part their country played in the project.

In mid-September Kunz finally heard from Bingham. The senator objected to giving Ellsworth the Congressional Medal of Honor because the flight of the *Norge* over the North Pole was not really an American enterprise. It brought little, if any, credit to the United States, and though financed by American capital, was not carried out in such a way as to promote the building of *American* airships and the recognition of *American* skill and resourcefulness in aeronautical and air navigation.[11]

In a further effort to persuade Senator Bingham, Kunz suggested that the United States government emulate Norway and the Royal Geographical Society by authorizing a medal for the *Norge* flight. But the senator's response was uncompromising. Ellsworth's financial help was not for the sake of America, he repeated, and no credit came to American aeronautical science or American aerial navigators. The senator had little patience with "wealthy Americans who bring more credit to foreign countries than to the land which nourished them and gave them the means which they use in their enterprises."[12]

Kunz was not pleased by this cavalier dismissal. Aware of the power of Byrd's long experience and extensive contacts and influence with political leaders in Washington,[13] he sent Byrd a comprehensive summary of Lincoln's participation in arctic exploration which had been prepared by an experienced editor, Kenneth M. Disbrow.[14] Byrd's response was heartening. He expressed high admiration and a strong conviction that Lincoln had not received the recognition he deserved from his country. Calling the flight one of the most remarkable exploits in all history, he promised to do all in his power to obtain justice.[15]

At this time Byrd was riding the crest of fame for an accomplishment to which he had no rightful claim. His flight, moreover, had no scientific value compared to that yielded by the geographical and meteorological observations gathered on the *Norge* flight. Unable to disclose his perfidy, he may have felt that literary atonement was better than none. In his 1928 book *Skyward*, he lavished praise on the *Norge* flight as "one of the greatest feats of exploration in all history . . . which will shine through future ages as the feats of Columbus, the Cabots, Magellan, and other great navigators of the past shine through our age."[16]

An interesting event early that year was a speech to Congress delivered by Representative Roy O. Woodruff of Michigan regarding congressional medals, an honor awarded to Commander Richard E. Byrd and Warrant Machinist Floyd Bennett for their North Pole flight. Byrd's citation read, "For distinguishing himself by courage and intrepidity at the risk of his life in demonstrating that it is possible for aircraft to travel in continuous flight from the now inhabited portion of the earth over the North Pole and return," a short, succinct tribute.[17] By contrast, ten of the sixteen pages of Woodruff's entire speech were comments, both factual and euphoric, centering on the scientific observations, accomplishments, and commercial significance of the first crossing of the Polar Sea, three days later, by the Amundsen-Ellsworth-Nobile flight. Added to the Byrd flight, declared Woodruff, the Amundsen-Ellsworth-Nobile expedition had "revolutionized all methods in Arctic exploration."[18] It was a fine tribute, but it contained no suggestion of an award for Ellsworth.

On December 6, 1927, however, Royal S. Copeland of New York introduced Senate Bill 815, proposing to present a Congressional Medal of Honor to Lincoln Ellsworth, "the distinguished American explorer, who by his conspicuous courage, sagacity and perseverance made his famous polar flight of 1925, and the transpolar flight of 1926."[19] This was encouraging. Furthermore, Vice President Dawes, Lincoln's cousin, and a powerful source of support for him in Washington, wrote Lincoln: "I still have your matter in mind and if it were not for one Senator there would be no trouble about it, in my judgment." He said he would do what he could with Senator Bingham, and assured Lincoln that his wonderful achievement deserved proper recognition from his government.[20] Lincoln forwarded this letter to Byrd with a scribble, "Really, Dawes is back of all the interest in this matter. Wouldn't it be a good plan for you to make known to him your interest? I know he would appreciate it."[21]

But Byrd was on a lecture tour, and when nothing happened immediately, Ellsworth prompted him further, sending two telegrams in late January 1928.[22] The first message related Dawes' information that Bingham was the only obstacle. "If you will write or see him I will be your debtor forever," Lincoln said. The second telegram, three days later, read: "I must rely upon you to try and get recognition for our flight." In mid-February he wrote Byrd. "I really haven't a lot of hope left as to recognition, but I'm not going to forget the men who helped me and took an interest. Those are *real* friends and you are one of them," he said. "From now on, I am going to call you Dick."[23]

Despite a crippling burden of lectures, fund raising, and planning for his own next expedition, Byrd swung into action, making time to advise on strategy and to implement it with letters and visits to influential members of Congress whom he knew personally. Hoping to soften Bingham's adamant position, Byrd addressed the senator in a masterful six-page letter flowing with tact, flattery, and facts. He described Ellsworth's career, his efforts to make it an all-American expedition, and how "the force of circumstances barred the way to him. . . ." He continued, "It is my humble opinion that Ellsworth's struggles, bound by his ultimate great achievement, should be rewarded by Congress." In conclusion, he wrote, "You and I also have aviation in common and these things give me courage to urge you in the strongest terms to allow Lincoln Ellsworth to receive some recognition."[24]

Two weeks later Ellsworth and Harold Clark went to Washington where they conferred with Vice President Dawes, Congressman Burton, Senator Copeland, and Senator Joseph T. Robinson, about a Congressional Medal for Ellsworth, or perhaps instead, a Langley Medal. This was an award granted by the regents of the Smithsonian Institution to a very small number of men who made significant contributions to the science of aeronautics—among them Wilbur and Orville Wright (1909) and Charles Lindbergh (1927).[25]

On April 2, 1928, Ellsworth thanked Byrd for what he had done in Washington, noting that "everything hinges on a letter that you are to write to Senator Robinson."[26] Byrd's letter, already in the mail, noted Ellsworth's successive efforts to reach the Arctic with airplanes: his talk with Peary, intercessions by Henry Fairfield Osborn, contact with Gilbert Grosvenor of the National Geographic Society, his request to join Amundsen on the "Maude" [*sic*], and attempts to get flying training before World War I. Trying to counter one of Bingham's major objections, Byrd emphasized that Ellsworth had made every effort possible to obtain backing in America, but without success. The *Norge* flight, "one of the greatest pieces of exploration in all history and one of the greatest flights on record," would not have been possible "without the initiative and accomplishment of Lincoln Ellsworth. His was a very great accomplishment and has earned him a place in history. His success was the result of long endeavor and years of preparation, and it seems a pity that our country has given him so little credit."[27]

Italia

Meanwhile Nobile was preparing for his own quest for fame. He felt demeaned by the treatment he had received since the *Norge* flight and by Amundsen's vicious public attacks. Determined to demonstrate his worthiness in the eyes of the world, he undertook to retrace the *Norge* voyage to the Pole by commanding his own expedition in a sister ship, the *Italia*.

After months of worldwide publicity, the *Italia* took off from Spitsbergen on May 23, 1928, for a voyage calculated to bring glory to Fascist Italy, Il Duce, and General Nobile. Early on the morning of May 24, radios around the world announced success. The *Italia* was over the Pole. Nobile first dropped the Italian flag, followed by the six-foot wooden cross especially blessed by Pope Pius XI for the occasion.[28] The crew, caught up by a combination of solemnity and jubilation, shouted "Nobile forever!" and "Long live Italy!"[29] After two hours of circling, they turned back toward Spitsbergen. The next day at 2:20 A.M., wireless messages from the *Italia* abruptly ceased. On May 26, polar experts gathered to organize and coordinate search efforts. Amundsen volunteered at once to head the relief expedition. Although he detested Nobile, he spoke of "the sentiment of solidarity which must bind men, especially those who risk their lives for the cause of science." In light of this sentiment and shared sense of mission, he declared, "our personal resentments must disappear."[30]

Matching words with action he at once set about thinking of men and equipment for the job ahead.[31] But he had failed to gauge the ramifications of the situation. In Italian eyes, ignominy had replaced glory. A splendid achievement had ended in disaster. Italian pride was shattered, Mussolini's dream in ashes.

In view of the unremitting scorn Amundsen had publicly expressed for Nobile, it was not surprising that Italy did not wish to take part in this Norwegian effort.[32] However, Amundsen's position in polar exploration required his involvement, and he was not to be thrust aside.

"Fifty thousand dollars needed relief expedition. How much will you contribute? When can you come?" he cabled Ellsworth.[33] Ellsworth had just undergone surgery. Deaf in one ear, he was under a doctor's care in New York after having both sinuses opened repeatedly due to an infection. Nevertheless, on June 1 he cabled Ambassador Henry Prather Fletcher in Rome that he was ready to start for the Arctic in search of Nobile if the Italian government so desired.[34]

On May 29, 1928, four days after the *Italia* fell silent, the U.S. Congress had voted a gold medal to Umberto Nobile, and also authorized the president of the United States to present a gold medal to Lincoln Ellsworth, "the distinguished American explorer, who, by his conspicuous courage, sagacity, and perseverance, made his famous Polar flight of 1925, and the transpolar flight of 1926."[35] Ellsworth wired Byrd: "In the passage of the bill yesterday, I am deeply conscious of my debt of gratitude to you for having made it possible."[36] His message to Harold Clark was more casual. "I hope Congress will remember it passed a bill," he wrote, "and not forget to give the medal."[37] The whimsy was not misplaced; he waited nearly three years longer for the presentation.

On June 2, a Russian amateur wireless operator in a village near Archangel reported hearing faint distress signals.[38] Six more days of anxious evaluation of similar messages were required to determine their origin and finally establish direct contact with the *Italia* crew.[39] Search plans gained momentum. The Russian icebreaker *Krassin*, which had been out of service for two years, was hastily readied for sea. With a plane on board, she headed north, where she soon became the center of an international search involving fourteen ships from Norway, France, and Russia, plus nineteen airplanes and seaplanes.[40]

Amundsen was determined to do what he could. He arranged with the French government for a seaplane and crew under command of Lieutenant Commander René Guilbaud. On June 18, Amundsen and Lief Dietrichson left Tromsö, Norway, on a search mission.[41] Their plane vanished. Hours passed, then days, with no word of its fate. The American legation in Oslo received a cablegram from Ellsworth on June 30 asking whether he could assist in any way in the search for Captain Amundsen and his companions.[42]

On July 3 the *New York Times* reported that Bernon Prentice, Lincoln's brother-in-law, had described Amundsen's act as one of the great examples of heroism and sportsmanship in aviation. He announced he would be glad to forward to Oslo all contributions to the relief expedition financed by the newspapers of Norway.[43]

How did it happen that Ellsworth—who only a few days before Amundsen disappeared had offered to join in the *Italia* rescue— delayed nearly a fortnight before offering to search for his fellow explorer and closest friend? Newspapers each day carried front-page stories of the *Italia* disaster, as well as the search. Nothing more came from Ellsworth. Harold Clark, ever protective of his friend's interests, felt obliged to tell Lincoln he was concerned about this continued inactivity. After this meeting, he wrote to Ellsworth's New York attorney, Charles S. McVeigh, describing how he had frankly explained his fears that Lincoln's apparent indifference would give rise to unpleasant public comment. He said that Lincoln did not agree with that point of view, and had resented his dealing with the situation so bluntly.[44]

Notwithstanding Ellsworth's indignation, Clark's initiative produced results. "Ellsworth Plans Amundsen Hunt. Offers Services In Effort To Trace Explorer Who Went To Save *Italia.*" On July 24, 1928, this headline ran in a special edition of the *Plain Dealer,* Clark's hometown Cleveland newspaper.[45] An announcement in the *New York Times* made public a cablegram Ellsworth sent to the American legation in Oslo, offering to search, and the mystery of Ellsworth's seeming lack of concern about his friend was at last explained. "When Captain Amundsen was first reported lost," the announcement said, "Mr. Ellsworth volunteered to go to his rescue, but an attack of sinus trouble confined him to the Presbyterian Hospital and prevented him from doing so. He has now been discharged and is ready at once."[46] This was not the only time in his career that pride in his reputation had kept Ellsworth from admitting physical debility.

In early September, hope for Amundsen vanished when a pontoon from his plane was found off the coast of Norway.[47] No other clue was ever discovered. Amundsen was lost over the land where, "when it comes time, I would prefer to die," Lincoln once wrote. From the depths of his grief welled up expressions of devotion to his mentor and fellow explorer. "This supreme adventurer who so often tempted fate . . . has at last paid the supreme sacrifice and journeyed into the unknown. . . . Beyond the last frontier—beyond even the outermost rim of discovery, toward that huge tract in the Polar Sea marked 'unexplored' lay my dreams! . . . they never could have found realization had not chance—or was it fate—brought us together?" Ellsworth spoke of intimacy that never dulled and the magic of Amundsen's personality. Beneath Amundsen's reserve, he perceived "the spirit and enthusiasm of a boy." He added, "He was not a happy man. No idealist ever is." A fragment of poetry concluded the tribute:

So SKOAL! Roald Amundsen:
The winter's cold, that lately froze our blood,
Now were it so extreme might do this good,
As make these tears bright pearls, which I would lay
Tombed safely with you till doom's fatal day;
That in thy solitary place, where none
May ever come to breathe a sigh or groan,
Some remnant might be extant of the time
And faithful love I shall ever bear for you[48]

On December 14, 1928, the bells of every church in Norway tolled from sunrise to sunset. Vast crowds stood bareheaded in the streets of Oslo and in every town in the Kingdom, silent for two minutes in memory of their great explorer.[49] Every flag flew at half staff.

As they dwelled on their national hero, the Norwegians extended generous recognition to Ellsworth for all he had meant to Amundsen and the Norwegian people. A message to him signed "Prime Minister

Mowinckel" ended, "The Norwegian government begs you to accept its grateful greetings."[50] A message from Frois Froisland, of the newspaper *Tidens Tigen* read, "I beg to convey to you, his best friend and most faithful companion, sincerest thanks and respectfullest compliments in remembrance of your inestimable services and unbreakable friendship for our national hero. Your splendid words commemorating Amundsen will be read all over Norway with deepest interest and sympathy."[51]

The story of the *Italia* disaster, subsequent rescue of survivors by plane and ship, and melodramatic but plausible allegations of cannibalism were headline news for many weeks. It had taken only two minutes for catastrophe to strike, for desperation to crush a sense of celebratory elation.[52] In the airship's crash, Nobile's leg was broken, three men were injured, and one died. On the ice, the five able survivors set up a tent, which they painted with red stripes, using aniline dye carried to mark the snow to attract a rescue party. One episode of the saga gives insight into how close the *Norge* had come to similar destruction, and how justified Amundsen's criticism of Nobile had been at the time. The *Italia* suddenly had begun to lose altitude. Engine power was increased, but the rapid descent continued, with a plunge from 1,500 feet to 250 feet within moments.[53] The ship "plunged like a shot bird," said survivor François Behounek, the Czech scientist who had been on board the *Italia*.[54] When the control cabin smashed on the ice, its ten occupants and their gear were flung out of the craft. Thus lightened, the balloon, carrying the rest of the men, soared aloft and was carried away by the wind. As the survivors worked to collect their belongings they saw a column of black smoke rising in the distance, where the balloon had drifted.

According to Amundsen, Nobile had nearly wrecked the *Norge* in the same way by carelessly turning the wheel that governed vertical control, without realizing the ship was speeding downward. Riiser-Larsen had sprung to the wheel just in time and by "a matter of inches" prevented the rear motor from smashing against the ice.[55]

In December 1928 Bowman sent a confidential letter to F. H. Hooper of the *Encyclopedia Britannica* stating that the American Geographical Society had decided to call the *Norge* flight "The Amundsen-Ellsworth Expedition," leaving off the name of Nobile. The Italian captain, he explained, had been hired and paid as a member of the crew; the airship was purchased outright from the Italian government, and the attachment of Nobile's name to the expedition was for Italian consumption only; Amundsen and Ellsworth had originated the expedition and provided for its financing.[56] Bowman conceded that it was appropriate to refer to Nobile's technical position with the expedition, but deftly suggested that the pilot's last expedition, entirely his own, should be the flight from which his record should crystallize, rather than from the successful Amundsen-Ellsworth flight, where he played a subordinate role.

An official Italian committee of inquiry held sixty sittings on the *Italia* disaster and on March 3, 1929, reported its conclusion to Mussolini: Nobile was responsible for the wreck. The committee censured the general, his broken leg notwithstanding, for having been the first to leave the ice floe.[57] Stripped of his rank, he spent the next few years in Russia.

For Ellsworth, this was a period of near despair, despite the concern and efforts of loyal friends to help him. "The thing seems hopeless," Ellsworth wrote Byrd about the proposed award of a medal. But at that very moment, a letter to him was in the mail from the vice president, and it was signed "your cousin, Charles G. Dawes." The Senate Committee on Commerce, said Dawes, had favorably reported the bill, when amended to award a gold medal instead of the Congressional Medal of Honor originally proposed.[58] A week later the Senate passed the bill.[59] The agonies were over at last. Ellsworth would have his medal, his country's recognition, and his self-respect.

A proposal by Vice President Dawes to award Ellsworth and Byrd the Langley Medal was frowned upon by the reviewing officer for the Smithsonian, H. I. Cone, who was also vice president of the Daniel Guggenheim Fund for the Promotion of Aeronautics Inc. Cone declared himself unable to find anything in "the gallant and heroic services" of either candidate that fell within the scope of the Langley Medal award to "those who distinguish themselves in advancing aeronautics by scientific investigation."[60] A few days later, however, it became evident that somewhere the exercise of persuasion had been convincing. Cone reversed his position and recommended awarding the Langley Medal to both men. In a separate memorandum he pointed out that Ellsworth's accomplishments and support had revolutionized arctic exploration by the use of aircraft in this work, and brought nearer the passage of commercial aircraft "over the Arctic areas heretofore inaccessible to man."[61] Disappointment soon followed. A specially appointed committee of distinguished experts advised Dawes that neither the achievements of Ellsworth nor Byrd came within the guidelines of the Langley Medal award.[62] More than a year later, however, the committee modified its decision and awarded the medal to Byrd.[63]

⁊ 7 ⁊

Friends in Need

1929–1930
Ellsworth was spared one ordeal endured by virtually every great explorer, with the possible exceptions of Nansen and those who were sent on government assignments—the constant, crushing need to obtain financial backing. Amundsen became embittered by financial woes and bankruptcy; Byrd wrote to John D. Rockefeller Jr., in tones of near despair; Wilkins hit the target with his comment that you can't succeed without money or political backing. Among the group, Ellsworth alone was free to go where he wanted without scrounging for money. The financial crash of 1929 rocked the industrial world, wiped out fortunes, and ushered in an era of extreme personal hardship for families throughout the United States. Lincoln had no conception of those realities. Life for the Ellsworth family went on as before. In addition to anything laid aside, he could count on $115,000 a year (more than a million dollars in present purchasing power) from trusts and bond interest.[1] He could now finance his own expedition, but it could not be said that he *enjoyed* his wealth. As his diaries, letters to family, and other writings all reveal, the only thing he truly enjoyed was escape. Escape to where, was the question.

He was torn by uncertainty. Had Wilkins' 1928 flight over the Polar Sea, from Point Barrow to Spitsbergen, ruled out the possibility of land or should further search be made? Or would Antarctica perhaps offer greater opportunities? He turned to Isaiah Bowman for advice. Excited at the mention of Antarctica, Bowman responded at length.[2] Knowing Lincoln's ambitions and temperament, he presented challenges calculated to kindle enthusiasm and galvanize interest into action.

"Here is the longest stretch of unexplored coast that there is in the world," he wrote, suggesting that Lincoln explore the African Sector, which spanned over 100 degrees, nearly one-third the circumference of Antarctica. "It is the biggest thing of its kind not only in Antarctica but in the Arctic as well." Taking off from a mother ship, a succession of photography flights by seaplane could penetrate 500 or 600 miles inland and then return to the ship, which would move along to a new point, where the process would be repeated.

"What a map we could draw! . . . How I would like to see you undertake it!" Bowman enthused. "It would be exactly suited to a man of your broad experience and your training in navigation." After making some observations about safety, Bowman glorified the opportunity with ringing words: there was no other work of such magnitude still waiting to be done. This show would represent the climax of Ellsworth's career. Whatever useful work he might do subsequently, he would never tackle a bigger job, for bigger jobs did not exist. To Bowman, the Antarctic was the place for Lincoln's next expedition. He estimated the cost at $250,000.

Ellsworth, then at Coronado Beach, California, had much to ponder. His future depended in part on what others were planning. As he studied the maps Bowman sent, his eyes were repeatedly drawn to the vast unmarked area between the Palmer (now Antarctic) Peninsula and the Ross Sea. Although riskier than Bowman's proposed short sorties, a 2,000-mile flight across that unknown expanse would surely prove more rewarding from a geographic viewpoint. And the bolder venture was more to his liking.

On the same day that Bowman wrote to Ellsworth, he also wrote Harold Clark: "I want to stay in touch with Lincoln for I feel that he needs the friendship of disinterested men who can advise him to his best interest. He has a great stock of energy that should be turned to good account. Moreover, I find him to be a likable character."[3] Clark needed no prompting; he was already trying to help. Responding to Lincoln's wish to secure a home that he could fix up in his own way, Clark offered three suggestions—Evamere Hall, James Ellsworth's old place in Hudson, Ohio; Fairacre, in Hot Springs, Virginia, on which

Clark secured a one-week option to permit Lincoln's consideration; and a property in Woodstock, Vermont, "a very unusual property," about which he enclosed various documents for study.[4]

Lincoln dismissed all three suggestions. He was drawn to the sound of ocean breakers pounding on the beach at Coronado, where he often stayed at the local hotel, and to nature's splendor in the Grand Canyon, the desert, and the awesome polar continents. "I shall give up altogether the idea of ever settling in the east," he wired Clark.[5]

Despite other preoccupations, Lincoln found time to compose and send to Hans Fay, Norwegian consul general in New York, a message of esteem for Fridtjof Nansen, "a hero of mine whose name is synonymous with high purpose and noble achievement. . . . No tale in all adventure so thrills me to read as his *Farthest North* from which came my first urge to go there."[6]

A month later, Lincoln was devastated by the death of the only person in the world with whom he felt comfortable and secure. On February 22, his beloved sister Clare Prentice died of pneumonia. To her he had confided his loneliness and ambitions, his secret agreement with Amundsen, his *coup de foudre* for Helene. Clare always understood, and gave comfort. She had rescued him from despair when James Ellsworth, by means devious and otherwise, sought to prevent him from joining Amundsen in an expedition to the North Pole. If Clare had not courageously confronted their stern father, Lincoln would never have gained a foothold in polar exploration. Coming so soon after the death of Amundsen, Clare's death was a crushing blow.

Fairfield Osborn, a longtime family friend, was quick to recognize this. He wrote Clark, "It seems more important than ever that [Lincoln] should be able to have some definite scientific occupation in addition to his business affairs."[7] Clark was in complete agreement with the suggestion and urgency of the need.[8] Within a year, the two combined with Bowman to get Lincoln seriously involved in Wilkins' submarine exploit.

The Lure of Lenzburg

At the time, Lincoln still had not decided what to do with the extraordinary Hapsburg castle in Switzerland that was part of his inheritance. He rather dreaded the visit he planned for the springtime of 1929—

"probably the only time I shall ever go to Lenzburg," he told Clark.[9] But Lincoln was a man swayed by moods. Two months later, in a letter to his niece, Clare Neilson, he wrote, "and there I stay forever, if I like it."[10]

Bowman's antarctic suggestions lay dormant while Ellsworth considered other projects. He told David Dietz of the Scripps Howard newspapers that he was thinking about establishing an air base in the Arctic to facilitate an air route from Europe to the Orient via the North Pole.[11] He told his niece that Wilkins wanted him to go on a submarine voyage to the North Pole.[12] His immediate trip was the one he would take to his inherited castle.

June 1929

It was a rainy day in June of 1929 when he strode through the streets of the tiny village of Lenzburg and gazed up at the ramparts and turrets of the castle that was his. Ever romantic, he made his first approach on foot.[13]

He had finished a week's climbing in the mountains and had left the inn where he was staying in Engelberg, resolved at last to grapple with the decision about where his home would be. He had never been drawn to the small Villa Aurora, in Florence, that he had inherited when his sister became owner of the larger Villa Palmieri. The gracious Italian setting lacked the drama to excite Lincoln's imagination and he found it bland.

But this—this stern fortress of Hapsburg rulers—just might be something he could understand. The castle stood proud and impregnable "on a commanding rock beyond reach of mine or battery."[14]

Closer now, he could look up and see rooks wheeling about the eaves. Ascending toward the castle, he skirted the flank of a hill once clad by vineyards, passed through the lower gate, and walked close to the ramparts to reach the entrance door—narrow, low, studded. There were chains on either side to raise and lower the drawbridge that spanned a deep breach, giving protection against attack.

Ellsworth rang the bell and waited. The door opened, and a man in shirtsleeves peered inquiringly at the visitor who stood before him, in a dripping poncho.

"I'm Mr. Ellsworth," Lincoln said.[15]

The man looked skeptical. A passport removed his doubts. The owner stepped through the doorway leading into a garden beyond. He looked at the enveloping walls, the steep roofs and slender chimneys topped with stately caps resembling small cottages.

The following day he felt a mixture of wonder and nostalgia. The spirit of his father permeated the great rooms. Ashes in the medieval fireplaces lay two and three feet deep. They had been left undisturbed after James Ellsworth had laid the last fire. His desk seemed to be waiting for the old man to sit down at precisely five o'clock and write in his daily journal.[16]

Accompanied by the steward, Ernst Bremer, Lincoln methodically took mental inventory: the well in the courtyard, ninety feet deep; the giant wheel near the entrance to hoist supplies in case of siege; the dungeon, with portions dating back to the twelfth century; Barbarossa Hall, commemorating Frederick the Red Beard who "paid his memorable visit to the castle, and on 20th February, 1173, entered into his inheritance,"[17] just as Ellsworth the explorer was now doing, 750 years later.

The hours and quarter hours were marked by a symphony of nearly a hundred synchronized clocks—striking, chiming, booming in concert with the bells of the great tower. It was as if James Ellsworth's famous collection was ringing a welcome for the heir.

From a tower window Lincoln looked contentedly out over the plain, and as the days passed, his tensions melted away. "I can truthfully say that the past ten days I have spent alone here have been the happiest in many a day," he wrote Clark. "It is really wonderful to think that all this peace and beauty belongs to me—so wonderful that I fear to awake and discover it all a dream. . . . The place makes up for a whole lot I have missed in the past five years."[18]

The letter, however, was a stream of consciousness—a series of conflicting reflections. Lenzburg, he wrote, "is the most wonderful place I ever saw. I like it immensely and shall make a home of it." But at once doubts arose. "When one is used to a lot of physical activity this sitting on a hill-top is slow death." He praised nature's extravagance on Lenzburg hill, "with tree and bird and insect life," adding, "All I ask is to stay right here—revel in all that surrounds me." Then contradictory thoughts arose. He had more to do in the Arctic, and the Grand Canyon always called. As so often, he drew on his impressive memory of poetry, this time quoting from Robert Service's "The Spell of the Yukon" to illuminate his feelings: "It's the beauty that thrills me with wonder, / And the silence that fills me with peace."[19]

To this Hapsburg fortress he shipped the things he most loved: blankets from the Plains Indians of the early American West; Frederic Remington's famous painting *Downing the Nigh Off Leader* and his bronze *Bronco Buster*; a Navajo blanket with threads of color that had been picked from the uniform of a slain U.S. soldier; a fringed deer-skin shirt as soft as velvet. On a wall of the library, heads of two moun-tain sheep flanked an elk's head with widespread antlers. A buffalo skull rested on each side of the hearth, more reminders of the Ameri-can West. Along with souvenirs of an African safari, there were bear-paw and beaver-tail snowshoes.

On a table in the center of the library lay a marble slab measuring some twenty inches square, one of Lincoln's most cherished posses-sions (which now, equally cherished, hangs over the fireplace in the author's library). During Amundsen's three-year voyage of discovery through the Northwest Passage aboard the *Gjoa,* this slab provided a sturdy, unshakable foundation for sensitive instruments set up on shore, preventing movement that might vitiate accurate recordings of magnetic observations. During the two years the expedition wintered over at King William Island, the slab provided a steady base for an unmoving camera: a continuous photographic record ran uninter-rupted for nineteen months on a slowly moving film.[20] When the expedition prepared to resume its voyage, Godfred Hansen, a lieu-tenant on leave from the Danish navy who was Amundsen's second in command, took the slab aboard and on its polished surface incised a map showing the *Gjoa's* route. "Instrument base from the *Gjoa* expe-dition to the conqueror of the Northwest Passage, from his second in command," reads the inscription, in Danish.

In his new home Ellsworth assembled his cherished books on nav-igation, astronomy, and life on the western plains. Photographs of galaxies hung on the library walls. "Cases of fossils were his library," reminisced his widow long after, recalling the four-foot case that housed the collection in Barbarossa Hall.[21]

To the extent that was possible for such a restless spirit, Lincoln tried to settle down, and made Lenzburg his home. Yet he was no more at rest than a storm petrel moving endlessly across the ocean wastes. This first visit to Lenzburg had been clouded with poignancy. "I lost my father and I lost Amundsen—two men who looked at things with the same eyes as mine—so I guess I shall have to travel it mostly alone through the rest of my life," he told Clark.[22] This fantastic reference to James Ellsworth as a man "who looked at things with the same eyes as mine" brings to mind Shakespeare's famous line in *Henry IV,* "Thy wish was father . . . to that thought." Lincoln hoped, however, that he would not remain in solitude.

July 1929

Some time before the end of World War I, he had proposed to a lovely young woman, Kitty Lanier Lawrence, who later married W. Averell Harriman. In her daughter Kathleen's imaginative words, he had "proposed one evening and went off to one of the poles next morning."[23] Kitty was now divorced, and Lincoln had invited her and her two young daughters to spend the month of July with him at the castle. Several times during their stay, he took the two girls to climb nearby Mt. Pilatus. Despite their awareness of his rugged qualities, wrote Kathleen, they were surprised some years later to hear it rumored that Lincoln, every night during his stay at the Lodge in Sun Valley, Idaho, would open all his windows and leave the bathroom door open with the bathtub filled with water, so that he could break the ice for his early morning bath. Neighboring guests complained because the cold air escaped under the doors and chilled them too. His snowshoe hikes were so rigorous, Kathleen said, that "few wanted to go with him after an initial jaunt," and he wondered why no one wanted to go on an overnight hike—sleeping in the open. "He was eccentric," ended the letter of recollection.

During Kitty's visit to Lenzburg, Lincoln again proposed marriage, and again the answer was no. She told her daughters that she liked him, respected him, but that they shared few interests. "Mary and Mummy and I all received pendant charms from Cartier [made specially] of ivory edelweiss (the everlasting flower for everlasting memories)," wrote Kathleen. On a scribbled note found after Lincoln's death were these forlorn words referring to the failed courtship: "Agree to disagree—that is, travel separate roads the rest of life, with nothing in common."[24]

Lincoln had fulfilled his filial duty to his father's memory by seeing to the privately printed publication of James W. Ellsworth's memoirs, largely a recitation of his achievements. He looked back on his financial successes and his art acquisitions, and proudly recalled his own civic leadership, stern benevolence, and victories over obstacles and over opponents—in short, repeated examples of getting his own way. Although Harold Clark described him as "an Apostle of righteousness and goodness," James Ellsworth's makeup contained little, perhaps, of the milk of human kindness, and no apparent capacity to understand his son's ambitions. Perhaps this digging into the past increased Lincoln's sense of aloneness. He no longer had his beloved sister Clare, nor his revered friend Amundsen, and his second proposal of marriage to Kitty had been rejected. Except in fantasy, where might he turn for solace?

He fell in love, became infatuated—with someone whom he could never meet. Her photograph shows a young woman so tender it melts the heart. Slim-waisted and trim, she had an enchanting smile with the tiniest suggestion of a dimple. Laughing eyes seemed to beckon the viewer to share a happy secret. Her face seemed to radiate kindliness and serenity. But this object of his devotion was the unattainable Tatiana, daughter of the czar of Russia. She was the dream of a lonely man, Lincoln's widow told the author years later.[25]

December 1929

At year's end, 1929, Ellsworth added to the list of activities he was considering. From the Grand Canyon, where he was enjoying his annual pilgrimage, he wrote his friend Gertrude Gavin, "I should like to go on that Labrador trip and may yet, but that submarine trip looms up big with me. I want to go back to the Arctic just once more."[26] But first he felt obliged to complete a geological collection destined for the American Museum of Natural History—more than a hundred specimens, mostly fossil algae, picked up at various Grand Canyon locations, which he carefully noted for the museum. Knowledgeably chosen to reflect the "story of orderly progress told by the rocks," the collection spanned from Archaen (Vishnu Series) to Lower Algonkian (Unkar Series) through Middle Cambrian (Tonto formation) and finally Carboniferous periods.[27]

~ 8 ~

Plans and Diversions

FOR LINCOLN ELLSWORTH, submarines never became an obsession—his dreams had always been of the bright white world of ice, not the darkness of the deep sea. Thus it was surprising that in June 1930, influenced by Isaiah Bowman's high regard for the submarine project, Ellsworth had contributed $20,000 to the newly formed Wilkins-Ellsworth Trans-Arctic Submarine Expedition, and had agreed to increase his total contribution to $100,000 *if needed.*[1] Now, seven months later, additional money was urgently needed, and Wilkins was still awaiting word of Lincoln's intentions. On January 18, 1931, Wilkins wrote Isaiah Bowman, at the American Geographical Society, saying that he needed to know within the next week whether Lincoln wanted his name associated with the expedition as coleader, a benefactor, or not at all. He also wanted to know if Ellsworth would join the expedition as coleader in charge of the scientific section, prepared to do part of the scientific work.[2]

Bowman responded the following day: "Ellsworth definitely declines to join you this year but talks of submitting alternative proposal for next year."[3] Wilkins replied that he was grateful for Lincoln's past help, but expected to proceed with his expedition this year. "Will gladly cooperate with him next year if required," he said.[4] Lincoln was now free, he thought, to devote full attention to his own unannounced plans for the Antarctic. He contemplated a flight from the Weddell Sea to the ice shelf of the Ross Sea, with Bernt Balchen as pilot. Wilkins, however, did indeed need his help.

A Persuasive Plea

Harold Clark thought Lincoln should sponsor the submarine experiment. At close to two o'clock one morning, Clark began a five-page letter to Lincoln that played on his sentiment and emotion. Wilkins desperately needed $50,000 to save his expedition from collapse. Clark said he could approach people to whom that sum was a "mere bagatelle," but before they were asked, he hoped Lincoln would provide it, on top of his earlier gift of $20,000. He reminded Lincoln that he had been extraordinarily privileged to link up with Amundsen and to blaze a trail that would carry his name through the centuries. Then Clark recalled Amundsen's anguish when he was forced to abandon his planned flight from Alaska to Spitsbergen. Now Wilkins faced a similar plight. Surely in helping Wilkins, Ellsworth would fulfill a role that Amundsen would have approved. Clark prodded Lincoln's conscience, pointing out that his father's resources had made possible the flights of 1925 and 1926. Then he intensified his fund-raising plea by suggesting that Lincoln had a philanthropic duty to back the venture. Wealth, Clark asserted, should be regarded as "a trust for the good of mankind." He further implied that Lincoln should use his talents to set an example, inspiring children he would never know, but who would be beneficiaries of his contribution. Clark regarded this opportunity to be almost as important as the one that opened up when Lincoln sought out Amundsen at the Waldorf Astoria. "Fifty thousand dollars, or several times that sum if needed would mean nothing to you, and [would] bring the happiness that comes from having a stake in something that is filled with vitality and romance," he concluded.[5]

The letter hit home. Ellsworth spent nearly all the following day with Clark and Wilkins, hammering out an understanding, formalized by two brief documents, signed and witnessed. One was authority from Lincoln to pay Wilkins, or upon his order, such amounts as Clark should request, not exceeding $50,000.[6] The second was a press announcement that "Lincoln Ellsworth . . . will make it possible to carry out this year the plans for the Arctic Submarine Expedition . . . to be known as the Wilkins-Ellsworth Expedition." The announcement also quoted from a statement Ellsworth had first made six months earlier: "I like Wilkins because he is of that virile pioneer type of the old American West that I have always so admired—men of great faith, courage and simplicity, who said little and did much. That is why I like him and have joined forces with him."[7] Satisfied, Clark returned to his Ohio law office.

Responding to Wilkins' letter of gratitude, Ellsworth said, "Probably it all gave me just as much pleasure as it did you. I do feel though that the honor of association is weighted more in my direction than it is in yours. It is an honor indeed to be associated with you, just to have our names together. Why? Because for sheer audacity in the attainment of one's ideals I know of none your equal, unless possibly it was Nansen's farthest north." As if he had just made a wondrous discovery, he continued: "It isn't so difficult to give money when you have it, but it's another story to get out and dig and slave and beg for it, and in the face of every discouragement carry on with your ideals. So you see there isn't so much credit to me after all."[8]

Harold Clark had orchestrated these events with extraordinary skill. He had pressed Lincoln relentlessly, yet subtly. To Bowman he later mentioned, with no explanation, the "remarkable spiritual experience" he'd had on January 29, "when Lincoln agreed to join forces with the Wilkins-Ellsworth Arctic Submarine Expedition!"[9] The expedition eventually took place, but without Lincoln.

At this time, Isaiah Bowman was maintaining his interest in securing information about Antarctica that would supplement fragmentary knowledge and replace hypothetical outlines on existing maps. He intended to arrange a planning session for Ellsworth and Clark with Wilkins, Balchen, and W. L. G. Joerg, who was cartographer with the Division of Maps and Charts, National Archives. Maps would be spread out "on which we can plan alternative routes," he wrote Ellsworth. In a deferential tone, he concluded: "If you wish anything further done by way of preparation, please command me."[10]

With his usual meticulous attention to detail, Clark took careful notes at the group's February 10 meeting, which he described as an intellectual feast.[11] He also found it full of surprises. He did not know that Wilkins had seriously considered a transcontinental flight across Antarctica, nor was he aware that Lincoln had come to know pilot Bernt Balchen well when he was at Spitsbergen for the *Norge* flight in 1926. The meeting opened a period of long collaboration between Ellsworth and Wilkins, sometimes troubled, but fruitful for both.

There was no need to address the inevitably hazardous character of the antarctic flight. Bowman, Ellsworth, and Clark already had gone over the dangers thoroughly. The real problem was transportation. With Balchen as pilot, Ellsworth intended to make a flight across the continent of Antarctica from the Weddell Sea to the Ross Sea, even though Wilkins warned that the chance of taking off from the Weddell Sea in any one year was fifty-fifty.[12] The problem was twofold: How would they get the plane and personnel to the starting point, and how would they retrieve the plane with Ellsworth and Balchen from the Ross Sea at the end of the 2,000-mile flight? Wilkins' experience with this problem had been sobering. When contemplating a flight in Antarctica in 1928, he had found that, should he have reached the Ross Sea, the cost of getting a large whaler to fetch him would have been $18,000 a day.[13]

Nevertheless, a message signed by Wilkins and Ellsworth was sent to Gunnar Isachsen of Oslo, prominent whaling fleet owner, asking him about possible charter opportunities.[14] "It is quite an undertaking to contemplate a flight across the antarctic continent," Lincoln told Clark, even though he had $250,000 available for the expedition. "Fortunately, I am in the hands of my friends to find a way. If they do my obligation can never be repaid." He continued with his usual self-doubt. "The question in my mind is why I have friends who are so interested. I hope that the opportunity may come to prove myself worthy of such friendship."[15]

To Wilkins he wrote, "There is nothing I would rather do than make that flight from the Weddell Sea to the Ross Sea. . . . But it don't [sic] look promising at the moment."[16] Then, with that streak of mysticism both men shared,[17] Lincoln's letter asked Wilkins for "something of yours that you have *carried* in your travels . . . that I can carry in my pocket . . . on my own journeys."[18] His request was in keeping with the sentimental gift he had bestowed on Wilkins several weeks earlier, symbolizing pioneer spirit. It was an ox shoe from the Jay Hawker expedition to the California gold rush of 1849, which he glorified in a three-page letter, describing 107 wagons pulling out of Salt Lake City headed for the California diggings.[19]

The broad scope of plans for the Ellsworth Antarctic Expedition would involve two divisions. The first would operate from Coats Land and focus on Ellsworth's proposed flight from the Weddell Sea to the

Ross Sea. The second division, operating from Little America under command of Dr. Laurence M. Gould, eminent geologist, geographer, and explorer, would establish a meteorological station, provide weather reports for the first division, lay an advanced base at the eastern end of the Queen Maud Range in case of emergency, conduct geological studies, and act as supporting party.[20]

For six weeks Lincoln and others on his behalf pursued an intensive search for a way of getting a plane and personnel to Antarctica for a transcontinental flight.[21] They soon found, however, that because of overproduction of whale oil, it was unlikely that any ships would be sent to the Antarctic in 1931 and 1932.[22]

The *Nautilus* at Sea

Four weeks after his cordial ox-shoe letter to Wilkins, Ellsworth seemed again submerged in anguish: "I am unspeakably weary of basking in the limelight of someone else's notoriety and long for the solace that the Great West always gives me until I can start something of my own."[23] The submarine *Nautilus,* overhauled and equipped, lay in the Brooklyn Navy Yard and invitations to the March 24 christening had been sent out, generating great personal visibility for Wilkins. Lady Wilkins, assisted by Jean Jules Verne, grandson of the famous author, was to officiate.[24] Ellsworth, a participant by name and generous financing, was perhaps in Wilkins' limelight—but hardly basking. Moreover, he had experienced such intense pressure to provide more financing for Wilkins that he felt abused. "I wish to impress upon you the sacrifice I really must make in order to contribute further to the Submarine Expedition," he wrote Wilkins after the christening. "But as I said to you if it must be done, it must."[25]

In contrast with Ellsworth's farsighted recognition of the expedition's potential, two weeks after the christening came denunciation of the project by Admiral Hugh Rodman, U.S. Navy, in Pathé News movie newsreels and newspaper headlines. With undisguised scorn, he asked what good could come from such a foolhardy attempt. "What benefit of any sort can be derived from it; what new data can be collected which can be beneficially utilized? Who cares seriously about the Arctic depths of unnavigable waters? And as for determining the set and drift of Arctic currents . . . I do not believe anything practical or useful can be obtained by diving under the ice."[26] This dismissal appears frivolous when measured against the reputations of the scientific organizations listed as associates on the letterhead of the Wilkins-Ellsworth Trans-Arctic Submarine Expedition: American Geographical Society; Carnegie Institution of Washington; Cleveland Museum of Natural History; Det Geofysiske Institutt, Norway; Woods Hole Oceanographic Institution.

Having stood by Wilkins in launching this pioneer venture, Ellsworth now returned to his own plans. Although his inquiries about possible transportation had been fruitless, he was unwilling to give up. He was fifty-one years old. For almost two decades, on the threshold of greatness, he had endured the frustration of seeking personal fulfillment in a world of exploration that no longer existed. But the lure of fame still drew him like a magnet, and his path was clear. The antarctic area over which he planned to fly was the last major portion of the entire earth that remained unknown—a vast empty white area on the map. Whoever was first in revealing its secrets would earn a permanent place on the roster of great explorers. Lincoln was determined to become that discoverer. It is little wonder that his close friends were making every effort to help him get there—ahead of Byrd's return to Little America in 1932 and recapture of headlines.

Because Riiser-Larsen was planning another South Pole expedition, Ellsworth saw a possible solution to his transportation predicament, even though it might mean sharing leadership. He suggested possible cooperation for an American-Norwegian flight between the Weddell Sea and Ross Sea, with the objective of scientific discovery.[27] Riiser-Larsen responded with a long letter describing his own plan. If he could get money enough, he would land in the Weddell Sea area. His expedition team would include two Eskimo couples, dogs and sledges, and a staff of scientists. He would take provisions for three years. With practical foresight, he urged Ellsworth to start from the Weddell Sea area, because if a flight took off from the Ross Sea and failed, it would be of no interest because of Byrd's expedition.[28]

As the *Nautilus* left Provincetown, Massachusetts, for her arctic voyage, Ellsworth cabled Wilkins, "urgent and confidential," that if his services would benefit the expedition, he would join immediately.[29] "I believe you know without the need for me to be demonstrative how very much I appreciate your confidence and your assistance," replied Wilkins. He referred to a letter just sent ashore with the ship's mail, urging Lincoln to join the expedition, even at the last minute, because "it would add greatly to the prestige and scientific accomplishment."[30] But it was not with a feeling of confidence that he ordered the *Nautilus* to sea that day. In a letter to Clark, he admitted his acute financial distress and lamented that Ellsworth was not able to assist further than the $90,000 subscribed.[31]

Meanwhile the American Geographical Society continued to try to locate a suitable vessel for Ellsworth's expedition. Bowman sought help from the U.S. Department of State so that the project might carry out important work in the Second Polar Year, an international program for meteorological work in high latitudes.[32] To no avail, Bowman made inquiry to the Norwegian Association of Whaling Companies. Robert Cushman Murphy sent a request to the owners of the famous British ship *Discovery* (first used by Robert Scott and later by Sir Douglas Mawson in the Antarctic), hoping it could be made available during that autumn of 1931 to convey Ellsworth, five or six associates, and two planes to the Weddell Sea.[33]

Two days after the *Nautilus* left Provincetown, the Hearst newspapers announced a polar rendezvous plan: "Zeppelin And Submarine Meeting At The North Pole."[34] A few days earlier the *New York American* had reported the "Zeppelin's Polar Dash to Meet Wilkins."[35] A special winch with wire cable and wire basket was being installed on the *Graf Zeppelin* so that a man could be lowered to the *Nautilus* or taken up from it and mail bags exchanged, if the famous airship succeeded in locating the submarine in the vast ice fields.[36]

The Hearst story described how sub and Zep would find one another. If the weather was clear, Wilkins would burn heavy black smoke bombs from the deck of the sub or from ice floes. If the weather was cloudy or foggy, he would send a captive balloon, painted black or red, above the clouds, to make the submarine's position visible. Attached to the balloon would be a special mirror to attract attention by reflecting sunlight.[37]

The *Nautilus* had not been at sea for long when serious mechanical and electrical failures began. For eleven days she overcame successive calamities, until Wilkins finally hoisted the international distress signal. The submarine was towed to Cork, Ireland, by the U.S. warship *Wyoming*.[38] Delayed for a month by the need for serious repairs,[39] she arrived in Tromsö, Norway, on August 9. Only Wilkins' fortitude and superb leadership qualities kept the enterprise from collapsing. On the day of departure from Tromsö, he issued a press release of guarded optimism: "Hopes high . . . firmly believe much will be accomplished."[40]

For almost a month the beleaguered vessel threaded her way through the floes, awaiting opportunity for subsurface action below the ice. The chance never came; the submarine's diving rudders were carried away. During all this time, undaunted by personal misery or the storm-created shambles below, Harald U. Sverdrup, head of Norway's Geophysics Institute, conducted significant research.[41]

Heroically optimistic, Wilkins dispatched a report on September 4. It began: "Battered, scarred and dented by tusks of ice, forward part of ice runners crumpled, drill mechanism shattered, hull leaking in two places. . . ." It concluded: "But we still believe that submarine most suitable vessel for future research in Arctic."[42] A press release summarizing the scientific achievements concluded with a single line of acknowledgment. "We are grateful especially to Lincoln Ellsworth . . . with his knowledge of the Arctic."[43]

Such brief recognition does scant justice to the man who perceived the greatness of Wilkins' undertaking and its potential for yielding knowledge about an unknown dimension of the polar region. Ellsworth's extraordinarily generous financing had enabled Wilkins to carry out the experiment and leave behind a record of preparations and activities to help "that someone who will some day make a transarctic journey beneath the ice successfully."[44] In 1957, twenty-six years later, Sverdrup's oceanic observations provided data used to great advantage by the U.S. Navy during the first extensive under-ice transit of the nuclear-powered submarine *Nautilus*.[45]

In 1924, Vilhjalmur Stefansson, a longtime believer in submarine exploration in the Polar Sea, devoted eleven pages of the *Northward Course of Empire* to the promising future of submarine travel beneath the ice.[46] Wilkins also had written a book before his experimental voyage in the *Nautilus*. Published in 1931, Wilkins' *Under the North Pole* was written to attract support and to counter the skepticism that he knew such an advanced proposal would generate. His introductory chapter began: "The Arctic has been crossed only twice in the history of the world, once by airship and once by airplane. The commander of the first airplane, Sir Hubert Wilkins, and the second-in-command of the first airship, Lincoln Ellsworth, have now joined to attempt the first crossing of the Arctic by submarine."[47]

The two partners in this undertaking shared a vision that reached beyond the allure of pure adventure, tempting as it was. Each had struggled in the Arctic for survival, and each recognized the need for reliable weather prediction if the dream of safe transpolar travel by air was to be realized. They believed their submarine voyage could demonstrate the feasibility of taking scientists anywhere in the Polar Sea, where they could establish stations on the ice for sending weather reports and carrying out research on such phenomena as ice conditions, ocean currents, density, and depths.

Destined for scrapping as previously agreed, Wilkins' *Nautilus* managed to reach Bergen Fjord in Norway.[48] There, on November 20, 1931, with American flag flying and sea valves opened, she sank for good in 200 fathoms of water.

Graf Zeppelin Mail Run

Hugo Eckener, commander of the *Graf Zeppelin,* had his own agreement with Hearst newspapers: $150,000 if *Nautilus* and *Graf* met at the North Pole and exchanged passengers and mail; $100,000 if they merely met there; $30,000 if they succeeded only in meeting somewhere in the Arctic.[49] Thousands of stamp collectors had paid for letters, postcards, and special covers (specially designed envelopes to be carried on the *Nautilus* or the *Graf,* and sold to the public to raise funds) to be cancelled at the roof of the world. Six hundred pounds of mail were sent to Friedrichshafen for the *Graf,* and 4,000 pieces of mail were sent for the submarine. By the time Eckener realized that *Nautilus* was in lasting trouble, it was too late to cancel his part of the flight. But the idea was not abandoned. He sought to arrange a rendezvous with a different partner, the Soviet icebreaker *Malyghin.*

As head of the American Geographical Society, Isaiah Bowman was the unofficial dean of polar exploration, and his counsel was often sought when a knotty problem arose. Eckener now requested that German diplomat William Von Meister ask Bowman whether Ellsworth might contribute $5,000 to such an arctic flight, and whether he might go himself or send a representative. Eckener explained his need to recoup. Due to the *Nautilus's* failure to rendezvous with the *Graf,* he would receive no revenue from the sale of news rights.[50] Bowman, having been so involved in getting Ellsworth to finance the submarine expedition, did not feel comfortable about the idea of approaching him, and replied accordingly. But, perhaps indicating his tacit approval, he added that "Von Meister can do so independently if he desires."[51]

Von Meister took the hint. A few days later a cable message from Eckener reached Bowman through Von Meister, inviting Ellsworth to make a contribution of $8,000 and to accompany the *Graf* as "Arctic expert for navigation," with the right to communicate to the Geographical Society any geographical discoveries.[52] Ellsworth accepted, and proceeded to Friedrichshafen in mid-July. While awaiting the *Graf*'s departure, he was startled to receive a cable from Bowman, who had dined in New York the previous evening with Bernon Prentice, Bernt Balchen, Laurence Gould, and Canadian bush pilot George A. Thorne. The group had met to discuss plans for Lincoln's antarctic proposal. They had agreed it was highly desirable that Thorne and Balchen meet Lincoln at Friedrichshafen on August 3 (the day of his anticipated return from the *Graf* flight) to confer on alternative proposals for transportation to and from Antarctica. This conference would permit quick action if Ellsworth's decision was favorable, and if the plan should be delayed, it probably would mean losing their present group of assistants and risking strong competition.[53]

Ellsworth was quite aware of the strong competition, knowing that Byrd was planning to return to Little America the next year. For months Ellsworth had searched in vain to find means of transporting to Antarctica seven men and an airplane for a flight across the continent from Coats Land to the Ross Sea. A stream of correspondence with ship owners all spring and early summer had produced no results.

The program that Bowman and the others had devised contemplated a main base at the Bay of Whales. Flights would be made over the unknown regions and coastline that lay between the main base and the Antarctic Archipelago. A rough map was appended showing the location of two depots where food and fuel would be laid down for emergency. The two depots would also be sites where geological ground studies would be made and soundings of ice would be taken by seismic methods. Scientific work at the main base would include observing the behavior of terrestrial magnetism and auroral light, as well as conducting radio research, which might reveal correlation between these phenomena. The provisional budget was $191,635.[54]

After his recent contributions to the *Nautilus* project, Ellsworth was in no mood to be pressured. "Prefer Thorne and Balchen do not come," he cabled Bowman, saying he had no future plans and did not wish to be forced into any decision such as the proposed meeting would require.[55]

The *Graf* left Friedrichshafen on July 24, carrying Ellsworth and fourteen other passengers, all scientists, with Eckener in command. Three days later, after stops in Berlin and Leningrad, she reached Franz Josef Land for a rendezvous with the Russian icebreaker *Malyghin*. The airship descended slowly until her bumper bags rested on the water between drifting ice floes. Captain Ernst A. Lehmann, second in command under Eckener, later described how a boat put out from the *Malyghin*, with a man standing in the stern. As the boat came alongside the airship's control car, Ellsworth stretched out his hand. The man in the stern was Nobile! "Both were visibly touched," wrote Lehmann.[56] The boat received a sack of mail from the *Graf* and returned to the *Malyghin*, Nobile waving good-bye. "The scene held an element of pathos that I can never forget," recalled Ellsworth. "The *Italia* disaster had made a different man of him."[57]

The *Graf* resumed its flight after only thirty minutes and cruised that afternoon over the Franz Josef Islands, which they recorded with a mapping camera. The aerial photography revealed that Albert Edward Island and Harmsworth Island, shown on all the charts, actually did not exist. The next day, flight over the little-known Nicholas II Land produced another minor geographical discovery: it was not one island but two, separated by a narrow channel. As if fearful of losing his lifelong image as a rugged man of the outdoors, Lincoln was careful to note that "this was real exploring despite its luxury."[58]

After the flight Lincoln went to Lenzburg, and a week later Balchen and Thorne appeared there, despite his initial reluctance to see them. According to Balchen's diary, they talked over with Ellsworth the proposal they had discussed with Prentice and Gould in New York. Ellsworth, however, said he was tired of all expeditions at the present time, and that in every undertaking he had been connected with, the only thing he had gotten out of it was to "give away considerable sums of money."[59] He told Balchen he wanted to rest for a while before making any decision. His interest increased, however, when Balchen and Thorne assured him he would be in charge of the expedition and told him of possibly solving the transportation problem by using the steamer *Volendam* to carry them south.

Ellsworth made no commitment, but asked them to get in touch with him immediately when he got back to New York.[60] "He showed a very bitter and antagonistic attitude towards R.E.B. [Byrd] based on several occurrences which gave reason for it," Balchen wrote.[61] Whatever it was that he had confided to Balchen, Lincoln remembered his pledge of loyalty to Byrd for helping with the medal. He made no public criticism. However, a strain in their relationship began to show in letters between the two, as they sparred to find out what the other was planning.

"Just in from Arizona and delighted to have your letter thought you had forgotten me. Do come to see me sometime," Ellsworth wired Byrd in mid-November 1931.[62]

A month later Byrd invited Ellsworth to come up to Boston and spend the day. "I would like a lot to see you," he wrote, "and I would like to give you any help that I could on any of your projects. I have felt that some of the people who were seeking your cooperation have not been doing so for your best good." Seeming to realize that Ellsworth's trust in him was faltering, Byrd continued, "Believe me, Lincoln, there is nothing in the world I would not do to assist you in any ambition of yours. You may be sure I have no ulterior motive." The letter closed, "My very best to you always. Your friend."[63]

Ellsworth replied promptly. "I am still contemplating the Antarctic with nothing very definite as yet. I wish we could talk it all over." He offered Byrd four dates for a possible meeting, and in his turn signed, "Your friend."[64] Byrd replied that he would come to New York if necessary, but would rather Lincoln visit him at his home.[65] "Impossible to come to Boston," replied Ellsworth, "should like to hear if you have anything in mind regarding the future. If you are not coming this way why not write me."[66] A letter from Byrd was already in the mail, but it was not what Ellsworth had in mind.

On Track at Last

"Be careful whom you tie up with," was Byrd's cryptic advice in his letter to Ellsworth at year end, 1931. "If you make a mistake, you may get into a lot of agony again just as you did in the Nobile expedition." The ostensible purpose of the letter was to offer help and cooperation: "My Dear Lincoln, from a number of sources I have heard that you would like to take an expedition south. I wanted to talk it over with you and offer any help I can give. . . . I am deeply interested in your success in anything you undertake . . . [and] I hope as the years go on I can prove this to you." Further assurances of cooperation were followed by a closing expression of admiration: "You have always been a sportsman and a gentleman and that is terribly rare these days where money, fame and ambition take good men and put them on the wrong track. May 1932 be your best year."[67]

In light of subsequent events, it seems that this letter was less a genuine expression of friendship than a fishing expedition, an attempt to learn what specific plans Ellsworth had in mind. What Ellsworth had in mind, of course, was a major flight across Antarctica, and he needed a plane, a pilot, and a ship. On April 18, 1932, on letterhead bearing the title "Ellsworth Trans-Antarctic Flight Expedition," he gave full authority to Bernt Balchen to discuss the engine, the airplane, and the wireless requirements for the expedition "and to draw up contracts for the purchase of such equipment."[68] On that same day, the *New York Herald Tribune* ran an announcement of Ellsworth's plans.[69]

Byrd was dismayed. Ellsworth had upstaged him. No longer would Byrd enjoy exclusive heroic visibility in the press. Furthermore, Ellsworth's expedition would divert public attention and might lower attendance at Byrd's lectures, which were an important source of revenue. Two days later Byrd wrote to his U.S. Navy colleague, Commander H. E. Saunders: "I think we should go down to the Antarctic this year. Ellsworth, my friend, has announced his plans to do exactly what I propose to do. . . . However, I do not see why I should not finish the job."[70] The job was ambitious, as Byrd had explained to his benefactor Edsel Ford in several conversations before his 1928 expedition: no less than a plan to "map out and explore the entire South Pole continent." At the time, Ford used those words in a letter to John D. Rockefeller Jr.[71]

Byrd's letter to Saunders included the seemingly irrelevant information that Ellsworth was taking Balchen with him. Balchen's defection to the Ellsworth Trans-Antarctic Flight Expedition was seriously troubling to Byrd, for he told "Savvy" (his nickname for Saunders): "since [Ellsworth] can pay Balchen more than I can, that is the answer."[72] However, that was not the answer. Byrd, it seems, was trying to deflect attention from the real reason. Balchen was shocked by the truth about the North Pole flight. In his autobiographical notes, he wrote that he "was not going down there again with Admiral Byrd." After all, Amundsen, Ellsworth, and Nobile "were the first to reach the North Pole by air."[73]

This rejection of Byrd's claim that he reached the North Pole was far from casual. But the world then believed this misstatement of fact and the National Geographic Society had affirmed it after reviewing Byrd's charts and navigation records.[74] Balchen had observed events in Spitsbergen in 1926, and he had flown on Byrd's transatlantic flight in 1927. It was on that flight that his feelings of distrust crystallized, as he saw Byrd repeatedly shape reports in a way that would allow him to claim credit for accomplishments that were not his own. Two years later, when he served as pilot for Byrd's flight to the South Pole, Balchen had insisted that a photographer-observer be aboard "to document who really flew the plane and the fact that the plane really reached the South Pole."[75]

In the early spring of 1932, Ellsworth was poised for action. He signed a contract with the Northrup Corporation for building and delivering an all-metal Northrup Gamma airplane, and made a payment of $12,500, half the purchase price of the craft. He also contracted for Balchen to start immediate work with the Northrup engineers and to test the finished plane. And he authorized Wilkins to search for a suitable ship.

By mid-May, before he sailed for Europe, Ellsworth's plans and his alliance with Balchen had attracted widespread public attention. To quell the growing fanfare, Ellsworth formally requested Balchen to refrain from making any statements or appearing in any moving pictures. Wilkins, responsible for organization and business affairs, had already agreed to honor a similar request. Any information about the expedition "must come directly and personally from me," Ellsworth insisted.[76]

Byrd was obviously concerned by the prospect of losing the exclusive attention of the press. Through an early letter, he had tried to divert Ellsworth from undertaking the dramatic 2,000-mile flight, ostensibly because of its perilous nature. Now he introduced a different reason to avoid such a challenge. He sought to persuade Ellsworth that since the country was in a serious economic depression, the public would resent seeing two expeditions spend large sums of money to go to the same place at the same time. Byrd regretted being in competition, he wrote, but could not leave his job in Little America half finished.[77] Clearly, he hoped that Ellsworth would abandon his own plan.

Zurich Meeting

On June 7, 1932, the people of Lenzburg heard the throb of engines overhead and, looking up, saw a giant dirigible. It paused above the castle overlooking the village. Hugo Eckener, in command of the *Graf,* was delivering a message to his friend Lincoln Ellsworth—a handwritten greeting attached to a stone dropped into the garden.[78]

Lincoln was in Lenzburg fulfilling the Swiss residency requirement for foreigners owning property in the country. He had arranged to improve his technique with the Leica camera by taking lessons from the renowned aerial photographer Walter Mittelholzer, who was manager of the Dubendorf airport in Zurich. One day his attention was diverted from photography when he caught sight of "a slender, long-limbed, dark-haired, brown-eyed young woman, very professional in a flying suit."[79] When the lonely bachelor "saw this vision again" on the following day, he asked Mittelholzer who it might be. "One of my students," replied the instructor, who soon introduced them. The woman who had caught his eye was Mary Louise Ulmer, whose father was Jacob S. Ulmer, a successful American banker and industrialist, of Philadelphia and Pottsville, Pennsylvania. Her mother was a sophisticated traveler, with whom Mary Louise had shared many trips in remote corners of the world. Two days after they met, Mary Louise accepted Ellsworth's invitation to breakfast at his castle.

Lincoln's first meal of the day was hearty fare, which he indulged in a manner bordering on ritual. Patterns were important—the eighteen-mile walk each day, one pipe a day—and breakfast was no exception. Always at hand was a pitcher of freshly squeezed orange juice. Strong black coffee was served with hot milk. A bowl of oatmeal with brown sugar and heavy cream was followed by eggs and crisp bacon. Finally, center of attention, there was honey in the comb from the Black Forest, to spread on coarse black bread. The talk that morning was of flying, of Lincoln's plans for his coming antarctic expedition, and of Mary Louise's adventurous life roaming in the Far East. She was not pretty, but had verve, the ability to enliven even the most routine topic. She negotiated ski slopes, she said, in order to get the schnapps at the bottom. But she was actually painfully shy. "Had to fight the feeling all my life," she told the author.[80] She hid her diffidence behind a cheery and entertaining manner.

Ten days after they met, Lincoln took her hand and said: "Mary, would you like to share your life with mine, because I'd like to share mine with you?" She said she would.[81] That was the extent of his proposal and her acceptance. Shortly thereafter he gave her the first of many presents: a gold brooch with two little birds sitting on an enamel branch. When the engaged couple returned to the United States, Lincoln paused from his travels long enough to produce two tangible manifestations of his devotion. He asked Mary Louise to choose a ruby, a sapphire, or a diamond from his collection of gemstones that he kept in Tiffany's vault. She chose the round diamond for her engagement ring. He also gave her a copy of his book *Search,* in which he wrote the czarina's poignant words to her husband, Czar Nicholas: "No more separations . . . and when this life is ended, to meet together in the other world to remain together for all eternity."[82] He then left New York to go to the West Coast, where his plane, *Polar Star,* was under construction.

Except for his close relationship with his sister, an affectionate feminine bond had been absent from Lincoln's life. Now, at age fifty-two, he had engaged to live, for better or for worse, with a woman in her thirties whom he had met only a few weeks before. Unaccustomed to giving of himself, or sharing emotions, he used gifts as symbols of his feelings and showered his fiancée with surprises.

Her delight and gratification were reflected in long letters to her "dearest Linky," filled with sweet nothings and expressions of concern for his health and happiness. In the first of these, she expressed interest in Lincoln's suggestion that she should resume flying lessons, acknowledging that at some time it might be useful even if she didn't pursue it constantly. "I know how trying it must be," wrote Mary Louise, "to have Mr. Balchen staying on and on . . . [and] yet nothing too much can be done to make [the plane] safe—more comfortable or better for you."[83] At this time Balchen was working in Los Angeles on Ellsworth's plane, with designer Jack Northrup and Northrup Corporation engineers. Balchen described it as an "entirely new aircraft, new design, which required an extensive series of test flights."[84]

As the days passed, Mary Louise became increasingly aware of the long separations that lay ahead, as well as the dangers her husband-to-be would face. Her letters took on a quality of yearning, and some express an intensity of sentiment that may have caused uneasiness in the lifelong bachelor, who was accustomed to total freedom. "I can never again be really happy without you," she wrote. And then, "To have a home with you!—that is thrilling enough . . . and we will be living in it together a long long time."[85]

She was glad he was enjoying Nansen's book, she told him in another letter, but added wistfully that three years seemed a long time to live on dreams. Lincoln had apparently tried to prepare his bride-to-be for the possibility of an extended separation. In 1896, after the *Fram*'s drift toward the North Pole, Nansen had written in *Farthest North,* "It is now three years since we left home." Perhaps trying to lighten her mood, she spoke of tentative plans to be married in Rome and mischievously suggested getting Mussolini to be a second witness at their wedding ceremony.[86]

Although Lincoln's side of this epistolary flow is missing, he apparently responded gallantly to her expressions of deep devotion, for Mary Louise wrote: "Your telegram was *so* beautiful . . . and I do believe the future is bright before us, but who could say it that way but you. It is only another proof of what a wonderfully beautiful soul you have Linky. Knowing and loving you have all through been like that."[87]

In late November, the rapturous mood was cooled by a polar chill. As if in sudden panic, Lincoln wrote his fiancée that when he got down to Antarctica he might "like it so much I'll want to stay there." She could not understand what he meant. "It is inconceivable to me," she told him, "that my life should not lie with yours. You see I love you and where you are how you dress wear your hair or act will not change that. . . . It was very saddening to find your letter so different from the others."[88]

What had happened to disturb Lincoln? Delivery of his plane that month would bring his dream within reach. Was he feeling shackled by the prospect of lifelong commitment? At year end, he followed his fiancée's advice to remain out there in the desert where he was happy—but he was not happy.

From his old haunt, the Furnace Creek Inn in Death Valley, he wrote not to Mary Louise but to his niece, Clare Prentice, noting that such places filled him with longing that could not be satisfied:

> It is as though I were formed of two beings from different spheres. The one is satisfied merely with the work and activity of the day. The other craves something else, something that is to be found somewhere in the west in the cloud kingdoms of the sunset, or in the dreamy splendor of the moon, or farther away in the trembling stars.
>
> How stupid and unsatisfying newspapers and interviews all become. Yet such is the price of ambition. That is why I have to pinch myself sometimes to keep going. It isn't easy when one loves the silence of the desert sunsets.

With a dramatic flourish, he concluded, "I am returning to Coronado tomorrow to go down on the desert and kill a sheep and have my Christmas dinner under a wild palm-tree."[89]

Clockwise from top left:

FIGURE 19. Tatiana, daughter of the czar of Russia. Although she was unattainable, Ellsworth was captivated by her charismatic beauty.

FIGURE 20. Mary Louise Ulmer and Lincoln Ellsworth at Lenzburg Castle, before they became engaged.

FIGURE 21. Lincoln Ellsworth and Mary Louise Ulmer on their wedding day in May 1933.

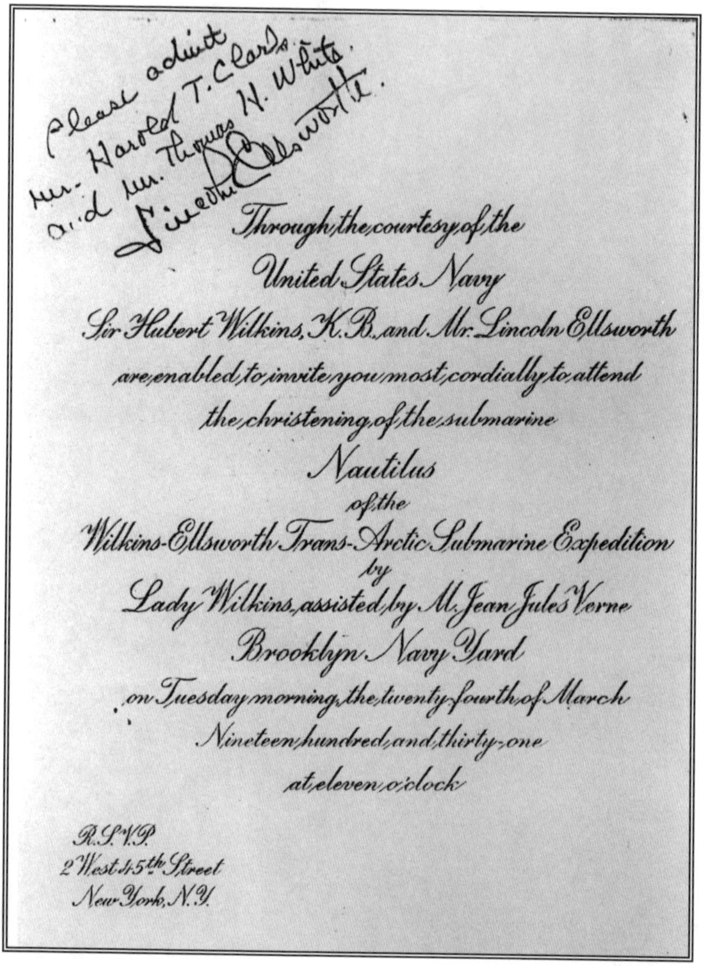

Please admit
Mr. Harold T. Clark
and Mr. Thomas N. White.
Lincoln Ellsworth.

Through the courtesy of the
United States Navy
Sir Hubert Wilkins, K.B., and Mr. Lincoln Ellsworth
are enabled to invite you most cordially to attend
the christening of the submarine

Nautilus

of the
Wilkins-Ellsworth Trans-Arctic Submarine Expedition
by
Lady Wilkins, assisted by M. Jean Jules Verne
Brooklyn Navy Yard
on Tuesday morning, the twenty-fourth of March
Nineteen hundred and thirty-one
at eleven o'clock

R.S.V.P.
2 West 45th Street
New York, N.Y.

FIGURE 22. Invitation for Harold Clark to the christening of the
submarine *Nautilus*, the vessel in which Sir Hubert Wilkins sought
to explore the North Pole.

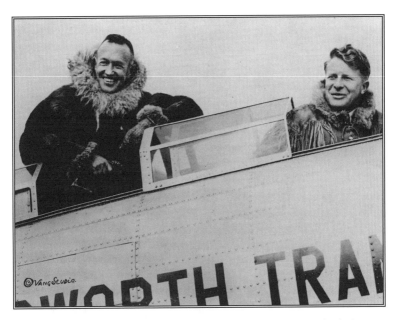

FIGURE 23. Ellsworth and Bernt Balchen aboard the *Polar Star*, built for Ellsworth by the Northrup Company for his first expedition to Antarctica.

FIGURE 24. Pilot Bernt Balchen, Lincoln Ellsworth, and Sir Hubert Wilkins.

FIGURE 25. Center, first row, Bernt Balchen, Lincoln Ellsworth, and Sir Hubert Wilkins with members of their crew.

FIGURE 26. The icebound *Wyatt Earp* on its voyage towards the Antarctic.

❧ 9 ❧

Antarctica—Maiden Voyage

BY EARLY 1933, organization of the Ellsworth Trans-Antarctic Flight Expedition had reached an advanced stage. Balchen acted as advisor and plane tester; Wilkins handled equipment and business affairs; and Ellsworth, momentarily preoccupied with his upcoming marriage, stood by with the checkbook. He was fortunate to have the services of Wilkins and Balchen, each preeminent in his field.

Exploration was not Balchen's primary concern. Rather, he was intensely interested in everything to do with the technical development, performance, and use of airplanes. "With him," wrote Ellsworth, "the performance of a plane was the whole thing."[1] Wilkins, on the other hand, was wholeheartedly committed to exploration for its own sake. He was a proven leader and organizer, experienced in polar survival, and he had accomplished outstanding flights in both the Arctic and the Antarctic. He possessed another quality exactly to Ellsworth's taste. "Had he lived in our West during the pioneer days," like Wyatt Earp, "he would most certainly have been a frontier marshal two-gunning some wild district into law and order," he said.[2]

After analyzing three alternative flights starting from the Bay of Whales on the Ross Sea, it was decided to attempt a nonstop flight to and from the Weddell Sea—2,900 miles altogether.[3] Two years earlier Ellsworth had been forced to abandon a similar plan because no vessel was available for transport to Antarctica. Now he had his own ship, which he named after Wyatt Earp, his gun-toting hero. Furthermore, he was better prepared to obtain, by aerial photography, information that would validate scientifically the importance of his undertaking. He was now ready to apply what he had learned from Walter Mittelholzer in the Swiss Alps, where he had studied and practiced mountain photography. Photographs would be the basis for maps. Moreover, wrote Ellsworth, "from a good photograph a geologist with a microscope can often determine the nature of rocks and mountains and therefore know something about their origin and history."[4]

Little was then known about the 5 million square miles of Antarctica. Some coastline had been charted, but the only major penetrations of the interior had been from the Ross Sea area: Scott, Shackleton, and Wilson in 1902; Shackleton in 1908; Amundsen and Scott on their harrowing trips to the South Pole in 1911; Byrd, in his 1928–29 flights.

If it accomplished nothing else, Ellsworth's flight might resolve two major geographical questions. Was Antarctica a single continent or was it divided by a channel between the Weddell Sea and the Ross Sea? And what evidence was there to show that a mountain range might stretch uninterruptedly across the continent, linking the Queen Maud Range to the mountains of Graham Land?

A statement prepared by the American Geographical Society announced that Ellsworth's flight was purely a voyage of discovery to determine the main outlines of the topography, record weather conditions, and take notes on the character of the ice surface. It explained that these data would provide the framework for detailed planning and mapping by future expeditions.[5] Some months later a press release focused on a more specific question regarding the structural relationships between East Antarctica and West Antarctica: What might be learned by determining the relationship of the flat-lying strata of *old rocks* (similar to those in Australia) in East Antarctica to the belt of *young folded rocks* represented by the Andes, the loop of islands beyond Cape Horn, and the Antarctic Archipelago—and at what point do these types of land meet?[6]

Ellsworth's deep interest in paleontology led him to accept as a fact that the mountainous islands of the Antarctic Archipelago were an extension of the Andes Mountains. In the years 1902 and 1903, members of the Swedish expedition to Antarctica, led by Baron Otto Nordenskjöld, had collected a large number of fossils showing that the primitive plant life of the Jurassic Age was identical in many respects to that of South America. This satisfied Ellsworth that at one time the climate of Antarctica had been subtropical and that in Jurassic times, Antarctica had been connected to the northern continents.[7] But a disturbing question remained. Since fossils of plant life from both areas were comparable, why had no fossils been found in Antarctica of four-footed land animals ordinarily associated with such an environment? Ellsworth voiced a daring but implausible hypothesis: Antarctica might have been cut off on all sides from the northern continents by a sudden gigantic convulsion, followed by such cold and ice that evolution came to a halt before the first land animals appeared.[8]

While these mysteries preoccupied Ellsworth, Balchen remained driven by his passion for aviation. He had worked for months with the engineers at the Northrup plant on matters of design and efficiency, until finally the time came for meticulous testing and preparation, as recorded in his journal entries during 1933:

> February 24, Fargo, N.D. Took equipment out on field and tried tent pitching and starting of motor with LE. Flew to Winnipeg and tested skis and engine on landings, etc. in cold weather for several days; tried various propeller pitches; trouble with oil leaks.
>
> April 6, Los Angeles. Worked on spare parts list, tried different setting for flaps [this was important, since the Northrup was fitted with specially designed flaps to cut landing speed].
>
> April 10, New York. Got from Ellsworth what he wants in Norway.
>
> April 11. Packed plane and parts (76 boxes).[9]

During the months of testing, Balchen looked into the capabilities of radio and navigation equipment, designed a new set of ski pedals, modified cold-weather equipment on the engines, and finally gave the Northrup a long-range test of fuel consumption by making a nonstop flight across the continent. After months of close involvement with the creation of *Polar Star,* as she developed from dream to drawing board to reality, Balchen had come to regard the ship with parental pride. Finally, on April 15, "Sir Hubert Wilkins and I and our airplane and my family" left on the SS *Stavengerfjord* for Norway.[10]

Although Ellsworth confessed to having no interest in flying—"used it only to do a job," he said—he proudly recalled Balchen saying that the *Polar Star* "stepped out three years ahead of world aviation,"[11] an opinion echoed by Wilkins, who called the ship the Rolls-Royce of airplanes. In May, June, and July, Wilkins was in Norway supervising refitting of the expedition vessel and, with Balchen's advice, selecting a crew.

And where was Lincoln all this time? On May 23 the fifty-three-year-old bachelor, stylishly attired in morning coat, with silk hat in hand, took Mary Louise Ulmer, some twenty years younger, as his bride. The service at the Little Church Around the Corner, in New York, was conducted by Lincoln's friend Bishop William Scarlett.

At the close of the ceremony the bride was startled to hear her husband ask, "When do I throw the veil?"

"Lincoln, this is a wedding, you're not at a football game," replied the bishop.[12]

The inside of Mary Louise's wedding band bore the inscription *"Semper Fidelis."*[13] No longer was Lincoln the lonely bachelor who had never known the feeling of being treated as an important personage. Mary Louise possessed an innate ability to say the supportive thing, often inconsequential, but always encouraging: "My, you have a wonderful sunburn" or "Don't you look fit!" She would compliment Lincoln on his haircut, necktie, and so forth, and her comments were genuine, not studied or uttered for effect. And so, late in life, Lincoln for the first time experienced the luxury of unstinting admiration. He and Mary Louise set off for a honeymoon of several months in the South Pacific, secure in the knowledge that arrangements for ship, crew, and plane were being completed under the capable direction of Balchen and Wilkins.

The expedition ship was a 400-ton wooden fishing boat, the *Fanefjord*, purchased in Norway and refitted there. She was sheathed from stem to the widest part of the hull, nearly amidships, with oak planking covered by three-quarter-inch steel armor plate for icebreaking.[14] On her sides appeared her new name, *Wyatt Earp*, chosen by Ellsworth in honor of his hero, the Tombstone, Arizona, frontier marshal who successfully confronted a truculent gang of lawbreakers, just as his namesake would confront the threatening ice pack. On July 20, 1933, under the command of Captain Baard Holth, she left Norway for the 18,000-mile voyage to New Zealand.

Unlike Ellsworth's previous expeditions, this one was entirely American. As the *Wyatt Earp* pulled away from the quay at Bergen for the first lap of her long journey, the Stars and Stripes flew from her foremast, and sirens and whistles clamored their good-luck message. Powered with a Bolinder semidiesel engine, the 140-foot ship had cost $23,000. This was about half the eventual cost of the little plane, thirty-one feet long, that was stowed in her hold, greased and wrapped in oil paper like a cocoon for protection against the corrosive sea air.

It was a tight squeeze to maneuver the *Polar Star* into the hold. From a blueprint of the ship, Balchen had laid out on a drawing board a scale model of the hatch and the hold clearances. He then drew a scale model of the fuselage and, on the drawing board, moved the model into the hold. It could be managed by raising the airplane vertically and lowering it down the hatch, then sliding it carefully in. "It went in there with 1½ inches to spare," Balchen recalled proudly.[15]

To fulfill technical requirements of the country of registry, the ship's manifest carried Balchen as storekeeper at a dollar a month—a somewhat whimsical figure in view of the agreement to pay him $14,700 for flying across Antarctica, in addition to a monthly salary. Wilkins was listed as purser, also at a dollar a month.

Byrd at this time was contemplating a return to Antarctica and sought to impress Bowman with his serious purpose. "I make a real effort to do really scientific work, and that means more men, more food and more equipment. If I were doing this thing alone, I believe I could get off with the greatest ease. Simply go down, make a few flights, and come back, and that is what the public would like best, but I am damned if I am going down there without getting some scientific information, because I don't feel warranted in doing so." Byrd closed with a backhanded thrust surely aimed at Ellsworth, who planned to produce significant results from a single flight: "I have not the slightest criticism of anyone else who wants to do things that way."[16]

Several weeks later Byrd sent Bowman a detailed list of the scientists and equipment he would take and the areas of proposed flight "over the unknown" in an effort to map with the mapping camera. He mentioned "other flights towards the Weddell Sea in several directions."[17] Whether by intention or oversight, he neglected to tell Bowman that these other flights would be "with a view to extending any discoveries made by the Ellsworth Expedition."[18] He said he had informed Lincoln Ellsworth of all his plans and that he would seek Bowman's advice as to what other work he would like to see done.[19]

Aboard the *Wyatt Earp*

From Las Palmas in the Canary Islands, where the *Wyatt Earp* made a stopover for water and fresh stores on the first leg of her journey, Balchen wrote his wife Emmy that everything was going well on board, with "really good guys," splendid food, and a fine ship. He was brushing up on navigation, he told her, and had installed the plane's radio set in his cabin so he could practice and "get really comfortable with it for the trip." Balchen closed with endearments and expressions of longing for his family, and told her that the roses she sent for the embarkation "lasted until yesterday."[20]

A month later he wrote a letter full of poignancy and longing, describing his dreams for the future—building a home in Norway, saving for their two-year-old son's education—and the wrench he actually felt when he separated from Emmy and Lillegut, and dared not show how much it hurt him to leave them both for so long. He assured his wife he would not take any unnecessary chances. His comments about Wilkins were not kind. He described a dinner party at Las Palmas where Wilkins had talked the whole time, and lied and bragged so terribly that someone finally asked what Balchen was doing on board the ship, because by then everybody believed that it was Wilkins who was going to fly the plane. Then Balchen seemed to give full vent to his own feelings of self-satisfaction. "He is a strange fellow," continued the letter, "fiddling around by himself all the time. Whatever he does, it usually ends up wrong. He is not liked by the crew on board. . . . I guess I will have to take more care of things."[21]

Magnus Olsen, reserve pilot for the expedition and second mate of the *Wyatt Earp,* saw Wilkins in a far different light. Worshipful is not too strong a word to describe his admiration. "I looked up to Sir Hubert as a dog does to his master," wrote Olsen, joyful at the prospect of following this "great man"—a wonderful leader whom the men trusted implicitly.[22]

In a letter to Emmy weeks later, Balchen showed no patience with Wilkins' searching mind nor with his many abilities. He criticized

Wilkins for "messing around" with the maps; for "messing around" with something he wanted to play with for a day. Wilkins didn't have a clue about basic principles of navigation or mechanics, he complained. And last but not least, he was "terribly messy." Listed with these supposed frailties was another of Wilkins' annoying traits: "He often gets new ideas."[23]

Balchen reported he now knew why Wilkins wanted to be part of the expedition. It was so he could "get hold of all the equipment and use it for staying on the Graham Land side over the winter."[24] While practicing his radio technique, Balchen picked up another startling bit of gossip from a Norwegian telegrapher who was with Byrd's expedition ship, in Panama. It seemed that Byrd might be planning a surprise by going over to the Graham Land side and flying from there to Little America.[25] In another message to Emmy, Balchen expressed his longing to be home and repeated his promise to take no unnecessary chances.[26]

On November 9, 1933, the *Wyatt Earp* reached Dunedin, New Zealand, where Ellsworth was awaiting his first sight of the little ship that would eventually voyage many hundreds of miles on his quest. "W. has become much nicer now that Ellsworth has joined us," reported Balchen in a letter to Emmy.[27]

For supplies, services, and concessions in price, Ellsworth owed thanks to many individuals and companies. Before leaving Dunedin he mailed several dozen brief letters of gratitude written from shipboard, each composed in a style meant to give the benefactor a sense of bonding with this faraway expedition. Ellsworth signed every note personally, and many closed with a gratifying (and quotable) endorsement: "We have found [this product] to be of the very best quality."[28]

On December 5, decks piled high with supplies and two tiers of petrol drums wired to the rails, the *Wyatt Earp* departed for the Ross Sea. Besides Ellsworth, Wilkins, and Balchen, the expedition included Magnus Olsen; Chris Braathen, motor mechanic; and Dr. Jorgen Holmboe, meteorologist, whose challenging duty was to make upper-air observations and to forecast flying conditions.

Dispatches calculated to pluck the heartstrings of the public were fired off to the *New York Times*. The first, bearing the imprint of Sir Hubert Wilkins, reported that a small biplane with Mrs. Ellsworth flew over the ship and "Mrs. Ellsworth waved and waved again to her husband who stood on deck visibly moved and sad."[29] Ellsworth sent the next dispatch three days later. "My memory of leaving Dunedin is vivid. Circling in a plane above the *Wyatt Earp*, my wife looked down upon my departure. I felt more than a twinge of sadness as I saw her disappear."[30] They had been married less than seven months, and considering the distinct possibility that they might never see one another again, twinge would seem to be a modest estimation of feeling. He might well have echoed Captain Ahab in *Moby-Dick*: "I widowed that woman before I married her," for up to the moment of his death, Lincoln's attention was directed unremittingly toward the realms of lonely splendor.

For days at a time on the trip south, the *Wyatt Earp* was all but buried under gigantic seas. Those stalwart enough to appear for meals, Ellsworth wrote, were often obliged to snatch crockery out of the air as the ship was flung about and battered. The jammed deck allowed no place for exercise. With no general cabin and a mess room so small it would seat only six at a time, those off duty retreated to their bunks to read or nap. Belying Balchen's sneer that Wilkins read only novels, Ellsworth remembered him as having his own small library of books on philosophy and medical matters, as well as a gramophone on which, in calmer weather, he played soft music in the evenings.[31] According to Ellsworth, Wilkins might also spend an evening pondering the provocative philosophy of Nietzsche.

In mid-December the ship reached the pack ice, and three days later got into a jam that could have finished the expedition right there. A colossal iceberg bore down toward them, crushing the ice in its path, building up pressure ridges, and tossing slabs ten to twenty feet thick into the air as if they were shingles. By frantic effort they managed to move out of its path, "but it was a couple of very exciting hours," Balchen recalled. More days of anxiety followed. Using six-foot saws, the crew cut and hacked, then dragged at the floes, until they made room to back and charge and recharge the ice. At last the ship butted her way through to open water.[32]

Tyranny of Ice

On January 7, 1934, early in the Antarctic summer, the *Wyatt Earp* arrived at the Bay of Whales, and the next day moored to the edge of the heavy bay ice. Crew members scrambled up a ladder placed against the ice wall. Ice anchors were swung ashore by derricks, where they were unhooked, placed on a sledge, and hauled farther from the water to be secured. Balchen took off across the bay ice on skis to find a possible landing and takeoff area.

During lulls in the weather, they were able to use the ship's crane to lower the plane onto the level snow that covered the ice. Engine runs and final checks were made, and a test flight on January 11 was successful. Everything was "GO." The *Polar Star* was ready for her long flight.

On the evening of January 12, heavy seas started to break up the ice where the little plane was secured. For safety, Balchen taxied her a mile toward the land. She was still not safe, but everyone was tired and hoped for the best.

However, early in the morning of January 13, a heavy rumbling, confused shouts, and pounding footsteps brought all hands racing on deck. To Olsen's ears, "ominous sounds like the tuning up of a mighty orchestra" thundered from far below the surface, the sound of "cracking, ripping and breaking of miles of thickly packed ice."[33]

Starting from the Barrier (a solid ice cliff edging the floating ice), a bank of heaving, upending slabs moved swiftly and relentlessly toward the plane, and within minutes the Bay of Whales changed from a flat, snow-covered plain to a hummocky tumult of churning ice. As if pushed by the knuckles of a giant hand beneath it, the ice shifted and the plane was nudged upwards. Emergency whistles shrilled, and nine men working on the plane scattered. The slab beneath the *Polar Star* smashed and she dropped, resting only on her wings.[34]

From the ship, men tumbled over the rail, leaping into the rescue boat, alternately pushing over the ice and paddling frantically toward the plane. "Never mind about the plane," shouted Ellsworth. "Get out and rescue those boys before anything else happens."[35] Noses were counted. All hands safe, the crew turned to salvaging the *Polar Star* from her precarious plight.

The *Wyatt Earp* struggled closer. Wires were secured to the plane and it was dragged, inch by inch, over the perilous ice until the derricks could hoist her aboard. "There was a deathly silence as the plane was lifted up"—a broken bird, skis fractured, left wing bent and damaged beyond repair. "Hardly one member of the expedition without tears in his eyes," wrote Olsen.[36]

The next morning a blizzard was screaming through the rigging, and for five days the ship lay helpless. Ice, stealthy in its massive approach, closed in. The crew became prisoners both of the ice and of their own darkening thoughts. Olsen feared that the continual sight of one another's faces "would eventually drive us crazy."[37] Finally, they dynamited their way to open water and set their course back to Dunedin.

"It was an expensive accident for me," declared Ellsworth, but he was determined to try again.[38] This time, however, the flight would be a one-way trip, starting from the opposite side of the continent and ending at Little America. The *Wyatt Earp* would be based on an island off the coast of the Antarctic Archipelago. In the good weather of October or November, the plane would fly to Little America and wait until being joined by the *Wyatt Earp* in January. He gave several reasons for the decision, but the most important was cutting the distance to be flown. This in itself would save enough weight in reduced fuel load to permit them to carry a tent, a sledge, and food supplies and camping equipment, without which, he had come to realize, it would have been foolhardy to "venture into the icy continent."[39]

The *Wyatt Earp* reached Dunedin on January 28, 1934, and for the first time on this plague-ridden expedition, Ellsworth experienced good fortune. A Texaco oil tanker, the *South Africa,* would be heading for Los Angeles after unloading fuel. Her Norwegian captain, Kjell Gran, agreed to transport the *Polar Star,* with Balchen and two other crew members, to Los Angeles, where the battered plane could be delivered to the Northrup factory in Inglewood for repairs.[40] Ellsworth and the others returned to their homes by steamer, with plans for the future still uncertain.

Balchen was "damned bored" waiting for a decision. Nevertheless, he was impressed by Ellsworth's dignity and courage in the face of crushing disappointment. "He takes the whole thing as a good sport," wrote Balchen admiringly.[41] He told Emmy that he couldn't desert when Ellsworth had been so fair to him, nor could he ask for more pay. On the contrary, he thought it would be fairer to get less in order to help him out with the great expenses he incurred. His new, mellow attitude extended even to Wilkins. "As time passes," he wrote, "I like him more and more. He is able when we are in the ice, and quite pleasant to deal with when one gets to know him. He has been really nice to me."[42]

The *South Africa* arrived in Los Angeles in the latter part of March, and Balchen delivered the plane to the Northrup factory for repairs. He was still on the payroll (at $500 a month for room and board, and no more until they sailed again for Antarctica). He was anxious to tell Emmy about his plans, but he could get no satisfactory commitment from Ellsworth in response to several telegrams. "I have been almost in despair because of this uncertainty," he wrote in mid-April. Forgetting his earlier expression of sympathy for Ellsworth's plight, he declared that he might have dumped the whole job if he had been able to afford to.[43]

For once, Ellsworth's indecision was not due to habitual procrastination or having too many irons in the fire. His dilemma was whether to go back by way of South America or New Zealand. He finally announced that the expedition would leave in early summer and the flight would start from the Weddell Sea. His confidence had been bolstered by the belief that Byrd's base in Little America would be occupied so that it could provide weather reports, which would substantially relieve the problem of flying into uncertain weather.[44]

Balchen escorted the plane on a steamer to Auckland, New Zealand, where he and the *Polar Star* were transferred to the *Wyatt Earp,* which then sailed for Dunedin after first stopping at Wellington to fetch Wilkins and the meteorologist. A letter to Emmy was reassuring: "fun to see the guys again, ship looked great; everything working smoothly on board, skipper pleased with the crew."[45]

Monotony of Waiting

"Amid ringing cheers of hundreds of Dunedins," reported the *New York Times,* the *Wyatt Earp* slipped her lines and put to sea at 10:15 A.M., Wednesday, September 19, 1934. On October 14, after weathering 4,000 miles of storm-lashed seas and a raging blizzard, she nosed her way into the harbor at Deception Island, site of an abandoned Norwegian whaling factory at the northern tip of the Antarctic Archipelago. "Wild willy-willies of wind swooped down from the high hill," wrote Ellsworth in a dispatch to the *New York Times*. Going ashore "the wind literally blew us off our feet and we had to cling to each other for support."[46]

For five days the *Wyatt Earp* strained at anchor as driving sleet coated her deck, making work impossible. At last the wind dropped, and the *Polar Star* and the huge case containing wings and tail assembly were hoisted from the hold, placed on shore, and dragged up the steep beach. Workers removed the protective covering that had sheathed the plane during the sea voyage, and Balchen and mechanic Chris Braathen commenced their chilly work of assembling the plane. Ten days later, the *Polar Star* was ready for a test flight. A fire pot was placed beneath the hood that covered the engine in order to warm it. Excitement ran high as the moment for takeoff drew nearer.

Without warning, snow squalls swept in and blanketed the sky. Balchen decided to test the engine on the ground. He climbed into the cockpit. The hood and heating pot were removed. He engaged the starter switch. The propeller made a half turn, stopped, quivered—and a crack erupted like a pistol shot. Lubricating oil, placed in the cylinders to prevent corrosion during the sea voyage, had frozen solid and one of the connecting rods had broken when the piston it was pushing was abruptly stopped by the mass of frozen oil.[47]

"A connecting rod was broken last night and no spare part can be found," Ellsworth radioed the *New York Times*. "It is a terrible price to pay in order to carry out my ambition, but I am determined to carry on until I succeed or see that there is no hope left to make the flight across Antarctica."[48]

By radio they ordered a replacement part to be flown to Magallanes, Chile's southernmost port, 900 miles from Deception Island, and on October 31, the *Wyatt Earp* set forth to fetch it. Ellsworth, Balchen, and three others stayed with the *Polar Star,* and during the anxious days awaiting the *Wyatt Earp*'s return, Balchen cooked for the party. Better than the professional chef aboard ship, thought Lincoln, admiring another of the varied skills of the man who would soon cause him bitter disappointment. Balchen was indeed versatile, a fine artist, a superb mechanic, and even a good sledge builder; but he was also "moody and temperamental," Lincoln found, and "subject to sudden fits of temper."[49]

By the time the ship returned to Deception Island and the *Polar Star*'s engine had been repaired and ground-tested, the snow on which she depended for takeoff had vanished. She was hoisted on board on November 27. The *Wyatt Earp* cautiously picked her way south through icebergs and menacing weather, searching for a level glacier or smooth shelf ice near shore where the little plane could be safely unloaded. In the De Gerlache Strait the expedition team looked up at vast cliffs and sheer ice walls of immense glaciers that rose 300 feet above the sea. Amidst the majestic beauty there was no takeoff site to be found. Heavy ice forced them back. They decided to venture into the Weddell Sea, notorious for its treachery and cruelty to ships. The *Wyatt Earp* reached Snow Hill Island and tied up to the ice barrier, which stood just slightly higher than the rail of the ship. Although it was late in the season to expect decent flying weather, Lincoln's December 5 dispatch to the *New York Times* announced that the *Polar Star* was "at last on solid ice from which she has a reasonably good chance of taking off with safety."[50] But optimism dwindled as days of gales and blizzards followed, creating an atmosphere of "settled gloom."[51]

Chafing over the delay, Ellsworth nevertheless turned the five weeks of waiting to good use by collecting fossils on the snow-free island incongruously named Snow Hill. He hiked across the island's high plateau to visit the hut of Baron Otto Nordenskjöld, which had been abandoned in haste thirty years earlier.

Gazing around the hut, which was guyed against the wind with cables at each corner, Lincoln was stirred by what he saw. What must it have meant, he wondered, to be holed up for two winters, with winds that sometimes screamed at ninety miles an hour?[52]

Everything remained just as it had been at the time of the baron's hasty departure. On the ground sprawled the mummified bodies of three white sled dogs, shot through the head. Boxes of clothing and food, including still edible chocolate, lay scattered about. There was even a pair of ice skates.

Nordenskjöld had also been interested in fossils, and slabs of fossils near the cabin now stirred Lincoln's imagination. Antarctica had been subtropical for a period of about 150 million years (between Carboniferous and Cretaceous periods). No explorer had found bones of any fossilized vertebrate other than birds. And no four-footed animal currently existed on Antarctica. Why was this? wondered Ellsworth. There was every reason to believe "that those ancient forests were populated by living moving things."[53] (Although he did not live to see his belief validated by empirical evidence, Ellsworth's faith was justified. Supported by National Science Foundation grants, in March 1982, scientists of the Seymour Island expedition found, for the first time in Antarctica, the fossil of a land mammal. It was the jawbone of a species of opossum related to the extinct marsupial family *Polydolopidae*, known from findings in Patagonia, Bolivia, and Brazil. The discovery in Antarctica provided a missing link in theories about continental relationships. In an article published in the *Antarctic Journal* in 1982, one expert referred to it as "perhaps the most important paleontological discovery ever made in Antarctica."[54] It has even been referred to as the Rosetta Stone of paleontology.)

From the Nordenskjöld hut, and from his other days of prowling on the island, Ellsworth brought back numerous specimens for the American Museum of Natural History, including a marine mollusk (ammonite) and marine snail (sea whelk) from Cretaceous times, indicative of warm temperate waters. He was proud to note that three of the twenty-eight species he collected had never been found in the Antarctic before.[55]

On December 18, 1934, the weather cleared at last. Snowdrifts buried the *Polar Star* up to her wings. Everyone turned to and dug her out. Balchen and Braathen saw to warming the engine, then climbed in to make a test flight. Hearts soared—and so did the plane. Ellsworth was so confident that he radioed the newspapers an advance story that was to be released upon receipt of a flash from *Wyatt Earp* that the great adventure had finally started.[56]

The flash never came. The next day the weather kicked up again, and eleven days of unremitting storms followed. Balchen wrote: "I have never in my life experienced any type of weather like what we had at Snow Hill Island. It was rain and sleet, low ceilings and snow squalls and fog in one succession, plus storms. It is hard to sit around day after day to wait."[57]

Ellsworth captured this feeling in a single sentence: "There is no adventure in the dreary monotony of endless waiting."[58]

But wait they did. Two years and a sizable fortune had been spent with no results, and successive disappointments were making Ellsworth nearly frantic. Seeking to escape the stigma of complete failure, Balchen and Wilkins suggested making an alternate flight over the Weddell Sea and back to cover an area that had not been seen before. But Lincoln was adamant: He had come down here to find out what lay in the gigantic unexplored area that was still blank on the map, and that was what he intended to do. He already had a name, James W. Ellsworth Land, and had brought a flag to drop when he claimed the unknown territory for the United States. No substitute flight would do. It was to be the transantarctic flight or nothing.

Finally, Ellsworth announced that if they did not get off by January 1, 1935, they would pack up and go home. Here was Wilkins' opportunity, the chance to accomplish the very flight he had hoped to achieve when he was at Dundee Island in 1928. Excited by the possibility of taking over leadership of a ready-made expedition, lacking only a moderate sum to continue functioning, Wilkins secretly radioed Bowman at the American Geographical Society, asking him to investigate whether new financing could be provided: "December 29, 1934 CONFIDENTIAL; Ellsworth tired waiting, is packing to return tomorrow. Have not yet proposed anything to him and not sure that he would agree to any proposal, also apart from what I might personally subscribe would need about $20,000 to carry on another year or $10,000 for rest of this season."[59]

On the day following Wilkins' message, a change in weather altered Ellsworth's frantic state of mind. He radioed the *New York Times*: "Now the nerve wracking strain of waiting is over. . . . The weather is good over the Weddell Sea and reported, through the courtesy of Admiral Byrd, to be fair at Little America."[60]

Fair or foul, Ellsworth was ready to go, although fully aware that disasters might strike. He had taken the precaution to radio code wireless signals to Byrd, brief messages that would be transmitted in an emergency. Each signal, consisting of only three letters, would provide information that would improve the chances for rescue or effective aid: the condition of the plane; injuries, if any, to Ellsworth or Balchen; fuel supply and so forth. "Fas," for example, meant "airplane damaged beyond repair," whereas "fsn" meant "repairs possible, supplies needed."[61]

Once again they dug the *Polar Star* out of snowdrifts, fueled up, and prepared for early morning takeoff. Once again the weather betrayed them. A heavy fog drifted in and blanketed everything. The falling barometer offered no hope. Two days later Wilkins sent Bowman a message canceling his takeover request: "Ellsworth unwilling transfer so unnecessary investigate further."[62]

Fearing to be trapped like Nordenskjöld or possibly crushed in the wind-driven pack ice, they had been preparing to load the plane on board and depart when Dr. Holmboe issued a new weather report. He predicted good weather at both ends of the route, though he warned there was the probability "that thick weather would force an early landing on the Weddell Sea end."[63] In the afternoon, the sky became cloudless.

According to Ellsworth, he said to Balchen, "Let's make a try." Balchen answered "All right" and immediately started to warm the engine.[64] Balchen's version is that he asked Ellsworth, "Would you like to make a flight?" and Ellsworth, believing they "were just joking said 'yes.' "[65]

"Flash," began an elated dispatch to the American press. Anticipating momentous and unprecedented success, Ellsworth wrote: "Balchen and I took off at seven this evening heading for the unknown. The great adventure so long awaited is at hand. The motor is warming up, and soon its roar will be breaking the silence that veils the earth's great unknown. . . . The opening of a continent for the last time in human history."[66]

They took off. But before they had been aloft for even an hour, they encountered a towering white cloud bank, which Balchen judged to be too high to fly over with the load they had aboard. He went into the murk to take a look underneath but found the ceilings were too low. "Couldn't see anything—the whole thing was white." He had only one choice, to turn around and get out of it.[67]

Was it really that bad? Or was he influenced by his responsibility toward Emmy and their little son Lillegut, his repeated promises that he would be careful, would take no unnecessary chances? Lincoln was furious. To him, the "squall ahead" that Balchen described was only a little wisp, with a glow of sun shining on either side. The two men returned to Snow Hill and landed after two and a half hours in the air. Watching Ellsworth jump angrily from the plane and trudge off through the snow, Wilkins asked Balchen what had happened. "Ellsworth can commit suicide if he likes," growled Balchen, "but he can't take me with him."[68] Communication between the two men had broken down completely.

Weeks before, Balchen had told Wilkins he would take off with a single companion only if the flight could be made nonstop, that he could not rely on the assistance of a single man in the event of a forced landing.[69] The radio operator at Little America had warned of probable thick weather at the Weddell Sea end of a flight, which suggests that Balchen may have agreed to "make one more try" in an effort to mollify Ellsworth, rather than with any real intention of reaching Little America.

Determined to salvage what he could from the shambles of his second expedition, Ellsworth tried to make the best of defeat in his next dispatch to the *Times*. "Ellsworth Finds Five New Islands" announced a headline, followed by reference to his revealing mountain peaks and fjords, and making discoveries that would considerably change charts of the vast ice-covered region.

Uncertain of his future but anxious to assure some lasting evidence of achievement that would honor his father's memory, he announced that he had assigned the name James W. Ellsworth Fjord to a large inlet feature, adjacent to five new islands not marked on the official charts.[70]

Although his expedition was provisioned for emergencies and food for two years, Ellsworth was aware of the Weddell Sea's reputation for treacherous passage, and he had no desire to risk a repetition of Nordenskjöld's experience. The season was getting late, and he abandoned all hope of further flight, expressing bitter disappointment at being unable to accomplish the transantarctic flight that year. "Only the weather is to blame," he said. "There are some men who are born to champion lost causes and I am one perhaps for I shall not give up."[71] He decided that as soon as possible they would head north to Montevideo. After four frustrating days of gales and blizzards, they finally were able to bring the *Polar Star* on board, and Ellsworth sent another dispatch to the *Times*.

Here, to fulfill his contract, he padded out news by resorting to the kind of descriptions so often found in his early journals: "the great, silent, purple-tinted ice-bound world . . . where in touch with the vastness of the unknown it is not difficult to sense the magnitude of the universe and the nearness of its creator."[72] He observed that "One also learns the lesson of patience, not the patience born of hours only, but that of days, weeks, even years."[73]

A week later the *Wyatt Earp* was still in the icy grip of the Weddell Sea. A small pool of open water surrounding her was closing rapidly as solid ice floes measuring many miles in each direction bore down, threatening to crush the ship. Escape seemed impossible and preparations were made to abandon ship. Each man checked his emergency pack that contained extra clothing and food for two weeks. They made sure that lifeboats were provisioned, and water casks filled. The atmosphere on board was tense, men's nerves almost at the breaking point.[74] Hour after hour the ship bucked and butted at the ice, then finally reached open water and set course for Montevideo.

Ever since Lincoln's 1926 letter of self-doubt, Bowman had been unstinting in his support and encouragement, and Lincoln, in his moment of defeat, had recognized the disappointment his friend would feel. "Awfully sorry not to have achieved what I set out to do," he radioed Bowman, "yet both success and failure are a part of life I suppose and better to have tried and failed than not to have tried at all."[75]

From Montevideo, a disgruntled Balchen wrote Emmy that Ellsworth

> will probably go down again this fall, but I am definitely not going with him again. Both he and Wilkins have been a big disappointment during difficult times. They both like to take all the credit they can get, but they are weaklings when things are going against them. They have made several attempts, in the most delusive way, to blame me for there being no flying this year.
>
> Where Ellsworth is these days I have no idea. Both he and Wilkins . . . can do whatever they want to now. I have cleared out my [things] and don't give a damn about them.[76]

⚜ 10 ⚜

A Job to Do

HAVING NO DESIRE to spend another year on Lincoln's project, Wilkins had tried without success to persuade him not to go south again. "Ellsworth is determined to go on with another attempt," he wrote a few months later to Aksel Holm, the Norwegian shipping agent responsible for hiring crew members for the *Wyatt Earp*.[1] Although Wilkins wanted to get on with his own plans, having a new submarine built for arctic work, he had not forgotten Ellsworth's loyalty and financial support when the *Nautilus* submarine venture was near collapse. Now he could reciprocate. "It has been a long drag for me," he told Holm. "However, I gave Ellsworth my word that I would help him do the job and it is not yet done and a promise is a promise after all."[2]

Ten days earlier, Wilkins had sought to persuade Balchen to become Ellsworth's pilot for a third attempt to cross Antarctica. Two good Canadian fliers could be found, he explained, but they lacked navigation and radio skills. With Ellsworth planning to leave the country in May, there would be no chance for him to meet a new candidate to see if they could work together. "There is no doubt you are the man for the job," Wilkins said.[3]

Ellsworth thought otherwise. He publicly stated that his greatest need was for men with the right attitude, and in his estimation, Balchen had failed that test the previous year. The search for a new pilot continued. The two Canadians being considered were both pilots with Canadian Airways. They were familiar with conditions of ice, snow, and ski landings, and comfortable in rough outdoor conditions.

Herbert Hollick-Kenyon had 6,100 hours on thirty-five different types of plane, with no crashes. He held a second-class navigator's license "up to the point where sextant work is the next step."[4] Little did he foresee the problems ahead when he added, "I have read theory of bubble sextant and think this would present no difficulty." The salary of $500 a month, plus a bonus of $2,000 to $3,000 depending on the expedition's success, was agreeable to the pilot. J. B. (Red) Lymburner applied for the second pilot position. He had 1,600 hours of flying time and was experienced in engine maintenance.[5] Wilkins accepted his application, warning that Ellsworth was not certain, even at this late date, that he would proceed with the expedition; he would decide definitely "by Wednesday."[6] Wednesday came, and the suspense ended.

"I am going back because I set myself a job to do, [but] the lure is not there any more," Ellsworth said.[7] However, the trip was more than just a job. Later he voiced the reason for it that was near his heart: "The memory of icy land and icy sea crowded with flat-topped bergs, delicately purple at noon, liquid gold when the sun declined to its midnight position. That mocking beauty called me back."[8]

He was confident that he had the services of two qualified pilots. Lymburner "had the ability to take a plane apart and put it together again with no parts left over," he told a reporter.[9] Ellsworth was able to relax and entrust Wilkins with the other arrangements, while he and Mary Louise took a trip to Lenzburg. His stay in Switzerland included two weeks of practice ice climbing. Then he and Mary Louise took off for Rio de Janeiro on the *Graf Zeppelin*. The South American jaunt included an outing in the jungles of Brazil with the legendary Sasha Siemel, famous for hunting jaguars with only a spear. Lincoln was about to fly to Montevideo to join his ship when word reached him that the *Polar Star* had had a mishap on a test flight.

When the *Wyatt Earp* reached Montevideo, Hollick-Kenyon had taken the plane ashore and tuned her up for a brief test flight. Only ninety gallons of gas were loaded. These were distributed among six fuel tanks, leaving two empty.[10] Lymburner described what happened:

Kenyon flew around for about twenty minutes, and for some reason known only to himself, he got fooling around with the gas-cocks and got it turned onto a tank that had hardly any gas in it, about this time he decided he would show off a bit . . . came down in a nice dive, and right over the airport at no feet the motor just quit. . . . He very expertly landed right on the fence between two fields and ran on into the other field . . . and I could have sat right down and cried. There was . . . a hole about three feet square in the under side of the right wing where it had struck a good substantial post. . . . Boy I was so mad when it happened that I could have bitten a chunk right out of the prop.[11]

"The motor just stopped," Hollick-Kenyon told Lymburner, but the next morning he admitted that *maybe* he "got mixed up in the gascocks."[12]

Kenyon, declared Lymburner, was a tinkerer. Fortunately the damage to the plane was not structural and was easily repaired. Despite his jealousy, Lymburner was fair. "I'm not criticizing Kenyon. He's a hell of a good pilot." He was also a very reticent man, according to television interviewer Len Chapple of the Canadian Broadcasting Company.[13] This reticence irritated the companionable and buoyant Lymburner, who described Kenyon as a loner who avoided company and preferred to sit alone at a table rather than join the others.[14]

Questioned by the author about Ellsworth's role, Lymburner made it clear that Wilkins was in charge of operations: "No question about that, he was the boss."[15] And that was exactly what Ellsworth wanted—to be free from all management details. But the limelight was another matter. Lymburner recalled that before they left Antarctica, they all had to agree to get off the ship before it arrived in New York for the anticipated welcome.

Persistence

For the third time the *Wyatt Earp* brought the *Polar Star* and the members of the Ellsworth Expedition to the shores of Antarctica. By November 18 they found on Dundee Island an ideal snowfield for takeoff, about 500 feet above the sea. Supplies and fuel were hauled up on sledges, the plane was test-flown, and they were ready for the great flight. Ellsworth spent the evening preparing his navigation chart for the next day—in case the weather permitted takeoff.

At estimated ground speed of 155 miles per hour, it would take fourteen hours to reach Little America, which was calculated to be 2,200 miles away. Lincoln plotted a great circle course between Dundee Island and Little America, marked off in fourteen equally spaced sections, each representing the estimated distance of 155 miles that would be traveled in one hour. The chart showed the latitude and longitude to be reached at the end of every hour. For each of these assumed positions, Ellsworth calculated the sun elevation and azimuth curves for the expected time of arrival. This would enable him to set his sextant quickly in the plane for the computed altitude of the sun at the given time, and thus determine if they were on course.[16]

Only the weather was left to chance. The plan assumed the flight could be made in a single jump, but survival plans for emergency had been worked out in detail. Loaded on board were 150 pounds of food. At 4,800 calories a man per day, it would last for five weeks. This was the estimated time it would take, trudging twelve miles a day, to reach landfast ice at the ocean edge and the nearest source of possible food—seals. Lincoln, who had observed the beneficial effect of chewing cocoa leaves on the high-altitude endurance of Peruvian Indians, stowed a pound of dried cocoa leaves in the *Polar Star*. As if to absorb the spirit of his frontier hero, he carried Wyatt Earp's cartridge belt with his belongings and wore the frontier marshal's gold ring. He also brought a small Bible with him.

Ellsworth left a detailed statement with Wilkins, telling where he intended to head in case of a forced landing at a site from which no further progress and no wireless communications could be made. Short of a fatal accident, radio failure seemed unlikely. In addition to the plane's own 100-watt radio and a portable generator for ground use, the plane was equipped with an emergency transmitter and receiver, operated either by hand or foot power.[17]

Should the *Polar Star*, in trouble, have passed latitude 75, longitude 75, an amphibian plane would be flown down to Magallanes, where it would be met by the *Wyatt Earp* and taken to Antarctica. Food caches would then be dropped, together with orange markers on long poles, at three locations the explorers might reach on foot. To permit communication between the men on the ground and the air crew, the plan spelled out a code of signals—orange strips of cloth in various designs, parachuted notes, and so forth.[18]

On the morning of November 20, 1935, Ellsworth's long-awaited opportunity was at hand. The weather was favorable. Lymburner and Braathen, the mechanic, made a final check of the plane and warmed the engine. Ellsworth and Hollick-Kenyon shook hands with the rest of the party, climbed over the edge of the fuselage, and squeezed down into their seats. They slid closed the canopy covers. Hollick-Kenyon started the engine, then gave her the gun, and at 0745 the *Polar Star* roared across the frozen surface of Dundee Island, on her way to Little America.

Ellsworth's elation was short-lived. Less than two hours later Kenyon passed him a note: "Sorry we have to go back—I have a fuel leak which may give worse trouble."[19] As the plane bumped over the frozen ridges on takeoff, the glass in a fuel gauge had broken, and the thin membrane of celluloid beneath was bulging under pressure.[20] After a total flight of three hours and fifteen minutes, they were back on Dundee. Trying to hide his disappointment, Ellsworth reworked his navigation chart for the next day. The ground crew hauled more gas up the slope to refuel the plane.

On the morning of November 21, the weather was again fair. "This time I felt in my bones we would make it," Ellsworth wrote.[21] They were airborne at 0800. The only means of communicating in the noisy cabin was by writing messages in Kenyon's flight log or in a small notebook, and passing them back and forth. There were questions and comments about wind drift, course alteration, mountains sighted—and frequent requests for Ellsworth to "try and get drift here." Once, fearful lest their common drinking cup be misused, Kenyon passed Lincoln a note saying, "Put the urine in your balloon [carried to use from surface camps to attract attention or indicate wind direction] and give me back the cup."[22]

Fuel diminished as they fought head winds. "Main rear tank dried up—31 gals hr," noted Kenyon, a sobering contrast to the preflight estimate of 25 gallons an hour.[23] Two hours later: "Second main front centre tank out at 1155," as the *Polar Star* yawed and pitched in the turbulence between high mountains. Fearful of smashing into a mountainside, they climbed higher. A great range appeared ahead, stretching at least seventy-five miles across their track, with higher peaks to the right and left.[24] Ellsworth snapped photographs with his small hand-held Leica camera. "This was the greatest hour of my life," he later exclaimed, "a mountain range of major importance and our eyes were the first to behold it."[25]

They continued to climb, but their ascent was slower getting up the pass. At 10,000 feet, they saw rocks only 800 feet below. They climbed higher. Kenyon watched the air-speed indicator readings drop: 130, 120, 118, finally 110.[26] He passed Ellsworth a message in the little notebook: "At 12,000 ft. cannot see any end to cloud." Lincoln was quite aware of the cloud bank towering into the stratosphere, but he was aghast to read "Am turning back."[27]

How could his dream be allowed to slip away once more? Yesterday Kenyon had turned back; today he was doing so again. The flag to be dropped on unexplored land lay at his side in the cockpit. Two expeditions had failed. And now, for the third year, success remained elusive. Only when they reached longitude 80 would they be over an area not yet claimed by any country—an area he would name James W. Ellsworth Land, his attempt at making amends, albeit late, for lifelong confrontation with his father. They must go on! This time he must succeed! "Can't you go to 80° so can drop flag," scribbled Ellsworth, and thrust the notebook forward over his pilot's shoulder.[28]

Kenyon had his hands full flying the plane in the rough air, sending messages to the *Wyatt Earp,* keeping track of course changes, and attending to fuel consumption as he changed from one tank to another. "Wait till I have time to get back to safety and figure it out—maybe—take some *sights* here" was Kenyon's answer.

An incredible exchange now took place as the two men passed the small notebook back and forth:

Ellsworth: "Say I dropped flag—"
Kenyon: "Do you mean here?"
Ellsworth: "At Long 80°"

Was Ellsworth tempted to risk making a claim that could not be proved? If so, Kenyon saved him from the kind of doubts that overshadowed Peary's and Byrd's claims that they had reached the North

Pole. Kenyon scribbled, "Well—we could say so—but I think with so many radio sets [on whaling ships] about here it would be difficult to prove afterwards. Let me work it out in peace. If we can't go now then we can another time."[29]

At 1435 Kenyon passed Ellsworth another note: "Couldn't get up the Strait—clouds and snow right to the bottom. I told ship we on way back. I've just had lunch. Have you?"[30]

Ellsworth's anger was immediately apparent when the *Polar Star* landed at Dundee. He stalked from the plane without saying a word—a replay of the scene with Balchen the previous year. Later he told Wilkins that he would try again the next day, but that he wanted to take Lymburner, not Hollick-Kenyon.

Wilkins dissuaded him. Lymburner was tired, he pointed out, having had no proper sleep for thirty-six hours while he attended to tuning the engine. Wilkins emphasized the advantage Kenyon had in knowing at least the first part of the route. Kenyon said it was all right with him if Ellsworth preferred to take Lymburner. Finally, Ellsworth, thinking of Kenyon's fine qualities as a flier, said, "No, Kenyon, I want you. . . . But next time we won't turn back."[31] This was not a fortunate prelude to a flight where survival would depend on mutual cooperation.

Flags Dropped

On November 23, at 0805, the *Polar Star* took off the third time for her great journey. An hour later, Ellsworth passed Kenyon the small notebook, saying, "Tell Lanz have named the range we discovered Eternity Range and three highest peaks Mts. Faith, Hope and Charity."[32]

From the start, Hollick-Kenyon's log records their progress and engine performance with meticulous detail. At every stage of the flight, it was vital to know how much fuel remained, and since consumption depended on many variables, an accurate measurement demanded recording the time and the prevailing conditions of each variable that applied. Was fuel mixture lean or rich, and over what length of time? Was flight climbing or level? For how long? At what RPM? What was the IAS (indicated air speed) and what was the temperature at the time of the IAS reading? The latter measurements were important because conversion charts show true ground speed in relation to IAS, with differences depending on temperatures. What was the direction and velocity of wind, and what sideways drift was observed? Was the engine delivering maximum power? From time to time Kenyon checked position with a punctiliously worded note requesting that Ellsworth take another drift sight.

After 500 miles of flying over the coast of Graham Land, which had been partially explored by Wilkins in 1927 and 1928, and with one tank of fuel already drained, they were again on the threshold of the unknown. Flying at an altitude of 11,000 feet, with the temperature at minus 18°C, Kenyon passed Ellsworth a note: "Have you a spare right-handed wool glove there?"[33]

The *Polar Star* climbed still higher, to 13,400 feet. "Cold HR [here] twenty two minus. . . . I can feel the height a little. Haven't much breath," reported Kenyon to the *Wyatt Earp*. (A few years later, during World War II, standard U.S. Air Force operating procedure required pilots to put on oxygen masks at 10,000 feet, to prevent diminished alertness from oxygen deprivation.) Mountains to the left were partly exposed, but ahead was a wall of clouds. Kenyon told the ship that he wanted to get under it (at noted time 1255). Fifteen minutes later he radioed, "If I cannot see a break soon I am going back." A quarter hour passed and Kenyon radioed, "Just asking L. E. what he wants to do."[34]

"He passes the buck to me," continued Kenyon, "says 'anything you like.' So what. Well, I am hoping there is a break ahead and to the right." He locked the transmitting key that automatically sent out continuous beeps so the *Wyatt Earp*'s radio operator would know the plane was not in trouble. A moment later he reported, "Can see a break." He passed a note to Ellsworth, "Well, it's opening up nicely ahead—better keep that camera and the sextant busy, eh?"[35] With ful-fillment of his life's ambition at hand, Ellsworth needed no prompt-ing. More than an hour earlier he had made a note: "1238 photo 7 to left of plane," which was the beginning of the stretch he named Eter-nity Range. The scientific justification for his years of effort depended on his bringing back photographs from which maps of this unknown area could be prepared, and he met the challenge. Between 1220 and 1308 he took seventeen photos, recording direction from plane and altitude.[36] Twenty-four more were recorded in the next six hours.

Kenyon's radio messages to the ship reported a big range to their right, another range to the left, and three big ones in the distance. He noted that the country in between the peaks seemed to be flat and looked like good landing, "but I am not landing now." Chattily, he reported that his pipe was going well but it took a lot of breath at that altitude to get it lit. He asked Lincoln whether he wanted to send any messages, and reported Ellsworth's response: "No msg till [we] get to 80. His heart seems set on it."[37]

Kenyon again mentioned the outlook for landing. "There are crevasses in places here but lots of places where one could land." They crossed the big range at about 10,000 feet, sometimes so close to a peak that they could see its sedimentary composition and stratification.

"One very high peak sticks through the clouds to left dead abeam—abt 120 dist maybe 150," noted Kenyon. A half hour later it was "highest peaks big NS range 11,000 feet," so dramatic that even the unemotional pilot was impressed. "Well, so this is the Antarctic—how do you like it?" he asked, passing back the log. "Yes, 100%," scribbled Ellsworth.[38]

It took three hours to cross lines of mountains on a long, slanting course. Ellsworth photographed range after range, continuing to jot down notes of the plane's altitude and the time of each photo. Using a pylorus to take bearings, he recorded, sometimes with a penciled diagram, the direction of each feature in relation to the flight path of the plane and whether it was on the left side or the right.[39] A mechanical failure had rendered his large mapping camera useless, and the sophisticated trimetrogen equipment, later used by Byrd on Operation High Jump, was not yet available. Consequently, he had to rely on his little Leica. These snapshots, as he called them, forty-one in all, measuring one by one and a half inches, proved crucial to the later construction of maps that were brilliantly produced by cartographer W. L. G. Joerg.[40]

But photographs were not enough. He had not yet dropped his flag. Fearful that something might occur to destroy his dream of claiming new land, Lincoln scratched a note to Kenyon: "How far from 80?" Although they had been flying for six hours, Kenyon replied cautiously. "I estimate about long 70 now, roughly two hours to 80—but unless we land and take a sight I would wait three—to make certain."[41] On they flew.

Bad news soon struck. The radio operator on the *Wyatt Earp* noticed that messages were becoming somewhat erratic, fading out, coming in again, fading, becoming fragmentary, until a final entry in his log: "Nothing heard after 1610."[42] The aircraft transmitter had broken down. On board the *Polar Star*, Kenyon calmly recorded the calamity: "Only thing to do is go on—we have another for land use."[43]

Somewhat more than three hours after Lincoln's question "How far from 80?" he asked for Kenyon's knife, presumably to cut the cord attached to a flag or flags. Then, "Guess I can drop my flag here." The next entry was a question. "O.K.?"[44] To release the flag Ellsworth had to pull back the sliding section of the small panel at the lower edge of the canopy, thrust the flag into the slipstream, and let go. Hollick-Kenyon's log noted, "1745—estimated Station 9." Beneath this entry are the words "Flags dropped."[45]

Ellsworth's diary, November 23 to December 15, 1935, recorded the entries of times and observations that he made throughout that day. At 509 the entry reads: "Long 80 dropped American flag and name [*sic*] the land up to 120 James W. Ellsworth Land. What a thrill!"[46]

It's surprising that "Ellsworth's Own Diary," as published in the *Journal of the American Museum of Natural History*, makes no reference to dropping a flag.[47] This was surely not an oversight. It is possible that by then Ellsworth realized there was no solid evidence that the *Polar Star* had reached longitude 80 at that time, and that he preferred to base his claim on action carried out at a position not subject to question. W. L. G. Joerg, cartographer for the Division of Maps and Charts, National Archives, noted in the *Geographical Review* that "no astronomically determined points were available" for the 1,600-mile portion of the flight between Dundee Island and the exact position of the second landing. *(See Map 3, page 249.)*

At 1800 hours, they sighted distant peaks. Visibility varied greatly because of blowing snow, and the surface below had no distinguishable features. Ellsworth often had to report that he was unable to determine drift. One hour and thirty-five minutes later, the peaks sighted at 1800 were now abeam, the nearest ones twenty-five miles away, the farthest seventy-five to eighty, about 12,000 to 13,000 feet high. Ellsworth was busy with his camera. He named the range Sentinel, and its central peak Mount Mary Louise Ulmer.

After twelve and a half hours in the air, and according to elapsed time and preflight calculations of position, they should have been approaching their final goal, the Bay of Whales. The strain and recurring anxieties of the long flight, as well as a feeling of expectation, undoubtedly clouded Hollick-Kenyon's judgment at this point. "Watersky," he reported, referring to a slight darkness of the sky often caused by reflection of water lying some distance ahead. Because their time in the air should have put them near their final goal, he estimated they were at station 12. But Kenyon was uneasy. At 12 there should have been no high peaks, yet 10,000-foot mountains were still in sight. He scribbled in the log and passed it back. "LE—I really have no idea where we are, but our course carefully steered should put us close in."[48]

It was essential to land to fix their position, and at 2155 they came down. ". . . Came down so hard," recalled Ellsworth, "I thought my teeth would go through my head."[49] Climbing to the ground, his first concern was to see if the fuselage had been badly damaged. Anxiously examining the body, he saw a slight crumple on each side where the wings joined the fuselage. Four or five small rivets were missing—something that happened on takeoff, maintained Kenyon defensively. In view of the unusually rough landing, Ellsworth thought otherwise.

Earthbound

November 23–24, 1935—Nineteen hours on the ground
After landing at Camp Northrop (Camp I), or "Camp Desolation," as Ellsworth called it, Kenyon drained the oil, then tried to establish radio contact with the ship. Ellsworth set up the tent and staked it down and stowed their equipment inside. Together the two men puzzled over the uncertainty of their position. What they discovered was not reassuring. According to elapsed time in the air (thirteen hours and fifty-five minutes) they should be near estimated station 13 (152°57′ west longitude). They took several sights and concluded they were at 104 west longitude, near station 10, alarmingly short of where they had anticipated, and 670 miles from their goal, the Bay of Whales.

"Very hairy after position fixed," wrote Kenyon.[50] Ellsworth seemed briefly to have lost all concern for the journey ahead. It was enough that they stood "in the heart of the only unclaimed land in the

Antarctic—in the whole world."[51] He named the area James W. Ellsworth Land, and called the area above 6,000 feet Hollick-Kenyon Plateau. This was the accomplishment of a dream, a celebration of achievement long sought.

Reality soon demanded their attention. They took sextant observations every three hours, but the results were wildly inconsistent. Ellsworth cranked the hand generator for the trail set, while Hollick-Kenyon tried to establish radio contact with the *Wyatt Earp*, following predetermined schedules for broadcasting. No reply. After nineteen hours of frustration, they took off, with "course set for Station 13."[52] Only thirty minutes later, low visibility forced them to land.

November 24—Two to three days on the ground

Ellsworth was dismayed about his navigation and intended to stay in camp (Camp Gamma, or Camp II) until they could fix their position beyond doubt. Thirty careful sun altitudes, taken over the course of three days, gave a varied spread of position. Kenyon transmitted repeated messages on the trail set, without any response. Balked and hopelessly confused, they finally took off in what they hoped was the general direction of Little America.

How is it possible that these two men elected to go blindly on rather than remain in camp until they uncovered the cause of their navigational predicament? Glin Bennett, a British clinical psychiatrist with a special interest in fatigue, offers persuasive answers. At times of great crisis, he suggests, tension may generate a level of anxiety that can hinder efficient functioning, and "when events are truly shattering, and the threat to life is too great . . . extreme reactions may follow and behavior may become totally disorganized."[53] For Ellsworth and Kenyon, this was such a time. After only fifty minutes in the air, heavy overcast forced another landing.

November 27–December 4—Eight days on the ground

They landed at their third camp (Winnipeg) in the nick of time. A blizzard struck and the temperature plunged to minus 25°C.[54] For three days, the two men shivered in their sleeping bags, crawling out only to transmit on their trail wireless and to fetch snow for cooking. One thing after another went wrong in this wretched blizzard camp. They listed their woes: no communication with the *Wyatt Earp* possible because both radio sets failed; cooking Primus leaks; sextant out of order; camp and plane half buried in snow; short of gas and might have to walk last stretch.[55]

Even so, they did not waste the days. They discovered the cause of their navigation difficulties. The index (lock nut) of their Bausch and Lomb aircraft sextant had somehow become unlocked. "Not known how long this may have been so," noted Kenyon's log. "Sextant reset approx. and awaits opportunity for checking. All previous sights now *doubtful*."[56]

There was no indication of how this disaster came about. Had the lock nut become loosened when the men passed the sextant back and forth during flight? Had Hollick-Kenyon, whose letter of application for employment admitted no previous experience with sextant work (and whom Lymburner called a tinkerer), fiddled with it? Should not Ellsworth, whose sole duties were navigation and photography, have discovered the defect? Whatever the cause, Ellsworth gave Kenyon full credit for discovering how to find the degree of error and thus enabling them to correct their previous observations.[57]

When the storm slackened on the fourth day, the men found the plane half buried in drifts. Kenyon shoveled snow away from skis and wings. Ellsworth, smaller in frame, was able to squeeze into the narrow tail of the plane between control cables and braces, where he spent the whole day with a bucket and a tea cup, scooping out the flour-fine snow that had packed inside around the controls and all the way to the tail.[58] "One of the worst days I ever spent," he wrote, "even a worse job than '25," he wrote, recalling his 1925 trip.[59]

Whenever the sun permitted, they interrupted their digging and took observations, putting the sextant bubble on the snow horizon and locking the index at zero. If they could determine the degree of error that had consistently invalidated previous figures, they could recompute all observations. After reworking their previous calculations they felt moderately confident of their position. It showed they had more than 500 miles to go.[60]

Ellsworth worried that Wilkins, unless he got word of their safety, would initiate the extensive search program they had agreed on. He also hoped that Byrd had by now reoccupied his station at Little America and might pick up any message. He prepared a message of reassurance, while Kenyon, as a last expedient, rigged the portable generator to the plane's radio for a final transmission effort. The December 2 message reported their latitude and longitude, and their intention to proceed to Bay of Whales if fuel supply held out (continuing on foot otherwise), and confirmed times previously agreed on for communication schedule. "No reply," noted the log, followed by the terse entry, "Repeated Dec 3."[61]

Ellsworth spent that next morning clearing away heavy snowdrifts. Then they put the canvas hood over the motor and placed the fire pot inside for forty-five minutes to warm the engine. They removed the hood and Kenyon activated the starter switch. They heard a weak whine and their hearts sank. The propeller failed to catch. Unfazed, Kenyon connected the radio battery to the starter; the motor caught, and they fought their way out of the drift. They loaded everything onto the plane and were about to leave when another storm struck. Wearily they unloaded and pitched the tent. It was at this point that Ellsworth first suspected that his left foot was frozen.

All the next day they struggled to free the plane from mounds of drifted snow, and late that evening they took to the air. Fearful of wasting fuel if they drifted off course, in a four-hour flight Kenyon asked Ellsworth six times to get a drift line, but, as usual, drift was not discernible because there were no ground objects to serve as markers on the white expanse. "Found more (30 mins 45 mins) gas in left centre tank," he noted, as they flew over crevasses where a forced landing would have meant certain death.[62] Then, with the surface below them almost at sea level, they knew they were close to their goal, and at 2310 on December 4 they landed to fix position.

December 4—One night on the ground

Ellsworth wrote of Camp Tranquille (Camp IV), "A beautiful calm night, the boundless snow field sparkling like diamonds."[63] In the morning they felt both anxious and hopeful when they took off. There was no margin for error: survival could literally depend on a mere cupful of gas. Kenyon's logbook recorded the flight:

Dec 5, 1935
Start 0900
1500–1520 RPM - 600 ft - IAS 125–130
landed 1005 Roosevelt Camp
all fuel in tanks consumed.[64]

Ellsworth declared, "the goal of four years of dreaming!"[65]

December 5–15

Camp Roosevelt (Camp V) and "Blind Wanderings." They had seen the open sea before landing, and estimated their position to be about four miles east of Byrd's base at Little America. The first concern was to get word to the *Wyatt Earp,* but the generator would not start. Repeated efforts to raise the ship with the emergency radio brought no results. Excitement and raised hopes gave way to anxiety. They didn't know how long it would take to locate the buildings of Byrd's base, where they expected to shelter while awaiting arrival of their ship. Would they be able to reach the base across the intervening crevasses?

Ellsworth summarized the next ten days as blind wanderings through the fog. After reconnoitering five miles west of the plane, they came to the edge of Bay of Whales ice and were encouraged when they "saw probable location Byrd camp" about six miles farther on. They returned to the plane, where Kenyon admitted with disarming frankness that he was out of condition and had had enough.[66] They continued to follow the schedule for radio transmission, cranking the hand generator for power, forlornly hoping their message would reach the *Wyatt Earp*.

As eagerly as their weary bodies permitted, they pulled the sledge parts from the plane and assembled them, preparatory to heading for the snow-covered buildings they had spotted. Plodding on snowshoes, they dragged the sledge, with sleeping bags, Primus stove, and food for fifteen days, intending to settle in one of the buildings at Little

America and then return to their plane to fetch tent, sextant, and other equipment. For seven hours they toiled over melting snow that clogged snowshoes, dragged at sledge runners, and soaked their feet.

In clear air and a featureless snowscape, distances are deceptive, and the shadowy buildings seemed no closer. The truth dawned. The buildings were blocks of ice! "Proved false scent and had to return 8 or 9 miles for tent and sextant etc," noted Kenyon.[67] By the time they had fetched these essentials and slogged their way back to the sledge, they had been sleepless for twenty-four hours and had traveled some thirty miles, carrying the sextant, tent, and tent poles on their backs more than a third of that distance. It was little wonder that Kenyon admitted being very tired when he dropped his pack and flung himself down on the wet snow. Ellsworth proudly denied fatigue, attributing his stamina to his long training on trails.[68]

On December 13, they dragged the sledge for weary hours, stopping at fifteen-minute intervals to knock the snow clumps from their snowshoes, then straining ahead again in the sledge harness. They were always thirsty, but faced the endless problem of fuel to use to melt snow for drinking water and cooking. They were about to camp when they heard a muffled sound like rising wind coming from beyond a long ridge. They reached the crest and looked down "into the black tumbling water of the Ross Sea."[69] It was the barrier edge. Fearful that the shelf ice might break off and dump them into the ocean, they pushed their weary bodies further, retreated a mile, and made camp as snow closed in and the wind increased.

Ellsworth later recalled "the confused, nightmarish memory" of those four days. His foot, now numb, looked like one huge water blister. He was bewildered by the effects of the impenetrable fog, which distorted depth perception, as they toiled across a surface often interrupted by crevasses and disorienting depressions. He felt a loss of balance, as if he might keel over. He drifted into long reveries about nothing at all. Once, he asked his taciturn pilot why he seldom spoke. Kenyon replied disarmingly that he had such a bad temper it was better to keep silent. Polar nerves for both of us, concluded Ellsworth.[70]

Shelter

December 15, 1935–January 16, 1936. Little America, Final Camp

As Lincoln had discovered, his companion was not one to waste words. Kenyon's log reported the end of their long search for Byrd's camp: "Arrived LA 1845 tired—place hard to find."[71] Ellsworth recalled topping a rise at the end of the day and looking down upon "the most desolate remains of past habitation I have ever witnessed . . . only a lot of masts and the stovepipes of buildings sticking out of the snow."[72] Digging through the snow beside a stovepipe, they found a glass skylight. They broke it, lowered a sledge rope through the opening, and slid down into the icy interior. It was the radio shack, dark and cold, with an adjoining bunk house. A large snowdrift covered the floor, but there was a stove and a bag of coal. Bleak as it was, they had shelter at last. They cleared out the snowdrift and got a fire going. Ellsworth pulled from his knapsack a small bottle of brandy that Mary Louise had given him to celebrate his crossing of Antarctica. The *Wyatt Earp* had carried it for three years. "Hollick-Kenyon took a sip and really smiled."[73] They cut a tunnel through the snow to the door of the shack. There, rummaging for food supplies and fuel, they found kerosene, two sacks of coal, a bag of hardtack, and some odds and ends of food. After two days, they had settled in. Kenyon's log for December 17 reported, "Had bath and change in morning, and cleaned up pots and pans. LE working on log. Found some good books, and a tin of Dill's tobacco."[74]

Hollick-Kenyon was also working on the log. He was determined to identify the causes of navigational error in the sights that he had recorded by himself and those that Ellsworth had also taken. Only when the answer was found could they be reworked to provide an accurate fix of their positions.[75]

The interests of the two made it natural to divide camp responsibilities as they did. Ellsworth undertook snow control, while Kenyon, who enjoyed food and cooking, became the chief food hunter. He prepared the meals and often praised his own cooking. Ellsworth valued food only for its energy-providing capacity. He was committed to physical activity, which Kenyon regarded only as a means to an end.

Accord on the division of labor did little to harmonize their relationship, however. Sometimes shared dangers create a close bond, and after what Kenyon and Ellsworth had been through together, one might expect they would have broken down the barriers of formality. Not so. Background and taste were at odds. Kenyon's log reflects the gap: he refers not to "Ellsworth's log," but to "Mr. Ellsworth's log."[76]

Lincoln was annoyed by Kenyon's "precise personal habits, shaving every day . . . melting snow for shaving water, and so on." He described Kenyon as the most fastidious man he had ever known on any polar expedition. Every night, if there was a chance to melt snow, the pilot always sponged down to his waist—in marked contrast to Balchen, "who had a fine Viking scorn for soap and water." Ellsworth himself was content to shave about once every two weeks.[77]

Their distancing extended to trivialities. Kenyon was always stoking the fire, and making the cabin much too hot for Ellsworth. An inveterate pipe smoker, he was delighted to find a carton of tins of Dill's Best Tobacco. Ellsworth had run out of his own favorite brand of New Zealand tobacco and tried some of the Dill. "How I hated it!" he wrote. Kenyon called Lincoln's New Zealand tobacco the worst he ever smoked. "Each man to his taste," muttered Ellsworth.[78]

How many anxious days of waiting would they have to endure? Even if the *Wyatt Earp* had set out when radio communication failed, it would take her six or seven weeks to cover the 3,000 miles from Dundee Island. Rested by December 20, they put on their snowshoes and, dragging the sledge loaded with a tent and bamboo poles, hiked to Ver-sur-Mer, Byrd's unloading base four and a half miles from Little America. There they pitched the tent and put up two orange-colored flags to attract attention when the *Wyatt Earp* arrived. Ellsworth left a note inside informing anyone who might find it that he and Hollick-Kenyon were at Little America.

Kenyon had found plenty of books in the camp and he read constantly, never speaking, his pipe incessantly gurgling. Ellsworth had left his glasses on the plane and was unable to read, although he worked on his log and reworked navigation sights taken during the flight.

Tension continued to increase between two men, who had little in common, other than the flight accomplished and the necessity of sharing quarters until relieved by the arrival of the ship. Kenyon's log reads almost as if Lincoln did not exist. Continuing to cook, he supplied his own cheering section, probably because praise by Ellsworth was lacking: "excellent bannock, and tossed it—not very high!—successfully!" "beans for breakfast very good indeed," "fine coffee for supper."[79]

On Christmas (which they had mistakenly celebrated a day early), "LE went out for walk—I celebrating by loafing," wrote Kenyon. Thoughts of home lay beneath their brave efforts to gladden Christmas with the extra bottle of brandy they had saved and a plum pudding found on a shelf. "Looking forward very much to arrival of *Wyatt Earp*," wrote Kenyon. He closed his day's log with "It would be reassuring to know that our families know we are here."[80]

Suffering from his infected foot and unable to read, Ellsworth lay hour after hour in his dark berth, his mind almost a blank. "I had long since extracted all the enjoyment from my daydream of the reception I should receive when I emerged victoriously into civilization," he wrote.[81] He was irritated by the intermittent gurgling of Kenyon's pipe: thirty minutes, then a swipe to throw out the juice, followed by the crunch of teeth on hard candy. One evening the sequence of gurgle, swipe, crunch was broken when Kenyon made "his second and last original remark" of their weeks on Antarctica. "Have you any dogs in your house?" he asked. Ellsworth said he hadn't, and Kenyon went back to his book. Another time, Ellsworth absent-mindedly allowed two matches to burn out in his fingers as he prepared to light his pipe. As he lighted a third, Kenyon said, "You must be president of a match factory." Ellsworth snapped back, "You use a good many more matches than I do."[82]

Little wonder that Kenyon, after such rebuff to innocent pleasantry, decided to forgo conversation! Mrs. Hollick-Kenyon once asked her husband why he and Lincoln never talked more. "We had such different backgrounds," he answered, "that it seemed better not to get too close."[83] Except for their involvement in this expedition, they had nothing in common and their backgrounds and personalities were completely dissimilar. In 1929, the year Ellsworth sailed from New York to claim his Hapsburg castle in Switzerland, Hollick-Kenyon sailed from England with wife and two small children to claim a small log cabin at Emma Lake, near The Pas, Manitoba. It was barely furnished and had no stove.[84]

An officer of the rescue ship *Discovery II* reported that the two "got rather severely on one another's nerves in that buried hut under the ice."[85] Neither man possessed "the gift of gab" and both were apt to retreat in stony silence. As Lowell Thomas put it, after interviewing Kenyon, "It was like trying to write a history of the Civil War by interviewing the statue of General Sherman."[86]

As time passed, Ellsworth's thoughts grew somber. Glands under his knee and in his groin had become swollen, and he realized he had a serious infection. "Will the *Wyatt Earp* never come for us?" he wondered.[87] And even if it did, when he returned to civilization, would his achievement be recognized in a manner befitting its importance? He was not famous, as was Amundsen; he had no public relations network to kindle public enthusiasm, as did Byrd. By the time he finally emerged into civilization, would the world even notice that he *had* emerged? He feared his plane was "doomed to remain there forever buried in the snow." What would become of all his flags and souvenirs and the thing he cared about most—the Wyatt Earp cartridge belt?

Lincoln succeeded in hiding the seriousness of his infection, for Kenyon's log for January 16 merely notes, "LE not feeling very well staying in bed." Later that day, from the cabin fifteen feet beneath the snow, Kenyon heard the roar of a plane. He scrambled up the shaft and discovered that a plane was circling.

Aid, Not Rescue

The story is told in the log of Flight Lieutenant E. R. Douglas, a royal Australian air force pilot who was on the relief expedition to locate Lincoln Ellsworth and Hollick-Kenyon after their transantarctic flight.

The *Discovery II* entered Bay of Whales the evening of January 15, 1936, and steamed parallel to the eighty-foot-high barrier face. Twenty minutes later the ship's officers reported sighting two orange flags and a tent a short distance in from the barrier. Knowing that Ellsworth carried orange signal strips in his plane, Douglas concluded that "they might possibly be living at 'Little America' [situated about 4½ miles south, over the barrier ice] and had erected this outpost as a signal to observers at sea."[88]

A Moth plane was lowered over the side, and after a half-mile run, Douglas got the machine into the air and headed for Little America.

"It was all I could do to keep the machine on course," he said, "because the glare from the ice merging with the reflected glare from the clouds made it impossible to see the surface." Then he saw a flag, and soon, radio masts. Circling, he observed an orange ground strip placed near what appeared to be the roof of a hut. "Imagine our delight when a man scrambled out from this roof and started to wave his arms."[89] Douglas dropped a small bag of provisions attached to a parachute. It landed about sixty yards from the man, who snowshoed across to it, picked it up, and waved again. In New York late that night, Mary Louise received a message from the *New York Times* that one man had been sighted. "But I want two!" she exclaimed.[90]

It was Hollick-Kenyon who had picked up the package. Ellsworth first assumed it had been dropped by the relief plane from *Wyatt Earp*, but Kenyon described a small Moth with pontoons. A message signed by Lieutenant L. C. Hill, commander of the British Royal Antarctic Research Society's ship *Discovery II,* instructed Ellsworth and Kenyon to walk to the tent at Ver-sur-Mer and meet a party of his men.[91]

Ellsworth's foot was so painful he told Kenyon to go it alone. Kenyon made off, saying he would be back in three hours, and Ellsworth crawled into his bunk. Despite a "little bother" getting across some shore cracks, Kenyon reached the bay ice edge, where he met the *Discovery*'s landing party and was escorted to the ship. The crew raised a cheer and gave Kenyon a "grand reception." He luxuriated in a hot bath, and the captain loaned him a change of clothes. He appeared "quite casual about it all," noted Douglas.[92]

Kenyon passed the hours by fascinating officers of the research ship with his conversation and then enjoyed a good sleep. Though the relief party was set to return and pick up Ellsworth, Kenyon assured them of his safety. For fourteen hours—not three—after the parachute drop, Ellsworth slept fitfully, shivering from fever. Finally the shore party went out and brought him back to the ship with all their gear in tow. "He appeared glad to be aboard," noted Douglas dryly.[93] Indeed! Swollen glands and inflammation in his leg indicated a serious condition, and his fever had climbed to 102 degrees.

Much as he deplored the characterization of the *Discovery*'s appearance as a *rescue,* Ellsworth sent Prime Minister Joseph A. Lyons a message thanking the government for its assistance. However, he devoted an entire chapter of *Beyond Horizons* to explaining that he was "not 'res-cued'—'AIDED.'"[94]

To uphold his reputation as an explorer, Ellsworth insisted that his antarctic expedition was self-sufficient; that the *Wyatt Earp* had been instructed to pick him up on or after January 22, and had actually reached the Bay of Whales on January 19, with a Northrup plane on board in case further search was needed. He enumerated the meticu-lous emergency plans that had been initiated under his direction and at his own expense. He quoted a long wireless message sent by Wilkins on December 10 to Australian Director of Navigation Captain J. K. Davis, stating that Ellsworth's own plans would meet all requirements until mid-January, and that no good reason existed to believe Ellsworth had not reached his goal at the Bay of Whales.

Wilkins, aboard the *Wyatt Earp,* reached the Bay of Whales shortly after the *Discovery*. His belief that there was no immediate emergency was based on reasonable deductions. The last wireless mes-sage received from *Polar Star* contained no suggestion of trouble. On the contrary, the ship had received encouraging words—"still clear." And later the plane's automatically transmitted signals came through, even though they did not convey a readable message.[95]

In a tone of wonder and admiration, Douglas' longhand diary and his official report describe the *Polar Star's* three landings and the hand-icap of bad visibility. "Knowing a little now about the flying condi-tions and the nature of the country, I think that their effort was one of the best flying feats ever to be accomplished," he wrote. While plans were being discussed for getting the *Polar Star* to the *Wyatt Earp* for loading, there was a good deal of visiting between the vessels. Douglas sized up Wilkins as a charming man, although undoubtedly a bit of a "stunt merchant."[96] On January 21, a spirited shipboard dinner was hosted on the *Discovery*. Ellsworth, his foot improved, Hollick-Kenyon, Wilkins, and Captain Olsen of the *Wyatt Earp* went aboard, sat down to a good dinner, and talked about things in general until after midnight, Douglas recalled.[97] Kenyon recorded being "enter-tained royally—returned about midnight—feeling very well!" Next day his log started, "Tired this morning."

Kenyon stayed to locate and fetch the *Polar Star,* then returned on the *Wyatt Earp*. Ellsworth remained aboard the *Discovery* to go up to

Melbourne to thank the Australian government for its efforts on his behalf. He would express particular thanks to Sir Douglas Mawson, the famous Australian explorer whose concern for Lincoln's safety included sending to the *Discovery II* his own sledge, borrowed from the Adelaide Museum. By the time Ellsworth reached New York, his leg had healed dramatically. He decided to give the *Polar Star* to the Smithsonian, reserving the right to use the plane should he require her for another flight.

F. D. Ommanney, scientific officer on the *Discovery II,* wrote: "Ellsworth, we thought rather a naif and childlike old boy who hadn't much idea why he was flying across the Antarctic or what he hoped to achieve by the feat."[98] Perhaps "naif," but certainly not ignorant of his purpose. Ellsworth had consulted repeatedly with Dr. Bowman since 1929, and more than once had stated in writing precisely what he sought to accomplish. What Ommanney perceived as uncertainty was more likely a sense of deep distress over a victory that was blighted by its characterization as a rescue.

During the voyage to Australia, Douglas expressed his regard for Ellsworth by making and presenting him with a model of the Moth plane, and with the parachute dropped at the Little America camp. The model was inscribed with names of the air personnel. But the true measure of Douglas' admiration for the explorer was his naming of his eldest son Ian Ellsworth. A generation later, Ian's son was christened Andrew Ellsworth. "So you can see," wrote Douglas' daughter to Lincoln's widow, ". . . the name Ellsworth is held very dear to us."[99]

Carrots and Sticks

During the early days of uncertainty regarding Ellsworth's fate, Byrd was on tour lecturing about his own recent expedition to Antarctica, but he wired Bernon Prentice that he was ready to consult or help in any way possible.[100] Less than two weeks later, Byrd wrote his friend Arthur Hayes Sulzberger, head of the *New York Times,* complaining that Wilkins had sent back disagreeable statements casting blame on him for not cooperating with Ellsworth in his difficulties. The letter contained four pages of explanation and disavowal, studded with accusations, innuendo, and self-pity, and ended in a threatening tone: "I would regret it enormously if I were forced into giving some facts to the papers that would be undignified and unworthy of all of us."[101]

"Up to my last expedition," Byrd told Sulzberger, "Ellsworth and I were great friends. I always liked him immensely regardless of his peculiarities, but I believe that his two failures down there on top of the North Pole episode, finally got under his skin." Byrd cited a number of instances when he had aided his fellow explorer and suggested that pride prevented Ellsworth from acknowledging any obligation. It was, Byrd concluded, utterly unfair for Wilkins to claim that Byrd had done anything to hold up Ellsworth's rescue. The next day, apparently concerned about his own reputation, Byrd wrote Sulzberger again, explaining that he had called Bernon Prentice twice and sent both a wire and a letter, but hesitated to become conspicuously involved because Ellsworth had left word that he did not want any help from Byrd or his men.[102]

Byrd's position was awkward. On his lecture tour, he was constantly bombarded with questions about Ellsworth from the audience and reporters. In quick succession, he sent Prentice three letters of self-justification. The first offered his services and listed items available (Curtiss Condor plane with skis, three teams of Eskimo dogs, camping equipment, etc.).[103] The following day he wrote two letters—one asked Prentice to assure Mrs. Ellsworth that "just as a member of the Polar Legion should feel," there was no one more anxious to do anything possible to help Lincoln. "The very evident feeling against me has greatly distressed me," concluded Byrd. "I don't understand it and I don't deserve it."[104] The other letter that same day offered to lend radio equipment, and referred to his effort to avoid personal publicity. It would be easy to get headlines, but poor taste.[105] These letters, with their curious blend of carrot and stick, seem to have accomplished their intended purpose. Prentice and Wilkins promptly expressed appreciation for Byrd's generous offers of assistance, as did Ellsworth two days later.[106]

Byrd told the editors of the *New York Times* that Ellsworth's flight would rank with the greatest, but this fell short of Vilhjalmur Stefansson's glowing tribute: "It is both the most spectacular and the most important ever made in the Antarctic."[107]

At year end Ellsworth received a telegram: "My dear Lincoln when I went down to breakfast this morning I was wondering where you were and was telling myself that it was a pity we had not had a visit since your return. I judge that you have been misinformed about a lot of things and so I was very glad indeed when I received your telegram at the breakfast table. Mrs. Byrd and I heartily reciprocate the New Year Greetings from you and Mrs. Ellsworth."[108]

Ellsworth gave generous credit to Wilkins for the expedition's success. "His conscientiousness had no limits. . . . The expedition and its great object came first with him, and nothing else—not sleep, food, or personal comfort—counted."[109] Nevertheless, Ellsworth remained aware of Wilkins' habit of stealing the limelight.

Although the reception in New York was disappointingly meager, the significance of Ellsworth's flight was not lost on the *New York Times*: "One of the great scientific achievements in the history of exploration," read an editorial. "[It was] the most important [flight] yet made in the Antarctic . . . unique because of the distance covered and the concentrated discovery that was packed into a three weeks' trip."[110]

At a ceremony on the White House lawn, June 16, 1936, President Herbert Hoover presented to Lincoln Ellsworth the special gold medal voted by Congress for "claiming on behalf of the United States approximately three hundred and fifty thousand square miles of land in Antarctica between the eightieth and one hundred and twentieth meridians west of Greenwich, representing the last unclaimed territory in the world."[111]

Though this honor should have been ". . . a sufficient crown for a career which began in such a fumbling fashion . . ." Ellsworth mused, it was not. "The old nostalgia" soon returned, leaving him as always, ". . . restless, unhappy in spirit." A few lines of poetry give wings to his thoughts:

Who has known heights and depths
shall not again
Know peace . . .
Who has trodden stars seeks peace no more.

FIGURE 27. Taken by Ellsworth aboard the *Polar Star*, this photo shows the Eternity Range as it appeared on the first flight, November 21, 1935.

FIGURE 28. The *Polar Star* amid snow drifts.

Figure 29. The *Polar Star* snowed in at Camp III.

Figure 30. Out of fuel at Camp V on December 9, packed for departure and search for Richard E. Byrd's Little America.

FIGURE 31. Ellsworth, arriving at Little America on December 15.

FIGURE 32. Prepared for a celebration, Ellsworth carried these bottles of cognac across Antarctica. He and Hollick-Kenyon autographed the bottle at right.

FIGURE 33. National recognition was finally Ellsworth's when he was awarded a special gold medal by Herbert Hoover, June 16, 1936, for his flight across Antarctica.

~c II ~.

Claiming Antarctica

AFTER THREE YEARS OF MARRIAGE, Mary Louise had yet to establish a home she could feel was her own. She was proud that Lincoln had prevailed over repeated setbacks and had been recognized for his achievements, even rewarded with fame. Now, she thought, they could find the home she yearned for and settle down. To that end, in December 1936 they went to Alberta, Canada, where they spent ten days looking over the EP Ranch. The ranch was being sold by King Edward VIII of England and, as the erstwhile king wrote in his memoirs, "Mr. Ellsworth was the last person outside of the Prime Minister and members of my Household to see King Edward VIII at Buckingham Palace on matters of general business."[1]

Mary Louise recalled that Lincoln and the king were close to a purchase agreement when oil was discovered on the ranch. When its price rose dramatically, Lincoln lost interest. He then found a 16,000-acre ranch with forests and waterfalls in the American West, and thought of buying it to create a refuge for animals. But Mary Louise envisioned a home somewhere in the East, where she had friends and roots, and she rejected the proposal. "I always had the idea that Lincoln wanted to bush me and put me off somewhere," she said. "I look back on it as about the most stupid thing I ever did."[2] One day she enthusiastically told Lincoln about a house she'd found in Maryland with a landscape that even would allow the eighteen-mile daily walk he deemed so necessary. Unimpressed, he responded to their differences in opinion on housing by never again raising the subject.

At about this same time, Mary Louise's hope for another domestic anchor was lost. Lincoln had warned her that they would not have children, insisting he would not have a son. But she thought adopting a girl might be possible, remembering how he had adored his sister Clare. To arrange a trial experience as foster parents without making a permanent commitment, they consulted Lincoln's cousin, Charles Dawes, who was head of the Cradle, an adoption agency in Chicago, and through him, they located a baby girl. Hoping Lincoln would become enchanted, Mary Louise had the infant brought to Hobe Sound, where they were staying in Florida. Although Lincoln admitted feeling somewhat moved when he felt the baby's tiny fingers holding his, he did not wish to be tied down by fatherhood.[3]

What Next?

Soon Lincoln again turned his attention to the Antarctic. "The polar regions leave a terrible restlessness in a man," he later said. "You simply cannot settle down to a humdrum existence."[4]

Isaiah Bowman, so close to Lincoln in earlier days, had left the American Geographical Society to become president of Johns Hopkins University. Because he was no longer available for consultation, Wilkins became Ellsworth's chief advisor. Sir Hubert was intent on building a submarine for arctic research, but he assured Lincoln in February 1937 that this effort would not interfere with his work for an Ellsworth expedition, and said "going with you either this year or next." However, he added, "I cannot afford—much as I would like to—to volunteer my services gratis."[5]

On Lincoln's behalf he looked into finding a suitable plane and reported that either Seversky or Bellanca could provide one comparable to the Northrup that would be satisfactory in range, speed, design, and cost. All too familiar with his friend's procrastination, he warned that if a trip was to be made that year, a machine must be ordered at once.[6]

By mid-May Ellsworth decided he would wait a year, but asked Wilkins to consult the Northrup Corporation, builder of the *Polar Star*, about building a plane—to determine price, instruments, and so forth. Wilkins wrote to company president Jack Northrup, asking when an order was needed to ensure a May 1938 delivery. "I will try to get Ellsworth to make up his mind so as to agree with the date you suggest," Wilkins concluded.[7] He apologized for bothering Northrup over just one machine, and continued, ". . . since you have met Ellsworth and know something of his ways, I feel sure you will understand. He is very loyal and so definitely honorable when he finally decides to do something that I don't so much mind the difficulties in getting things in order."[8]

Northrup responded that he thoroughly appreciated Wilkins' difficulties in assisting Mr. Ellsworth. "He visited us for a short time early this spring, and it was very apparent at that time that he did not have the slightest idea what he wanted to do with regard to further polar exploration."[9] Northrup said delivery of a plane would take at least eight months from date of order, at an outside cost of $60,000 for the airplane and all equipment.

Meanwhile, Wilkins wrote Hollick-Kenyon asking whether he would be willing to go south again for three short flights inland from the Enderby coast, or "(though a remote possibility) making a trans-Antarctic flight to the Ross Sea."[10]

Hollick-Kenyon replied that he would like to accompany Ellsworth; that Lymburner would be a satisfactory second pilot; and that "business associations and proven ability" prompted him to require $750 monthly, $5,000 for transantarctic, and $1,500 for any flight more than 100 miles inland from the sea.[11] Displeased with this response, Ellsworth cabled Wilkins: "Of course am not considering any trans-Antarctic flight as Kenyon mentions in telegram. Afraid he won't suit with present opinion of himself."[12] This indignant denial is curious, because Wilkins had already told Hollick-Kenyon that one possible obligation would be a transantarctic flight.

In a later interview Ellsworth said—with surprising bravado, considering the extreme danger—that the expedition, weather permitting, would take off, "draw a bead on the Bay of Whales, 2,500 miles away, and shoot for it."[13] Danger was not a deterrent to the fifty-seven-year-old explorer. After all, he had returned only two years earlier from an equally hazardous flight. Why, then, did he deny that he was thinking of a transantarctic flight? Perhaps he was following the tactics of his 1925 expedition with Amundsen, when the two explorers publicly disavowed any intention of flying all the way to Alaska, while they secretly determined to do just that. This gave them an opportunity to stun the world if conditions allowed them to accomplish the spectacular flight; at the same time, it protected them from the stigma of failure should they not achieve their goal.

Despite a telegram from Ellsworth that read, "Are ship repairs necessary?" preparation of the *Wyatt Earp* continued under Wilkins' supervision.[14] Selecting a plane was even more important. Cold-weather flying was still on the threshold of innovation, and Ellsworth's pioneering flight across Antarctica had been spectacular. Now, as a new plane was considered, the question of improving on the *Polar Star*'s performance naturally arose.

Hollick-Kenyon was asked for advice on this point. The Canadian flier, now operations manager of a new venture, Skylines Express Ltd., offered a number of suggestions. His 1935 experience with Ellsworth led him to recommend a Northrup machine of the same layout as *Polar Star,* but with a more powerful engine, an "H" type Wasp, that had the advantage of automatic lubrication of some moving parts. He explained the need to fit the plane with a constant-speed propeller to increase efficiency for high-altitude takeoffs. The pilot proposed streamlined skis to lessen wind resistance in flight, although he recognized this would cause landing problems. He suggested several improvements for navigation instruments, and set forth detailed recommendations on radio and emergency sets, and for a reliable portable power source for transmission. Kenyon's confident, flourishing signature on the letter tells much about this pilot, whose aim was efficiency and safety, regardless of personalities. "While [Lymburner] did not seem to like me personally," wrote Kenyon, "it would certainly be desirable from the point of view of the expedition to have him," because of his familiarity with the work and the machine in use.[15]

Financing the expedition seemed daunting after Wilkins prepared an estimate of £120,000 needed for all costs, including those for reconditioning their ship and building a new plane.[16] The July 1 deadline for decision came and went. On July 2, 1937, Ellsworth assured Wilkins he would soon wire him the "last word, awfully sorry to have kept you waiting."[17]

Ellsworth and Wilkins shared a deep psychological bond and similar outlook on life, and each man was useful to the other. However,

Claiming Antarctica 223

Lincoln's tolerance for being upstaged had its limit. With justification, as it later proved, he anticipated that Wilkins' charisma and dramatic submarine proposal would draw press attention away from his own expedition. As they both prepared to return soon from Cherbourg to New York, Lincoln had no intention of being overshadowed. He wired Wilkins, "Prefer we do not sail on same ship."[18]

Nevertheless, Lincoln was uncomfortable about repeatedly interrupting Wilkins' submarine project. On July 21 he told Wilkins by wire that if he was willing to return to California and draw up plans, awaiting Lincoln's decision until September 1, okay; otherwise sell the *Wyatt Earp*.[19] Lincoln must have spent a restless night, for the next day he sent another message: "Hope you decide to return."[20]

This was followed a few days later by a pathetic note from Ellsworth: "It is only 50-50 whether or not I shall decide to go to Enderby Land. I wish my enthusiasm was more, but it isn't; it brings nothing afterwards. The thing is I can find nothing else and so I just keep clinging on hoping for better but it don't [*sic*] seem to come."[21] Here, once again, was the self-doubt that pervaded Lincoln's thinking, although it was seldom apparent to others.

"I am sorry that you don't feel more enthusiastic about the Enderby Land trip," Wilkins replied at the end of July, "because after all this talk about the Russians in the Arctic the public will be glad of something from the South again!" This letter discussed planes that might be available, and the "false reports—mere guesses" by the press about Wilkins' plans. He strongly encouraged Ellsworth to make one more antarctic trip and concluded, "I can no more see you settling down and tied to a 'home' for the next year or so than I can see my way to be content in 'civilization.' "[22]

One talked-about Russian venture in the Arctic failed but produced more distractions. On August 14, 1937, Russian flier Sigismund Levanevsky and five companions were lost on a flight from Moscow to Fairbanks, Alaska, while attempting to demonstrate the practicability of linking east and west using an arctic route. Wilkins was asked to help search for them, and he responded by making numerous flights between September 1937 and March 1938. The effort received generous newspaper coverage.[23] He was still caring for Ellsworth's interests, but, always alert to the importance of remaining in the public eye, he made the most of his current prominence. When asked to give up the search, he announced that he would continue his effort to take a submarine to the Arctic.[24]

In September Ellsworth received a commission as lieutenant commander in the United States Naval Reserve.[25] This seems puzzling since he was too old for active duty and at the time was planning another flight in Antarctica. But in light of his activities for the State Department less than a year later, it seems that the commission could have been a strategic move to prepare for any service that might be asked of him.

"Probabilities of Outbreak of War"

This was the stark title of a voluminous file of documents, dated from March 17, 1936, to August 30, 1939, that was preserved by the U.S. Naval Attaché in London.[26] Germany had withdrawn from the League of Nations in 1933; in 1934 Adolf Hitler became chancellor and president of Germany; and by 1936, at a great rally in Nuremberg, Hitler announced his Four-Year Plan. Its objective was clear: "1. The German army must be ready for war in four years' time. 2. The German economy must be ready for war in four years."[27] The optimism of Sir Neville Chamberlain notwithstanding, the United States and its closest ally, Great Britain, regarded outbreak of war as certain.[28] By 1938 Europe was in growing disarray. That year a German expedition—perhaps for the purpose of demonstrating worldwide power—even went to Antarctica. A number of flights were made that resulted in a large land claim.[29]

Even though the threat of war loomed larger, Ellsworth continued to pursue his personal plans. He had purchased a single-engine Northrup Delta suitable for flights over Enderby Land. Yet his mind constantly turned to the more glamorous possibility of mapping the coastline of the terrain he had claimed for the United States in 1935, which would allow establishing a better claim. For this he would need a twin-engine amphibian. In early May he radioed Wilkins: "Approximately how far from ship necessary to fly to find land off Ellsworth Land. How many flights necessary. Would any work down there establish better claim. Answer immediately."[30]

Wilkins had talked with Ellsworth many times that winter and fully understood the temptation to undertake the more dramatic flight. However, he warned that it would mean flying for at least 300 miles over broken pack ice where a forced landing would be fatal— "there would be not even a chance." If Lincoln chose the "great gamble," continued Wilkins, Lymburner could see about disposing of the Northrup and acquiring a Grumman. Such a change, he warned, would add about $18,000 to the expense.[31]

While awaiting Ellsworth's decision, Wilkins went to Norway in May to engage crew members for the *Wyatt Earp* and interview some of the fifteen applicants for the captain's position. He also had to oversee final reconditioning of the ship, for which he showed appropriate concern about cost.[32] Lincoln finally made up his mind and cabled Wilkins that although he would prefer the Ellsworth Land flight, he had decided against it because of the additional cost and because he needed a topnotch pilot who understood navigation; instead, he would go to Enderby Land and make a single 500-mile flight inland with no coastline mapping.[33]

Wilkins took exception to the disparagement of Lymburner's navigational ability. "I think you are a little hard on Lymburner," he told Ellsworth. "He is certainly a much better pilot than Kenyon— for Kenyon . . . won't fly in bad conditions." As for navigation, Wilkins contended that Lymburner knew as much as Hollick-Kenyon did when he was hired; that Lymburner would have three months to practice on the way south; and anyway, Ellsworth would be doing the navigation.[34]

In late June 1938, uncertain of his finances, Ellsworth wrote Dr. Gilbert Grosvenor, president of the National Geographic Society, outlining two proposals and saying it now seemed impossible to carry out either plan adequately without assistance.[35] Three days later he telephoned to ask for the society's decision regarding its participation. He explained that he must buy a new plane costing about $25,000 and his ship must leave from New York in mid-August, only seven weeks away. Worried about the "uncertain conditions" of the world, the society declined to give him any immediate assurances.[36] But the lure of the icebound continent was strong, and Ellsworth continued to plan.

In early July he went to New Hampshire to build up endurance by hiking in the White Mountains, but at fifty-eight, he was no longer able to force himself as he had in earlier days. He was briefly hospitalized for overexertion in Morrison Hospital at Whitefield, New Hampshire. Unfazed, he announced plans two weeks later for a mountain-climbing trek through the Abadares Range in Kenya, before he would join his ship in Dunedin on October 10.[37]

That autumn, major press attention for Ellsworth's upcoming antarctic expedition focused on Wilkins, rather than on its leader. "Please stop press notices and photographs yourself in connection [my] expedition," Ellsworth cabled.[38] When the request brought no results, he cabled again three weeks later: "Extremely irritated publicity given your connection with my expedition."[39] Another message followed: "Think advisable we do not stay same hotel. Appreciate suggestion immediately."[40] Wilkins' response was equally terse: "Having much work *Wyatt Earp* propose living aboard."[41]

In August of 1938, Ellsworth started a five-week safari in Nairobi. During this period, the *Wyatt Earp* arrived in Cape Town. Highly confidential matters were afoot; Ellsworth had become involved in a devious arrangement with the United States Department of State. It was so certain to cause international confrontation that related memoranda and correspondence were not declassified until the early 1950s. Still unresolved when Ellsworth set out on his fourth expedition to Antarctica was the basic question posed in 1930 by Under Secretary of State Boggs in a memorandum to the acting secretary of state: "What territories are the United States and other countries entitled to claim based on exploration, occupation and asserted claims?"[42] Attempting to answer this and related questions in 1938, a fourteen-page State Department memorandum, classified strictly confidential, cited recent antarctic activities of various countries: Great Britain's 1933 claim on behalf of Australia to a sector embracing 115 degrees of longitude, including the area known as Wilkes Land, which had been discovered by the official American expedition under Lieutenant Charles Wilkes, 1839–40; various claims made by nations under the sector principle; and anxious inquiries from the Japanese embassy and the Norwegian legation in Washington regarding American intentions. Lincoln Ellsworth, an American citizen, has just sailed on an expedition to take him to Enderby Land, and perhaps across the South Pole to Little America.[43]

"The Soviet Union is pursuing a vigorous polar policy," wrote Boggs, "to establish its authority in the Arctic sector which it claims."[44] This was a modest statement in view of the contemporaneous boast of Russian flier Mikhail Vodopyanoff that the world would "rotate on a Bolshevist axis" when the Russians established a scientific camp at the South Pole as they did at the North Pole.[45]

Boggs proposed a "practicable procedure" for laying claim to all lands and islands in the polar regions to which the United States is "entitled to assert a claim because of discoveries, explorations and other acts of officers and men of official American expeditions and of American citizens."[46] He suggested that the United States take the position that it cannot acknowledge in advance sovereignty based on the so-called sector principle supported by Great Britain, the Soviet Union, Canada, Australia, New Zealand, and, apparently, France, because it "is not an established principle of international law."[47]

Prior to this memorandum, Mary Louise Ellsworth's brother, Joseph Ulmer, had visited the State Department on Lincoln's behalf to convey his interest in making claims to new territory in the Antarctic on behalf of the United States "if it were desired that he do so"; Ellsworth's plans could be influenced by suggestions as to areas the department would consider most desirable to explore "from the point of view of claiming or establishing American sovereignty." Ulmer was told that the department could not make suggestions of this character to a private expedition.[48]

Despite this disavowal, Secretary of State Hull gave explicit instructions to James Orr Denby, the American consul in Cape Town, to inform Mr. Ellsworth "in strict confidence, that it seems appropriate for him to assert claims in the name of the United States as an American citizen, to all territory he may explore, photograph, or map which has hitherto been undiscovered and unexplored, regardless of whether or not it lies within a sector or sphere of influence already claimed by any other country." Hull also suggested dropping notes or personal proclamations attached to parachutes, containing assertions of claims identified by latitude and longitude, and subsequently making public the text of such claims. Ellsworth should, of course, be warned not to disclose government knowledge or approval. Hull's letter did not directly ask Ellsworth to communicate with the State Department. It merely suggested that "if he should care to communicate to the Secretary of State a report of his expedition, particularly in relation to areas visited and claims asserted, the Department would be pleased to receive such a report."[49]

On September 26 Ellsworth arrived in Cape Town after his five-week stay in Nairobi. When he called on Denby, they discussed at length the department's confidential instruction. According to the consul's report to the State Department—worded with highly meaningful ambiguity—Mr. Ellsworth "took serious note of the Department's observations and is in accord with the principles set forth." Denby summarized Ellsworth's plans to make several flights into the unknown interior toward the South Pole, or perhaps a single flight from Enderby Land directly to the Bay of Whales, if he found it possible to take off with sufficient fuel to make the 2,000-mile flight. Ellsworth told Denby that he regarded his undertaking as a mapping flight, but (remembering fossils of the sea life he found on his 1935 expedition) added a practical note about the "good probability of oil on the Pacific side of Antarctica." He also mentioned "future possibilities" of both iron and copper found on the coastline by Sir Douglas Mawson, the Australian explorer.[50]

As to the delicate question of claiming land he would fly over, Ellsworth realized that the Australian government had already claimed all of the land south of his projected flight path. However, nobody had seen the interior beyond the coastline, so he professed not to know how far inland the Australian claim extended.[51] Neither did the State Department, but one thing was agreed: trouble lay ahead if their official plot became known, so it continued in secret. When Ellsworth asked for a copy of the State Department's instruction about claiming land, the consul refused. His instructions were that Ellsworth was to be thanked for his willingness to cooperate, but because of the highly confidential nature of the August 30 instruction, "and the Department's desire to avoid any possibility of its contents coming to the knowledge of any person not an American citizen," a copy must not be given him, only "on plain paper the substance . . . so paraphrased as to give no indication of its source."[52] Throwing Ellsworth to the wolves, so to speak, should the instructions be found out, the memorandum disavowed any intention of suggesting to Ellsworth the extent of claims he might assert in the name of the United States as an American citizen.

As instructed, the American vice consul (Arthur L. Richards, act-ing for Denby's temporary replacement, John S. Richardson Jr.) handed Ellsworth a paraphrase typewritten on plain paper. It was so worded that it could not be identified as coming from the State Department or involving any particular individual. Apparently Lincoln relished his involvement in this clandestine undertaking. The consul reported that Ellsworth had been disappointed over the absence of enthusiastic support by the department, though nonetheless "fully aware of the reasons for the government's reluctance to take a more def-inite stand."[53] He left, having given assurance that he would do all that he could to further American claims in any territory he might visit. Thus, with secret State Department encouragement, private citizen Lincoln Ellsworth set out to assert claims on land that he knew his Aus-tralian shipmate and expedition advisor Hubert Wilkins regarded as Australian.

Secret Purpose

As the *Wyatt Earp* left Cape Town, South Africa, on October 29, 1938, Lincoln sent the first of many dramatic press dispatches. "With her decks covered with drums of fuel and the little Aeronca scouting plane fastened to the hatch my ship the *Wyatt Earp* is ready. . . . The area to be visited this year is the last great land mass in the world to be recon-noitered."[54]

Soon the great southern ocean grew angry, and for two weeks they drove through heavy storms, then through lashing snow and sleet. Winds of fifty miles an hour whipped wave tops into spray which raked the ship from stem to stern and "rattled like heavy hail as it dropped almost solid then froze to the sails and rigging." Finally they reached the edge of the pack ice. The wind dropped, storm clouds cleared, "Bright and colourful aurora australis shot back and forth. . . . Then suddenly we entered a curtain of ice crystals hanging in the sky . . . visibility was nil . . . the sudden stillness of the air was awesome."[55]

After three weeks of living with his secret, Ellsworth was not at ease in the role of undercover agent. One day he informed Wilkins that the State Department had requested him to claim any land he might visit in Antarctica. "Before leaving New York," Wilkins wrote in his report of the incident to his government, "[Ellsworth] had published a statement (which I helped to prepare)" in which he said he would not claim any land while on this expedition. It seemed unlikely that Lincoln would go back on such an assurance. Nevertheless, Wilkins felt uncomfortable and questioned Lincoln at the time of his shipboard disclosure. If ever someone was caught on the horns of a dilemma, this was it. Ellsworth had not actually been asked to make claims on behalf of the United States, but the confidential memorandum he was given at Cape Town left him no alternative. He promised to show Wilkins that document at some later date, Wilkins reported.[56]

Ahead lay several hundred miles of ice-choked ocean before they reached the solid ice barrier of the Antarctic continent. For forty-five days the *Wyatt Earp* battled the ice. At one time, for thirteen days the propeller never turned, while they awaited a favorable wind to loosen the solid pack ice that held them prisoner.

Their patience strained after sixty-five days at sea, and on January 3, 1939, the small Aeronca plane was sent out to search for solid land-fast ice from which a flight with skis might be made. The surface was too honeycombed.[57] Only one hope remained: to take off from floating ice, if a suitable expanse could be found. The long-range Northrup was brought on deck for assembly, and Ellsworth had to make a difficult decision. Pontoons would be safe if the thin ice gave way on take-off, but disastrous in the event of a forced landing over the crevassed surfaces of their coming flight.[58]

"I have chosen to be ready in the morning and use the ice and skis," announced Ellsworth on January 5.[59] As the weather looked promising, he sent his wife a radiogram: "Off at 4 A.M. tomorrow (approximately 6 P.M. today EST), Mary, on one single straight line flight due south. . . . With a total visibility of four hundred miles inland it will show whether any great mountain system traverses this side of Antarctica." Aware that this might conceivably be the last word she would ever receive from him, he closed: "To you, all the love I have."[60]

They prepared to lower the Northrup to the ice, but at the last moment clouds rolled up and obscured vision over the barrier.[61]

Prevented from flying, Lincoln had to live another day with his secret. But it was time to produce the memorandum he had promised to show Wilkins and to tell Wilkins his specific plan. On January 7 he showed Wilkins a copper cylinder that he had prepared at Cape Town, and a memorandum stating that an explorer should claim for his country any territory that he actually explored, "irrespective of whether it lay within an area already claimed. . . ." Ellsworth declared that he intended to claim the area from the ship's position (latitude 69 south longitude 77 east) and 150 miles each side of his line of flight and to the South Pole.[62]

Wilkins had pointed out that that part of the Antarctic was already claimed by the British by right of discovery, followed by transfer to the authority of the Commonwealth of Australia, and he advised Lincoln to limit his claim to the new area actually seen and explored during flight. Ellsworth finally agreed to this and asked Wilkins to prepare a record.[63] Wilkins expressed his opinion that Ellsworth's act "would, if taken notice of in official circles, do little more than bring about a definite decision as to the legality of claims based on the 'Sector' principle." Nevertheless, Wilkins was troubled. Allegiance to native land eclipsed his role as advisor to Ellsworth, and he decided to protect his country's interests.

The expedition had a small boat fitted with a Johnson outboard motor, and while awaiting clear weather for flying, Lincoln had gone ashore on some of the islands in the vicinity and "made some most interesting geological discoveries—veins of copper, traces of lead or zinc."[64] Wilkins decided to do the same. He had been authorized by his government, while acting as technical advisor to the Ellsworth Antarctic Expedition "in a portion of Australian Territory," to enter upon, explore, and report. On January 8, 1936, the day after Ellsworth's disclosure, Wilkins did just that. With J. H. Lymburner as a witness, he landed on the northernmost island of the group marked as Rauer, flew the flag of the Commonwealth of Australia, deposited the flag and a record of the visit in a small aluminum container, and collected four cases of geological specimens. On January 9 he repeated the formality at another location, again with Lymburner as witness. He was pleased that this time the landing was more solid: on part of the mainland of Antarctica.[65]

Twenty-four hours later the situation on board the *Wyatt Earp* seemed hopeless. Large icebergs threatened to crush the ship, and the floe they had counted on for a flying field had been shattered.

Lymburner took up the Aeronca seaplane and after two hours of scouting, returned and reported that he had seen a location that might be possible. The ship at once set out to reach it, threading her way among hundreds of icebergs until she came to the edge of some flat ice which looked "fairly suitable." Hopes rose, but quickly dwindled. The surface was riddled with potholes. The plane would be wrecked on takeoff if they tried to carry a full load of fuel. They found a short runway that would permit takeoff with a very small fuel load, but this would limit them to little more than three hours in the air, instead of going out for four hours and return.[66]

While they pondered this dilemma, the wind rose to almost a gale, and it became impossible to lower the Northrup plane onto the ice. With sinking hopes, they watched sections of ice break off from the edge of the flat area that offered the only hope for takeoff. Wilkins made the most of the delay. For the third time he took action to bolster Australian rights to the coastline of the area that Ellsworth intended to claim for the United States. He landed on the mainland and flew a large Commonwealth of Australia flag and then deposited it together with a record addressed "To Whom it May Concern." It recited the rights of the Commonwealth of Australia to "administrate" the area, specified latitude and longitude, and recorded placing the document as evidence of having put foot on the Antarctic mainland in several places and upon several of the islands, and having flown and left the Australian flag.[67]

On this occasion Lymburner was not a witness. He was waiting for the flight with Ellsworth to claim that same land for the United States. About noon, the wind died down, and Ellsworth realized that it was now or never. The big plane was lowered onto the ice and taken up for a test flight. Then, ready for departure, they loaded fuel for a three-hour flight and emergency provisions for five weeks, and took off. For the first fifty miles as they flew inland from the coast they looked down at great open crevasses that shut out all possibility of a safe emergency landing.[68]

This was not the first time that Lincoln had deliberately chosen a brave all-or-nothing commitment to maximum achievement rather than a plan offering greater chance of survival in emergency. He had pioneered an unimaginably daring flight across Antarctica, involving four landings en route. He had always expressed the hope that, when the time came, his ending would be in the icebound wastes that had so long enchanted him.

Ellsworth's plane returned after a flight of two hours and forty minutes, and a jubilant announcement was sent out to the world. Eighty thousand miles of country "never seen before by human eyes has today been added to the known area of the world's surface, and, following a precedent set by earlier discoverers I have claimed the area I have explored for my country the United States of America."[69]

Lymburner made it sound very simple: "They flew in to where Lincoln Ellsworth decided they were far enough towards the Pole to drop the cylinder, opened the window, flung out the cylinder and called the boat and told them the words of the claim to make it official and then they turned around and went back to the boat and that was the end of the flying trip."[70] According to Ellsworth's public announcement, the record he dropped read as follows:

To Whom It May Concern:
Having flown on a direct course from latitude 68.30 south longitude 79 east to latitude 72 south longitude 79 east I drop this record together with the flag of the United States of America and claim for my country, so far as this act allows, the area south of longitude 70 and to a distance 150 miles east and 150 miles west of my line of flight and to a distance of 150 miles south of latitude 72 longitude 79 east which I claim to have explored.—Date: January 11th, 1939
(signed) Lincoln Ellsworth[71]

Growing Unrest—Turmoil Erupts—Positions Harden

Six years earlier Balchen had told his wife that Wilkins wanted to be a part of Ellsworth's 1934 expedition so he could get hold of all the equipment and use it for staying through the winter.[72] Perhaps he might now fulfill such a hope.

Wilkins radioed a confidential message to the secretary of the Department of External Affairs in Canberra, urging Australia to establish a winter base in order to offset Ellsworth's claims. He had found a safe harbor, and by purchasing Ellsworth's equipment, the entire cost to carry out the proposal would be £15,000.[73]

All this time, continuous consultation had been taking place among top-echelon U.S. Department of State officials who sought to increase American power and influence in Antarctica and fend off new claims wherever possible. One experienced observer, Magnus Olsen, dramatically predicted that whichever nation first unraveled the mystery lying below that frozen continent would rule the world. U.S. Under Secretary of State Sumner Welles addressed a seven-page confidential letter to President Roosevelt, analyzing the principles relating to acquisition of polar sovereignty and calling attention to "the positive steps to preserve their territorial rights which have been and are being taken by other countries pursuing vigorous and acquisitive Polar policies." Welles' letter warned of measures being taken by the Soviet, British, Canadian, Australian, New Zealand, French, and Norwegian governments, and the recently expressed interest of the German and Japanese embassies in Washington. He said that these activities (along with strategic and national defense considerations, and interest in aviation, fisheries, and potential mineral and fuel sources) indicated the need for "early and serious consideration of the measures which should be taken by the United States to assert its claims, before the successful assertion of such claims was prejudiced through further undue delay."[74]

Illustrating recent positive action by the State Department, Welles informed the president of the strictly confidential letter of instructions to Denby, the American consul in Cape Town, regarding the antarctic expedition then being undertaken by Lincoln Ellsworth. Welles suggested five steps that might be taken in connection with safeguarding American claims, and proposed, if the president concurred, that representatives of Departments of War and Navy and State meet to formulate concrete suggestions. A map showed "James W. Ellsworth Land" and on the opposite side of the continent an arrow noting that Lincoln Ellsworth was then en route to Enderby Land (December 1, 1938) and "plans extensive exploration on the Antarctic continent, 1938–9."[75]

President Roosevelt replied the very next day. He suggested getting a congressional appropriation to send to two separate South Polar regions an expedition every autumn to remain until early spring when it begins to get dark; one would place men ashore at Little America, the other at the region south of the Cape of Good Hope then being explored by Ellsworth. Byrd and Ellsworth would be consulted on estimates of cost.[76]

At the president's direction, a meeting was held to plan procedure. It was agreed that attention should be directed chiefly towards Marie Byrd Land and the territory in the Enderby Quadrant then being explored by Ellsworth: Heard Island, Ellsworth Land.[77] A second meeting a few days later identified four possible U.S. claims in the Antarctic for location of American settlements. Lincoln Ellsworth's exploration was mentioned in connection with two of them: [1] Heard Island, "because of its use as a point of approach to that portion of the mainland which has recently been explored by Mr. Lincoln Ellsworth." [2] "An area to include the territory recently claimed for the United States by Ellsworth."[78]

Ellsworth's activity at this time generated more turmoil among nations than did Byrd's, despite the greater magnitude of the latter's expeditions. To be sure, Byrd's Little America base was located in the area of Great Britain's Ross Dependency Claim, but after the South Pole flight in 1929, Byrd's activity had been directed at the area to the west—an area still unclaimed. Thus, his activity caused relatively little concern among nations. Ellsworth, on the other hand, might—and did—swoop anywhere. For other countries his current expedition raised questions that did not pertain to his 1935 flight, where some 1,200 miles of the course was over territory unclaimed by any nation, and where the coastline had never been seen or approached.

While deliberations were taking place in Washington, Norway hurried to protect its whaling interests. The U.S. secretary of state received a detailed memorandum saying that at a cabinet meeting on January 14, 1939, Norwegian sovereignty was declared over the region lying between 17 west and 45 east longitude. The message referred to the desirability of Norway establishing control over "a broad stretch of mainland with the adjacent sea," and said that the foreign minister of Norway "had telegraphed to the United States to verify the exact location of the territory claimed by Ellsworth and had found that it was already occupied by Australia."[79]

In a quagmire of uncertainty, Boggs and Cumming of the State Department traveled to Boston to get Byrd's advice about the president's suggestions for settlements in Antarctica. The necessity for secrecy was stressed as they prepared a list for study of places that might be occupied by the United States, including Ellsworth Land and the area recently explored by Ellsworth close to Wilkes Land.[80]

In early February, Commonwealth officials sent a report to the Australian Cabinet pointing out that the region claimed by Ellsworth had been claimed for Australia when it was explored by Sir Douglas Mawson in 1928.[81] Ellsworth seemed almost to enjoy the commotion he had stirred. Here he was at the center of top-level diplomacy involving the president of the United States, and so sensitive to international relations that documents were strictly confidential. He issued a feisty statement saying he welcomed a dispute over his claim, as it might be a stimulus to interest in and settlement of the polar lands.[82] Furthermore, he contended, the basis of claims recognized by governments was the land seen by the eye or within range of the eye. On the same day as Ellsworth's statement, Secretary of State Cordell Hull sent to President Roosevelt a report that representatives of the Departments of the Navy, War, Interior, and Treasury, plus Byrd, had agreed that it would be feasible to establish scientific parties at Little America and at "some point yet to be selected in the area of the so-called Australian quadrant recently explored from the air and claimed for the United States by Mr. Lincoln Ellsworth."[83]

Now a few months short of age fifty-nine, Ellsworth momentarily felt less pushed by the fire of ambition, and in February he sold the *Wyatt Earp* to the Australian government to be used to raise the Australian flag over Antarctic territory claimed by the Commonwealth. But the void was unbearable. He could not endure the thought of retiring from exploration; nor, it seems, could he contemplate the constrictions of domestic involvement. Two weeks later he announced that in 1941 he intended to pass the entire winter at the South Pole with two companions to carry out continuous scientific observations.[84]

Other nations were assuming a less equivocal position than the United States. "Let the Rising Sun be unfurled over the South Pole," was the clarion call from Tokyo, advocating annexation of territory in the vicinity of the Bay of Whales, where Lieutenant Nobe Shirase landed in January 1912, named two bays, and traveled for some days on the Ross Ice Shelf.[85]

From Berlin came an announcement that the German Antarctic Expedition of 1938–39 had discovered and mapped 135,000 square miles of land (between 4°50′ west, 16°30′ east, and as far south as 72°23′), and that Germany had "reserved all rights to the territory over which its planes flew, dropping swastika flags every twenty miles along the borders of the regions and hoisting flags at several points."[86] Norwegian Foreign Minister Halvdan Koht immediately challenged the claim, declaring that the territory claimed by the German Antarctic Expedition was "properly explored, mapped and photographed by land, sea, and air by the Lars Christensen expeditions in 1937 and 1939," and was under Norwegian sovereignty by government resolution of January 14, 1939.[87]

Nevertheless, in March the Australian counselor of the British embassy in Washington, D.C., called on the State Department's Pierrepont Moffatt, chief, Division of European Affairs, to discuss Ellsworth's claim. Taking a bantering tone, the Australian inquired, "Have you been claiming any more of our territory lately?" Underlying the banter, however, was serious concern lest the United States take steps to support Ellsworth's claim. Moffatt replied with dignity that the U.S. did not recognize any foreign claims to antarctic soil. "I hope Wilkins won't be tried for high treason," remarked the Australian as he took his leave.[88]

In mid-April Ellsworth visited the State Department. Anxious to forestall further international apprehension about the consequences of Ellsworth's claim, Moffatt suggested that the press be informed about the visit and that the official position be reiterated, namely, "thus far the U.S. has recognized no Antarctic claims of other governments and that although it has not formally asserted any American claims, it has always, in communications with other governments, reserved such rights as it or its citizens possess in that region."[89]

Two days after his conference at the State Department, Ellsworth wrote Secretary Hull that in order to avoid conflict between his own claims and previous ones, he deliberately waited until he had flown sixty miles inland from the coast on his flight of January 12 before asserting any claim to terrain for the United States. Then, assuming the role of an expert, he set forth in detail why the Antarctic was significant, and quoted Sir Douglas Mawson extensively regarding economic considerations. Apparently unaware of the State Department's decision that establishing bases in the area recently explored by him was not worth the possible advantages, Ellsworth concluded, "The foregoing notes are respectfully submitted to the State Department for whatever action the Government may see fit to take on the claims which I have made in Antarctica."[90]

The next day the *New York Herald Tribune* carried an article featuring Ellsworth's report that the "Antarctic May Be Rich in Ores."[91] It also reported that State Department officials and Dr. Ernest Gruening, director of the Division of Territories and Possessions of the Department of the Interior, conferred with Lincoln Ellsworth in anticipation of an international conference to settle conflicting claims of other countries. According to a State Department memorandum of the conference, Ellsworth learned about studies by various branches of government and intimated he was willing to supply some of the necessary funds.[92] Like a warhorse made restless by lack of battle, he was tempted to go further than that, for the next day he cabled Wilkins: "Confidential. Appreciate inquiring immediately, if ship similar to *Wyatt Earp* for sale in Norway for Antarctic and price."[93] Before leaving for the West some weeks later, Ellsworth made sure that Secretary Hull knew where to reach him in case he cared to communicate.[94]

Disturbed by Germany's militaristic posture, the State Department sent President Roosevelt a memorandum that began: "There is strong reason to believe that we will have the Germans in the Antarctic ahead of us in the regions in which we are interested if we do not act quickly to forestall them."[95] The department's reason for urgency was certainly justified by the tone of a passage it quoted from an issue of the *Four Year Plan,* a periodical published by the Nazi Party in Berlin.[96] Another German source explained that the 1938–39 expedition "has created the grounds for German participation in future international arrangements concerning the question of sovereignty in the Antarctic."[97]

At this time Congress was being asked to appropriate $340,000 for a U.S. government expedition, and a memorandum from State

Department to Senator James F. Byrnes, referring to other nations claiming Antarctic territory, deplored the fact that "while two Americans, Admiral Byrd and Lincoln Ellsworth, have discovered large areas there and claimed them for the United States, our government has been inactive."[98]

German newspapers attacked the United States for imperialism, referred to its "cloven hoof," and quoted the opposition of the Argentine press to the U.S. efforts.[99]

Long afterwards, the German counterpart of the U.S. Board on Geographic Names disparaged Ellsworth's claim, commenting that when Ellsworth in private capacity "claimed a large territory at the 79th meridian east as 'American Highlands' by throwing down flags, this procedure was called a 'new and unaccepted principle' in the journal of the Scott Polar Research Institute at Cambridge."[100]

On July 17, 1939, Mr. A. C. E. Malcolm, second secretary of the British embassy, called on Mr. Hugh S. Cumming Jr., Division of European Affairs, U.S. Department of State, to learn about U.S. plans to locate bases in Antarctica, and inquired whether an American base would be established in the area in the Australian Antarctic territory recently claimed for the United States by Lincoln Ellsworth. Alert to preserve a fallback position if necessary, Cumming's reply was somewhat evasive: this was not one of the areas "currently identified" for locating a base.[101]

Three days after the "cloven hoof" article, a memorandum from President Roosevelt was sent to the secretary of state, saying, "I think it can be made clear to Argentina that the primary and really sole objective of the American expedition to the Antarctic is to prevent any claims by any [European] nations for the wide sector of the Antarctic continent line, roughly south of the American continent. It is, therefore, an expedition solely to protect the ultimate rights of the twenty-one American Republics in this sector."[102]

A few days later, Roosevelt sent an even more challenging suggestion to the State Department: study of a new form of sovereignty, i.e., a claim to the sovereignty of the whole sector lying south of the Americas in behalf of, and in trust for, the American Republics as a whole. "That is a new one," concluded the president's memorandum. "Think it over."[103]

It is not surprising that this imaginative suggestion was greeted by foreign nations with scorn—an attempt to acquire territory without the reproach of aggression.[104] Disapproval extended as far away as Central America, where an editorial in a Honduras newspaper expressed concern about Byrd's coming expedition. It referred to the Monroe Doctrine, and to Lincoln Ellsworth's "reclamo" to the west of the 80th meridian.[105]

Oblivious to a finding that 62 percent of Americans thought a European war would be started by the Germans and 52 percent thought that the United States would be drawn in,[106] Ellsworth continued to focus on what had again become the burning objective of his life. Byrd was soon departing as head of a government-sponsored expedition to Antarctica. Why shouldn't Ellsworth go again? He sent Wilkins a telegram: "Would make flight Elizabeth Land to Ross Sea if possible find suitable ship."[107]

Three weeks later, the long-simmering warnings of impending war burst into reality. Germany invaded Poland on September 1, 1939. Undeterred by complaints of other nations, on November 25 President Roosevelt issued instructions to Byrd, including "delineation of the continental coast line between the meridians 72° West and 148° W and the consolidation of the geographical features of Hearst Land, James W. Ellsworth Land, and Marie Byrd Land."[108] *(See Map 3, page 249.)*

The president's instruction was a logical step toward consolidating American claims to the only area of Antarctica where preexisting claims had not been asserted.[109]

ᴐᴇ 12 ᴈᴑ

Dreams Only

WAR SWEPT INTO THE WATERS of Antarctica in 1941, when a German commerce raider, the *Pinguin,* seized two Norwegian factory ships loaded with oil. Four months later, the *Pinguin* was torpedoed by HMS *Cornwall.* The German ship sank, with all hands on board. Ellsworth's plans for further exploration of Antarctica were perforce abandoned. Battles notwithstanding, however, he thought there must be places beyond the reach of war that could satisfy his restless urge for discovery. He gave free rein to his imagination.

From his expedition in the mountains of Peru in 1924, he recalled hearing tales of adventurers scaling a mountain known as El Misti, seeking treasure said to have been stored at its summit by Indians. Earlier parties had found remains of stone walls within El Misti's volcanic crater, which had inspired speculation about sacrifices in pagan times. In spite of his scientific discipline in some areas, Lincoln's romantic nature took command. At times he suspended disbelief, so that he might be lured by the legend of buried Inca treasure, or accept as established fact that an assemblage of ashes dug up in Death Valley had come from the campfire of the Jay Hawker party. Whether arising from imagination or childlike credulity, his quest was that of a boy at heart. He believed because he wanted so much to believe. He speculated whether the stone foundations in the crater of El Misti might represent the burial site of a king.

With the opportunity to travel, together with the money to finance an expedition, he was in a position to set out on a new adventure. He presented a proposal to investigate the ruins to a well-known

Peruvian archaeologist, Dr. Julio C. Tello. Dr. Tello agreed, and an expedition was organized.[1]

Mounted on mules, the eleven-member party left Arequipa on July 26, 1941, and, after an overnight stop, reached the edge of the crater, having climbed to an altitude of 5,852 meters.[2] The technical portion of the expedition's report, written by the team's junior archaeologist Mejia Xesspe, records location and measurements of five sets of stone ruins and, probably to no one's surprise, says, "Pits dug at various places about these structures gave only negative results. . . . No other artifacts were found to throw light on the age and nature of these structures." The report concludes, "We do not feel justified in adding further speculations about the origin of these ruins to those already on record."[3]

In the spring of the following year Lincoln was dismayed when the U.S. Navy placed him, as lieutenant commander, on the retired list because he had failed his physical checkup. Having devoted his life to staying in top condition, he refused to accept retired status as anything but temporary. He had been extremely nervous during the physical, he wrote Harold Clark, so of course his blood pressure jumped high. Also, his eyesight was one point below passing. "Nevertheless," he declared, "I am more fit than most men. The examination just came the wrong day."[4] Still confident of his physical condition and forgetful of his age, he seems to have taken no warning from his hospitalization three years earlier, when he was treated for exhaustion after hiking in the White Mountains of New Hampshire.

He told Clark that he and Mary Louise were still hunting for a home, someplace where they could be self-sufficient on the land, and he asked for suggestions.[5] But a home was not what was closest to his heart.

"Oh, for some excuse to get back to the Polar Regions again!" opened a letter to Wilkins in May of 1943. "Do try to think of something that gets us out into God's free air again!" it ended.[6] He wrote Harold Clark the same day, "I am out here recuperating, after a concussion." Then he added, "I am still a Lieutenant Commander in the Navy, and hope to be reinstated in September."[7]

The cause of his concussion is mysterious. Mary Louise told the author long afterwards that he had fallen off a bridge into a ravine while returning in the dark to his hotel room in Guaymas, Mexico.

But she offered no details as to how the accident happened, only that he had been found in the morning, with his suit caked with blood and bruises on his neck.[8] Upon his return to the East that autumn, he had a myelogram at the Neurological Institute of the Presbyterian Hospital, in New York, to diagnose the extent of possible injuries. The procedure remained vivid to Mary Louise, because immediately afterwards, he insisted on walking back to their apartment, several miles from the hospital—presumably to prove to himself that he was all right.[9] Only his wife and a few close friends recognized the early consequences of his accident. As a result of his serious fall, recalled Harold Clark, Lincoln's mind at the time was "in quite a confused state," adding that he was, nevertheless, fixated on problems of the Antarctic.[10]

In a speech before the American Polar Society on its tenth anniversary, in December of 1944, Lincoln closed with the declaration, "Of course I am going back again, to the fogbound coast of James W. Ellsworth Land."[11] There he planned to erect a permanent weather station, he announced, to be manned by different young scientists each year, to investigate the high mountain ranges over which he had flown in his crossing of Antarctica.[12] This dream was not to be realized.

After the war, Ellsworth formulated plans with Wilkins for another expedition, to extend over three years at a cost of $150,000. Its purpose would be to "locate and survey the influence of the South Magnetic Pole, to winter at the Geographic South Pole for the maintenance of magnetic and atmospheric electric observations and meteorological observations, and to investigate the physical properties of the polar ice cap at various depths at the Pole."[13] Ellsworth was to be in command, with Wilkins participating in preparing and carrying out the plans.

Nothing came of this scheme, and more than a year later Wilkins wrote Clark that he realized Lincoln could never again go to the Antarctic.[14] It was not hard for Wilkins—similarly moved by a questing spirit—to imagine his old friend's suffering, which was made more poignant by Lincoln's outward gallantry and stoical attitude. Wilkins was determined to help. He devised a plan to try to direct his friend's interest toward other concerns, to give him "something to think about."[15] With an initial contribution of his own and donations from others, he set up the Lincoln Ellsworth Fund within the Arctic Institute of North America. Lincoln expressed pleasure that his friends had seen fit to thus acknowledge their interest in him, but his attention remained riveted on his personal dream.

"Will return south next season if details can be satisfactorily arranged," he radioed Wilkins.[16] This kind of message was exchanged frequently, as the two explorers played their parts in a fantasy that ended only with Lincoln's death three years later. The onset of Lincoln's last illness was in December 1948,[17] and was attended by "special difficulties" in California, which Mary Louise explained "in the greatest confidence" to Harold Clark.[18]

Lincoln's increasingly pathetic condition had become obvious to others. A letter to the headmaster of the Hill School from a classmate who had kept in touch with Lincoln over the years, stated that he had suffered two "attacks" (presumably strokes). The classmate said that Lincoln "seemed far from his usual spry self." He also wrote, "It seemed to me that I would be helpful if I wrote an obituary note for the Alumni Record for use when required. . . . How few," he added, "with great means at their disposal, would have followed their 'vision' as he did? Not many!"[19] This admirer enclosed his write-up with the letter, a final tribute to his boyhood friend.

Stroke or not, Lincoln's dream remained alive. To Harold Clark he wrote: "I shall never give up the idea of trying to get back to the Antarctic again—it is the thing that keeps me going on and hopeful. You know one has to have something to build on."[20]

A year later, Wilkins wrote Charles McVeigh, Lincoln's attorney in New York, "I wish to goodness we could find something that Lincoln *could* do and which would interest him. The Antarctic potentialities will 'wear thin' before too long."[21] On the same day, continuing with the compassionate playacting Ellsworth's friends had agreed on, he wrote Lincoln a long letter comparing the capabilities of different planes suitable for the antarctic job.[22]

For those trying to provide comfort, Lincoln's illness became increasingly difficult. Mary Louise found the ordeal unbearable. Helplessly, she watched his trim figure become swollen, his face puffy, and his keen blue eyes dim. Lincoln was long accustomed to walking eighteen miles a day. Now his firm stride gave way to a tentative shuffle.

From boyhood, the little self-confidence he possessed had hinged upon his pride in physical prowess. Now, although an object of pity, he was resolute in his own mind about returning to the land of his dreams.

During his long illness, Lincoln was nursed by a devoted caregiver named Carol Whittaker. Understanding and competent, she played along, needing no reminder that "our one big problem is this Antarctic question." Miss Whittaker, however, was not alone in tending to Lincoln's needs. In her role as liaison between Mary Louise and Ellsworth's advisors, Marion Goff bore the brunt of the complicated planning. Sir Hubert, she recalled, sent Lincoln a letter discussing antarctic plans. She was supposed to write Lincoln's doctor and tell him that "Mr. Ellsworth is making all preparations for his contemplated trip to the Antarctic next May." Then Miss Whittaker was to arrange for Mrs. Ellsworth to tell Miss Goff to get in touch with Wilkins, and tell him that Mr. Ellsworth was getting ready.[23]

"I'll do my best to keep him pacified," wrote Miss Whittaker, who played her assigned role in the fabrications. But she admitted that "He knows in his mind—when he is lucid—that he cannot go." She spoke admiringly of his courageous nature.[24]

From Miami Beach, Mary Louise wrote Harold Clark, describing Lincoln as "belligerent about having Miss Whittaker with him. He has always been a free soul who chafes under captivity."[25] A few months later she wondered "how much he realizes in his heart," adding, "he is so gallant he would never say."[26]

"As time passes," she told the author more than thirty years later, "I realize he was a very rare and special and dedicated person—not an easy life but a dedicated one for me. And at least he had a goal—and lived it every day."[27]

On May 26, 1951, Lincoln Ellsworth died of a heart attack.

Ten words on his gravestone in Hudson, Ohio, capture the essence of a lonely spirit, who from childhood through old age dreamed and prevailed:

> To strive, to seek, to find
> and not to yield.
> —Alfred Lord Tennyson, "Ulysses"

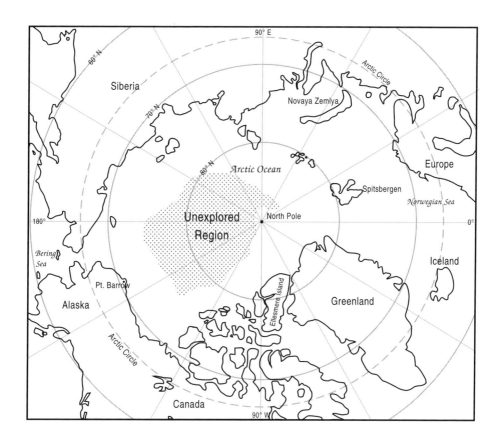

MAP 1. As late as 1945, uncertainty remained regarding the possible existence of land in the unexplored region of the Arctic shown here.

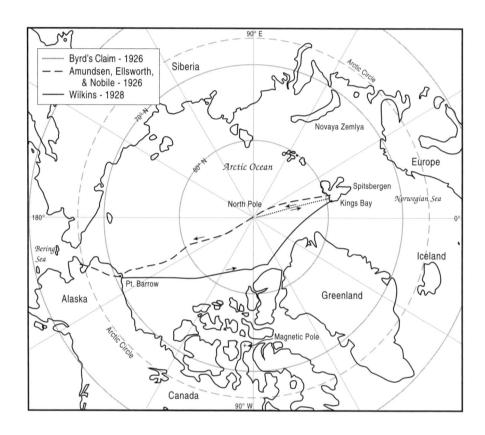

Legend:
- Byrd's Claim - 1926
- Amundsen, Ellsworth, & Nobile - 1926
- Wilkins - 1928

90° E

Siberia

Arctic Circle

70° N

Novaya Zemlya

80° N

Arctic Ocean

Europe

Spitsbergen

North Pole

Kings Bay

Norwegian Sea

180°

0°

Bering Sea

Iceland

Pt. Barrow

Alaska

Greenland

Arctic Circle

Magnetic Pole

Canada

90° W

MAP 2. North Pole routes taken by Byrd, the Amundsen-Ellsworth-Nobile Expedition, and Wilkins.

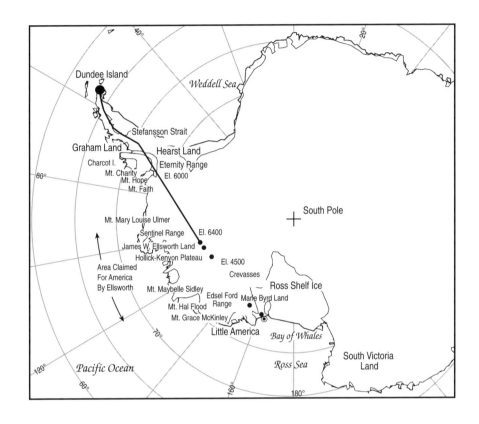

Map 3. First transantarctic flight from Dundee Island to the vicinity of Little America base at the Bay of Whales.

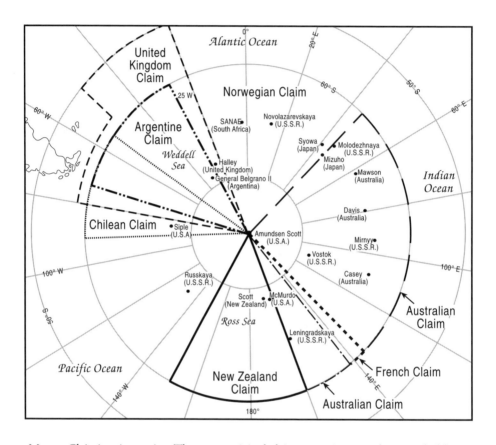

MAP 4. Claiming Antarctica: The seven original claimant nations are shown in bold print; others have asserted their claims over the ensuing years.

Epilogue

BY THE 1920s the legendary figures of polar exploration—
Nansen, Sverdrup, Amundsen, Peary, Scott, Shackleton,
Stefansson—were followed by men with different outlooks and expectations. The early heroes endured cruel hardship over long periods:
Nansen's crossing the Greenland ice cap, and the three-year drift of his
ship *Fram* in the Arctic Ocean; Sverdrup's four uninterrupted years
mapping Ellesmere Island and the unexplored islands to the west;
Amundsen's three-year traverse of the Northwest Passage in the tiny
sloop *Gjoa* and his attainment of the South Pole; Scott's tragic fate
after reaching the same goal; Peary's eighth attempt to reach the North
Pole; Shackleton's incredible 800-mile voyage from Antarctica to
South Georgia in a small open boat, on a search for some means of
rescuing his crew, after his ship *Endurance* was crushed in the ice;
"Stef," comfortable in "the Friendly Arctic," living off the land for
months at a time.

The new breed of explorers of the 1920s was no doubt motivated
by the same feelings as earlier pioneers: quest, curiosity, sense of
adventure, testing of self, opportunity for personal advancement,
desire for admiration and glory—that heady elixir of recognition and
world acclaim. But one thing was different. Now the talk was of flying, and, increasingly, of scientific purpose beyond filling in white
spaces on the map.

During this period there were three major aspirants for polar
fame: Byrd, Wilkins, and Ellsworth. Besides being a naval officer, Byrd
had powerful political connections—longtime personal friendship
with Franklin D. Roosevelt; an influential nephew, Senator Harry
Flood Byrd; recognition by members of Congress with whom he had
worked on behalf of the U.S. Navy. Ellsworth had the advantage of

personal wealth. Wilkins had only his own daring vision and extraordinary self-confidence.

The still unknown expanse of polar regions attracted these men. Each held dreams of exploring by air. Byrd and Wilkins were both pilots, but Ellsworth, in middle age, entered a totally unfamiliar field of activity. Nevertheless, for two decades his presence and imagination and money had a profound effect on polar exploration from the air.

Ellsworth's flight with Amundsen in 1925 was the first major success using airplanes to explore the great unknown areas of the north.

Fifty-seven years later, the Division of Polar Programs, National Science Foundation, wrote of Ellsworth's highly significant exploration and discoveries. They noted that until another flight in 1956, his 2,200-mile flight across a portion of Antarctica in 1935 was the longest flight and the only transcontinental flight in the history of Antarctica.

During the quarter century after Ellsworth's flight across Antarctica, the area he had claimed for the United States was identified successively as James W. Ellsworth Land, then simply as Ellsworth Land, and then Ellsworth Highland. The latter name satisfied neither geographers nor Lincoln's widow. Cartographers found it useless as a geographic reference because it failed to indicate the limits and extent of the areas included.[1] Determined to correct this situation, in 1960, the Advisory Committee on Antarctic Names (of the U.S. Board on Geographic Names) undertook a careful study of aerial photographs of the Sentinel Range and a flat-topped range to the south,[2] both discovered by Ellsworth on his 1935 flight.[3] This resulted the following year in a decision to adopt the name Ellsworth Mountains for the group comprising the Sentinels and all adjacent mountain peaks that could be considered as belonging to this new entity.[4]

Maps of Antarctica now show the Ellsworth Mountains—an area extending approximately 480 nautical miles north-south and 240 nautical miles east-west, a roughly rectangular area having north-south limits of 77°00′ N and 85°00′ S, and east-west limits of 75°00′ E and 100°00′ W at the parallel of 80°00′ S. Now they are known familiarly as the Ellsworths, much as one would refer to the Alps or the Rockies.

In 1988 the U.S. Postal Service issued a set of stamps commemorating four men who contributed significantly to discovery in

Antarctica: Nathaniel Palmer, Charles Wilkes, Richard Byrd, and Lincoln Ellsworth.[5]

In 1935, when Ellsworth was waiting in Antarctica to be picked up by his expedition vessel, he and his pilot Herbert Hollick-Kenyon were the only two humans on the entire 5-million-square-mile continent. By 1991 there were approximately three thousand people on the continent and the number of research stations had grown to sixty-eight. "This had little to do with science. It was politically inspired," explained Alfred Fowler, head of the Council of Managers, National Antarctic Program Committee. If there were mineral riches to divide, "countries wanted a seat around the table."[6]

Few moments in polar exploration have proved so astounding and so profoundly dramatic as the spectacular disclosure on May 9, 1996, of Byrd's erasure in his 1926 flight log.[7] The news altered history and the measure of the men who competed for the spotlight on the stage of polar exploration.[8] Had Byrd not claimed the first flight to the North Pole, Ellsworth would have received a measure of the glory, fame, lecture tours, and major publicity, and he would have been accorded the heroic stature which Byrd enjoyed. But just as important for Ellsworth personally, he would have received the recognition he deserved in his quest for accomplishment that he could truly call his own.

Notes

Introduction

1. Ellsworth letter to Gavin, 5 December 1929, Beekman Pool collection.
2. Ellsworth letter to the author, 26 April 1930.
3. *New York Herald,* Paris, 18 June 1930, Beekman Pool collection.
4. Ellsworth letter to the author, 26 April 1930.
5. Pool diary, 22 July 1930, Beekman Pool collection.
6. Ibid., 31 July.
7. Lincoln Ellsworth, *Beyond Horizons* (Garden City, N.Y.: Doubleday, Doran & Co., 1938), 239.
8. Pool diary, 2 August 1930.
9. Ibid., 18 August.
10. Ibid., 19 August.
11. Niagara Falls, 184 feet; Grand Falls, 245 feet. In 1965 Grand Falls was renamed Churchill Falls, after Sir Winston Churchill, but today it no longer exists. The water flow, diverted by forty miles of earth and rock-fill dikes, is now retained on the plateau above in reservoirs, covering 2,567 square miles. From there it is channeled to a point near the river below the rapids and falls to create a drop (gross head) of 1,060 feet at a power plant, where the access shaft to the power house is equivalent in height to a 94-story building (*Churchill Falls News,* 24 August 1968, published by Churchill Falls [Labrador] Corporation, Ltd.). Enough electricity is produced to satisfy three cities the size of London. (Notes for D. J. McParland, President and Chief Executive Officer, Churchill Falls (Labrador) Corporation, Ltd., at press conference, London, 14 September 1968, 11.)

In 1839, Hudson's Bay Company employee John McLean was the first white man to see the Falls, which he encountered while seeking a route for trade canoes from Ungava Bay to the Atlantic Ocean. Proceeding "gaily on our downward course," he wrote, "one evening the roar of a mighty cataract burst upon our ears, warning us that danger was at hand." He described the spot as "one of the grandest spectacles in the world," but the seemingly impassable obstacle of the Grand Falls ended hopes of getting to the coast. He described the river's roaring and foaming, its maddened course, and how he and his companions felt "the solid rock shake under our feet, as we stood two-hundred feet above the gulf" (John McLean, *Twenty-Five Years' Service in the Hudson's Bay Territory* [London, Richard Bentley, New Burlington Street, 1848], vol. II, 75–76). Trying again two years later, he discovered a bypass along a string of small lakes *(Northern Quebec and Labrador Journals and Correspondence, 1819–35* [London: The Hudson's Bay Record Society, 1963], vol. 24, 75).

12. Ellsworth, *Beyond Horizons,* 240.

13. Pool diary, 22 August 1930.

14. Ellsworth, *Beyond Horizons,* 237.

15. Ellsworth letter to the author, 23 November 1930, Beekman Pool collection.

Chapter 1: The Long Road North

1. Grouitch letter to Ellsworth, in National Americana Society, *The Ellsworth Family in Two Volumes;* vol. 2, *Lincoln Ellsworth,* ed. Howard Eldred Kershner (New York: National Americana Society, 1931), 1. Subsequent references to *The Ellsworth Family in Two Volumes* are annotated as *Ellsworth Family.*

2. Ellsworth, *Beyond Horizons,* 7.

3. Mary Louise Ellsworth, taped interview with author, 23 August 1978. Transcript in Beekman Pool collection.

4. *Ellsworth Family,* vol. 1, 28 (reminiscences by James W. Ellsworth, 13ff.); Ellsworth letter to Clark, 25 May 1943, copy in Beekman Pool collection.

5. Ellsworth, *Beyond Horizons,* 33, 34.

6. Ibid., 6, 8, 35.

7. Page Smith, *The Rise of Industrial America, A People's History of the Post-Reconstruction Era* (New York: McGraw-Hill Book Company, 1984), 492ff.

8. Ibid., 505.

9. Ellsworth, *Beyond Horizons,* 9, 10.

10. *New York Times,* 23 April 1895.

11. Paul Chancellor, *The History of the Hill School, 1951–1976* (Pottstown, Pa.: The Hill School, 1976), 12.

12. James W. Ellsworth letter to Harlan N. Wood, quoted in J. F. Waring, *James W. Ellsworth and the Refounding of Western Reserve Academy* (Hudson, Ohio: Western Reserve Academy, 1961), 12. Subsequent references to *James W. Ellsworth and the Refounding of Western Reserve Academy* are annotated as *Refounding of Western Reserve.*

13. Chancellor, *The History of the Hill School, 1951–1976,* 40.

14. Mary Louise Ellsworth, taped interview with author, 23 August 1978.

15. *Ellsworth Family,* vol. 1, 59.

16. Wylie letter to Wendell, 14 February 1927, Hill School Archives.

17. Brownell letter to author, 25 September 1978, Beekman Pool collection.

18. Meigs letter to James W. Ellsworth, 9 August 1900, in *Ellsworth Family,* vol. 2, 3.

19. Ellsworth, *Beyond Horizons,* 40–41.

20. Theodore Roosevelt, *Ranch Life and the Hunting-Trail* (New York: Century Co., 1888), 15ff.

21. Ellsworth, *Beyond Horizons,* 41.

22. Ibid.

23. Ibid., 49.

24. Ibid., 55.

25. Ellsworth, *A Diary of a Few Wanderings Written in Abstract Moments.* Diary entry 12 June (Seattle, Washington, 1905), NA.

26. Ibid., 19 August.

27. Ibid., 22 September.

28. *Ellsworth Family,* vol. 2, 2.

29. Mary Louise Ellsworth, taped interview with author, 23 August 1978.

30. Ibid.

31. Professional Record, American Society of Civil Engineers, Lincoln Ellsworth, November 1905 to April 1906; *Ellsworth Family,* vol. 2, illus. facing 24.

32. Ellsworth, "Diary and Notes, Grand Trunk Pacific Survey, 1906," 6, 7 April 1906, NA.

33. Ibid., 9 April, 10 May.

34. Ibid., 15 May.

35. Ibid., 6 June.

36. Ibid., 11 June.

37. Ibid., 23 June.

38. Ibid., 28 June.

39. Ellsworth, *Beyond Horizons,* 63.

40. Professional Record, American Society of Civil Engineers; *Ellsworth Family,* vol. 2, illus. facing 24.

41. Ellsworth, *Beyond Horizons,* 69.

42. Ibid.

43. Salvatore Cortesi, *An Historic Italian Villa* (Rome: Editrice Nationale, n.d.), 2.

44. Quoted by J. F. Waring, *Refounding of Western Reserve,* 15.

45. Ellsworth, *Beyond Horizons,* 73.

46. H. L. Ferguson diary, "Over the Andes, Colombia," 1909; Lincoln Ellsworth, H. L. Ferguson, 8 January 1909, Ferguson family papers.

47. Ellsworth, *Beyond Horizons,* 81–82.

48. Wally Herbert, *The Noose of Laurels: Robert E. Peary and the Race to the North Pole* (New York: Atheneum, 1989), 283, 285; also 242–58. In a chapter titled "The North Pole or Not," Herbert analyzes actions and communications relating to Peary's claim. A page of Peary's diary entry for 6 April 1909 commences, "The Pole at last!!! The prize of 3 centuries, my dream and ambitions for 23 years" (*Noose of Laurels,* 248). But Herbert points out that this is a loose-leaf page inserted in the diary, and could have been inserted later.

On 11 September 1909, the *New York Times* published a message from Peary declaring that Cook had not been at the Pole on 21 April 1908 or at any other time; that he "has simply handed the public a gold-brick" (*Noose of Laurels,* 285).

49. Ellsworth, *Beyond Horizons,* 28.

50. J. F. Waring, *Refounding of Western Reserve,* 10.

51. Charles Breasted, *Pioneer to the Past: The Story of James H. Breasted* (New York: Charles Scribner's Sons, 1947), 349.

52. Leaflet describing plaque, Beekman Pool collection. Quoted by Winfield S. Downs in "Lincoln Ellsworth, Civil Engineer and Explorer," *Americana Illustrated* 21 (January 1927), 6.

53. Edmund O. Hovey letter to Ellsworth, 29 October 1912, *Ellsworth Family,* vol. 2, 26.

54. Ellsworth, *Beyond Horizons,* 88–89.

55. Ibid., 90.

56. *The Times* (London), 15 February 1913.

57. Roland Huntford, *Scott and Amundsen: The Race to the South Pole* (New York: G. P. Putnam's Sons, 1980), 317, 319. Subsequent references to *Scott and Amundsen: The Race to the South Pole* are annotated as *Scott and Amundsen.*

58. *New York Times,* 8 March 1912.

59. Huntford, *Scott and Amundsen,* chapter 31, 509 et seq.

60. Goddard letter to Osborn, 6 January 1914, AMNH, New York.

61. Ellsworth letter to Wissler, 30 December 1913, AMNH.

62. Ibid.

63. Osborn letter to Sherwood, 24 March 1914, AMNH.

64. Ellsworth letters to Osborn, 30 March, 30 April 1914, AMNH.

65. Ellsworth, *Beyond Horizons,* 92ff.

66. R. A. Harris, "Some Indications of Land in the Vicinity of the North Pole," paper read before the Philosophical Society of Washington, 9 April 1904, *National Geographic Magazine* (June 1904), vol. 15, 255–61; map 256.

67. Vilhjalmur Stefansson, preface to *Race for the Pole* by John Edward Weems (New York: Henry Holt, 1960), 29.

68. Ellsworth letter to Osborn, 8 October 1915, AMNH.

69. Ibid.

70. Osborn letter to Ellsworth, 16 December 1915, AMNH.

71. Ellsworth letter to Osborn, 7 January 1916.

72. Ellsworth letters to Osborn, 11 January 1916; 13, 27 February 1916; 13, 15, 19 March 1916; AMNH.

73. Osborn letter to Ellsworth, 16 March 1916.

74. Ellsworth, *Beyond Horizons,* 103–106.

75. Ellsworth journal, "Astronomy Notes—1920," NA.

76. Ellsworth letters to Walcott, 7 December 1920; 9, 20 January, 15, 18 February, 7 March, 25 April 1921; 11 January 1922, Arch. Record Unit 45, SIA.

77. Ellsworth, "News from the Stars," 1921, Arch. Record Unit 45, SIA, NA.

78. Ellsworth, "Nature and Religion," 1923–24, signed and inscribed to his father, Christmas 1923, NA.

79. F. J. Pettijohn, *A Century of Geology 1885–1985 at The Johns Hopkins University* (Baltimore: Gateway Press, 1988), 45, 68.

80. Ellsworth, "The Wonder of the Universe," 1924, NA.

81. Ellsworth, "Foundations of the Universe," 1924, NA.

82. Mary Louise Ellsworth, statement to author, September 1972, recorded by author in scribbled note at Hotel Carlyle, New York, N.Y.

Chapter 2: The Big Trip

1. Ellsworth, *Beyond Horizons,* 125.

2. J. F. Waring, *Refounding of Western Reserve,* 59.

3. Mary Louise Ellsworth, taped interview with author, 23 August 1978. Transcript in Beekman Pool collection.

4. Ellsworth, *Beyond Horizons,* 111. Quoted from a collection of poems first published as *Das Narrenschiff* ("The Ship of Fools") in 1494, about a crowded boat of buffoons in a stormy sea.

5. Ellsworth letter to James W. Ellsworth, 27 September 1924, NA.

6. *New York Herald Tribune,* 7 October 1924.

7. Roald Amundsen, *My Life as an Explorer* (Garden City, N.Y.: Doubleday, Doran & Co., 1928), 120.

8. Ellsworth, *Beyond Horizons,* 91.

9. Amundsen diary, 8 October 1924, trans. Lars O. Melemseter, UB. This diary was in the form of an ongoing letter to his wife.

10. Ellsworth letter to James W. Ellsworth, n.d., but indicates mid-October 1924, NA.

11. James W. Ellsworth letter to Lincoln Ellsworth, 27 October 1924, Yale.

12. Ellsworth, *Beyond Horizons,* 127.

13. Ibid., 128.

14. Norwegian Consulate, New York, telegram to Ministry of Foreign Affairs, Oslo, 11 November 1924, UB.

15. Ellsworth, *Beyond Horizons,* 129.

16. Ibid., 131.

17. Amundsen diary, 1, 17 November 1924.

18. Ibid. For a record of Amundsen's progressive friendship with Ellsworth, see 13, 31 October and 3, 6, 9, 11, 14, 29 November 1924.

19. Ibid., 20 December 1924.

20. Ibid., 14 November 1924.

21. Ibid., 20 December 1924.

22. Hans Fay telegram to Noreg, 27 December 1924, UB, trans. for *Polar Extremes* by Lars O. Melemseter.

23. Aero Club telegram to Thommessen, 2 January 1925, UB, trans. Lars O. Melemseter.

24. *Ellsworth Family,* vol. 2, 60. See also Ellsworth, *Beyond Horizons,* 130, 133.

25. Ellsworth, *Beyond Horizons,* 115.

26. J. R. L. Anderson, *The Ulysses Factor* (New York: Harcourt Brace Jovanovich, 1970).

27. *Ellsworth Family,* vol. 2, 60–62.

28. Ibid.

29. Harold T. Clark, confidential report of investigation relative to Roald Amundsen, February 1927, Stef.

30. Clark, "Episodes of the Amundsen-Ellsworth Arctic Flights," talk given at the Cleveland Museum of Natural History (Cleveland, Ohio: 14 December 1928), 15.

Subsequent references to "Episodes of the Amundsen-Ellsworth Arctic Flights" are annotated as "Episodes."

31. Ellsworth letter to James W. Ellsworth, n.d., NA.

32. Clark, "Episodes," 16.

33. Ellsworth, *Beyond Horizons*, 134.

34. Clark, "Episodes," 17.

35. *New York Times*, 2 February 1925.

36. Clark letter to Ellsworth, 4 March 1925, Stef.

37. James W. Ellsworth letter to Lincoln Ellsworth, 7 March 1925, NA.

38. Ibid.

39. Ellsworth, *Beyond Horizons*, 17.

40. Unidentified newspaper clipping, n.d., Stef.

41. Ellsworth, *Beyond Horizons*, 136.

42. Helene Mathilde Fenger-Eriksen letter to her sister, Bertha, 6 April 1925, trans. for *Polar Extremes* by Professor Per Tryde, Copenhagen; see also letters to author from another sister, Grete Larsen, 20 April, 4, 5 July 1985, Beekman Pool collection.

43. Ellsworth, *Beyond Horizons*, 137–39.

44. Amundsen diary, 4, 6 April 1925.

45. Ellsworth letter to Clare Prentice, 8 April 1925, Beekman Pool collection.

46. Roald Amundsen, et al., *Our Polar Flight* (New York: Dodd, Mead & Co., 1925), 15.

47. Amundsen diary, 16 April 1925.

48. Ibid., 18 April 1925.

49. Ibid., 28 April 1925.

50. Amundsen, et al., *Our Polar Flight*, 146, Riiser-Larsen.

51. Ellsworth, *Beyond Horizons*, 151–52.

52. Ibid., 153–54.

53. Ibid., 152.

54. Amundsen diary, 15 May 1925.

55. Ellsworth, *Beyond Horizons*, 147.

56. Ibid., 153.

57. Ibid.

58. Amundsen diary, 18 May 1925.

59. F. M. Keller, "North to Eighty-Eight Degrees," *Americana*, vol. XXI, no. 1. January 1927, 39(2).

60. Amundsen, et al., *Our Polar Flight*, 226, Dietrichson.

61. Ibid., 158–59, Riiser-Larsen.

62. Ibid., 35–36.

63. Ibid., 223, Dietrichson.

64. Ibid., 60.

65. Ibid., 107, Ellsworth.

66. Hjalmar Riiser-Larsen, *Great Norwegian Expeditions* (Oslo: Dreyers Forlag, special edition printed for American-Scandinavian Foundation, New York, n.d.), 182.

67. Amundsen, et al., *Our Polar Flight*, 47, Amundsen.

68. Ibid., 109, Ellsworth.
69. Ellsworth, *Beyond Horizons,* 159.
70. Amundsen, et al., *Our Polar Flight,* 110, Ellsworth.
71. Ibid.
72. Ellsworth, *Beyond Horizons,* 161.

Chapter 3: On the Ice

1. Except where otherwise indicated, the events and emotions described in this chapter are drawn from the diary kept by Roald Amundsen 22 May–15 June 1925: "Dagbok Fra Polflyvningen," translated for *Polar Extremes* by Erik J. Friis, former editor and publisher of the *Scandinavian-American Bulletin,* UB.
2. Ellsworth diary Amundsen-Ellsworth Expedition, 24 May 1925, AMNH.
3. Amundsen, et al., *Our Polar Flight,* 116, Ellsworth.
4. Ibid., 116.
5. Ibid., 117.
6. Ibid., 117–18.
7. Ibid., 65.
8. Ellsworth diary Amundsen-Ellsworth Expedition, 27 May 1925.
9. Ibid., 31 May 1925.
10. Ibid., 29 May 1925.
11. Ibid., 31 May 1925.
12. Ellsworth, *Beyond Horizons,* 172.
13. Ibid.
14. Ibid., 174.
15. Ellsworth diary Amundsen-Ellsworth Expedition, 2 June 1925.
16. Amundsen diary, 3 June 1925.
17. Ellsworth diary Amundsen-Ellsworth Expedition, 3 June 1925.
18. Ibid.
19. Amundsen, et al., *Our Polar Flight,* 128, Ellsworth.
20. Ellsworth diary Amundsen-Ellsworth Expedition, 4 June 1925.
21. Amundsen, et al., *Our Polar Flight,* 71, Amundsen.
22. Amundsen diary, 4 June 1925.
23. Ellsworth diary Amundsen-Ellsworth Expedition, 5 June 1925.
24. Ellsworth, *Beyond Horizons,* 178–80.
25. Amundsen diary, 5 June 1925.
26. Amundsen, et al., *Our Polar Flight,* 69, Amundsen.
27. Amundsen diary, 6 June 1925.
28. Amundsen, et al., *Our Polar Flight,* 131–32, Ellsworth.
29. Ibid.
30. Amundsen diary, 8, 9 June 1925.
31. Ellsworth diary Amundsen-Ellsworth Expedition, 10 June 1925.
32. Amundsen, et al., *Our Polar Flight,* 76, Amundsen.
33. Ellsworth diary Amundsen-Ellsworth Expedition, 10 June 1925.

34. Amundsen diary, 10 June 1925.

35. Amundsen, et al., *Our Polar Flight,* 76–77, Amundsen.

36. Amundsen diary, 14 June 1925.

37. Ellsworth gift to author, Beekman Pool collection.

38. Amundsen diary, 15 June 1925.

39. Ibid., 16 June 1925.

40. Amundsen, et al., *Our Polar Flight,* 339, leaves from the diary of Fredrik Ramm, journalist on expedition vessel *Fram.*

41. Bernt Balchen, autobiographical notes, Accessional Microfilm, Record Group 401–97. Annex 1:1, 2, 6, NA.

42. Amundsen diary, 29 June 1925.

43. Ibid., 4 July 1925.

44. Ellsworth, *Beyond Horizons,* 191–92.

45. Ibid.

46. Ellsworth letter to Clare Prentice, 8 April 1925, Ellsworth family papers.

47. Dagfinn Davle, Norwegian Artillery Captain, letter to Ellsworth, 4 July 1925, Yale.

48. Signed "From a young Norwegian lady," letter to Ellsworth, n.d., Yale.

49. Helen Olausen, president, Norwegian National League, letter to Ellsworth, 5 August 1925, Yale.

50. T. Dannevig letter to Ellsworth, 4 May 1927, Yale.

51. Amundsen, et al., *Our Polar Flight,* 59.

52. Gunvor Dietrichson letter to Ellsworth, 18 July 1925, Yale.

53. Morris Markey, *New York Evening World,* n.d., quoted in *Americana* (The American Historical Society, Inc., Somerville, N.J.), vol. XXI, no. 1, January 1927.

54. Clare Prentice letter to Ellsworth, 25 July 1925, Yale.

55. J. F. Waring, *Refounding of Western Reserve,* 77.

56. Clare Prentice letter to Ellsworth, 25 July 1925.

57. Amundsen, et al., *Our Polar Flight,* 144, Riiser-Larsen.

58. Roald Amundsen and Lincoln Ellsworth, *Air Pioneering in the Arctic: The Two Polar Flights of Roald Amundsen and Lincoln Ellsworth* (New York: National Americana Society, 1929), 55. Subsequent references to *Air Pioneering in the Arctic: The Two Polar Flights of Roald Amundsen and Lincoln Ellsworth* are annotated as *Air Pioneering.*

59. E. R. Hope, "Geotectonics of the Arctic Ocean and the Great Arctic Magnetic Anomaly," *Journal of Geophysical Research 64* (April 1959), 408, 410–23; discusses the discovery of the Lomonosov Range in 1948 and its effect on the tides.

60. Ellsworth letter to Grosvenor, 31 October 1927, NGS.

61. Ellsworth notebook, 107 pages, 25 May–13 June 1925, NA.

62. Amundsen and Ellsworth, *Air Pioneering,* 56.

63. Ellsworth, *Beyond Horizons,* 194.

64. Amundsen, *My Life as an Explorer,* 132.

65. Ibid., 134.

66. Ibid.

67. Kopo Furmaregistret, 17 August 1925, UB. The Aero Club was headed by Dr.

Rolf Thommessen, owner and editor of the daily newspaper *Tidens Tigen* in Oslo. He was assisted by Major Sverre of the Norwegian air force and Alf Bryn, who served as secretary.

Chapter 4: Undeclared Race

1. *New York Times,* 20 January 1924.
2. *New York Times,* 13 September 1923.
3. *New York Times,* 18 January 1924.
4. *New York Times,* 20 January 1924.
5. Associated Press, 10 November 1924, Washington, D.C.
6. *New York Times,* 15 February 1924.
7. *New York Times,* 25 February 1924.
8. Richard E. Byrd, *Skyward* (New York: G. P. Putnam's Sons, 1928), 140.
9. Bernt Balchen, autobiographical notes, 1930, Accessional Microfilm, Record Group 401–97, supplement, NA. Quotes Byrd's claim of achieving certain goals "through his influence in political circles." See also "Introduction to Preliminary Inventory of the U.S. Antarctic Survey Service" (Record Group 126), 1955, NA, containing records showing that Byrd had "direct access to the White House."
10. Ford telegram to Rockefeller, 20 March 1925, RAC.
11. Walcott letter to Fosdick, 24 March 1925, RAC.
12. Rockefeller telegram to Ford, 24 March 1925, RAC.
13. Ford letter to Rockefeller, 31 March 1925, RAC.
14. Byrd letter to Ford, 4 April 1925, RAC.
15. Ford letter to Byrd, 6 April 1925, RAC.
16. Byrd, *Skyward,* 143–65.
17. *New York Times,* 22 August 1925.
18. Byrd letter to Ford, 23 January 1926, EI.
19. Ellsworth telegram to Amundsen, 12 August 1925, UB.
20. Amundsen telegram to Ellsworth, 13 August 1925, UB.
21. Ellsworth telegram to Amundsen, 14 August 1925.
22. Amundsen telegram to Ellsworth, 15 August 1925.
23. Ellsworth telegram to Thommessen, 1 September 1925, UB.
24. Agreement between il Regio Governo Italiano and Norsk Luftseiladsforenings, Amundsen-Ellsworth Expedition, 1 September 1925, UB. The contract called for making such modifications to the airship as might be found necessary, and specifically, for installing a device on the nose for fastening a ship to a mooring mast and replacing water tanks with fuel tanks.
25. Amundsen letter to Ellsworth, 6 September 1925, Yale.
26. Ellsworth telegram to Aero Club, 23 September 1925, UB.
27. Thommessen telegram to Amundsen, 14 October 1925, UB.
28. Amundsen letter to Thommessen, 17 October 1925, trans. Lars O. Melemseter, UB.
29. Raestad telegram to Amundsen, 20 October 1925, trans. Lars O. Melemseter, UB.
30. Amundsen letter to Raestad, 20 October 1925, trans. Lars O. Melemseter, UB.

31. Amundsen, et al., *Our Polar Flight,* 238.

32. Amundsen, "Dagbok Fra Polflyvningen," 28 May 1925.

33. Amundsen letter to Ellsworth, 27 November 1925, Yale.

34. *Aftenposten,* 19 December 1925, trans. Lars O. Melemseter.

35. Thommessen radiogram to Ellsworth, 30 December 1925, UB.

36. Aero Club radiogram to Ellsworth, 15 January 1926, UB.

37. Ellsworth radiogram to Aero Club, 16 January 1926.

38. Aero Club radiogram to Ellsworth, 20 January 1926.

39. Agreement between Aero Club and Colonel Umberto Nobile, 16 January 1926, NA.

40. Amundsen, *My Life as an Explorer,* 146, 148.

41. Aero Club telegrams to Ellsworth, 23 January, 10 February, 15 February 1926.

42. Amundsen, *My Life as an Explorer,* 165.

43. Bryn letter to Riiser-Larsen, 24 February 1926, trans. Lars O. Melemseter, UB.

44. Riiser-Larsen letter to Bryn, 12 February 1926, trans. Lars O. Melemseter, UB.

45. Norwegian legation, Rome, telegram to Thommessen, 13 March 1926, trans. Lars O. Melemseter, UB.

46. Norwegian legation, Rome, telegram to Ministry of Foreign Affairs, 14 March 1926, trans. Lars O. Melemseter, UB.

47. Gottwald, Horgen, et al., telegram to Thommessen, 13 March 1926, trans. Lars O. Melemseter, UB.

48. Thommessen telegram to Riiser-Larsen, 13 March 1926, trans. Lars O. Melemseter, UB.

49. Helen Stibolt, memorandum, n.d., UB.

50. Thommessen telegram to Bryn, 15 March 1926, trans. Lars O. Melemseter, UB.

51. Agreement signed by Amundsen, Ellsworth, Thommessen, and Nobile, 28 March 1926, Museo Storico-Aeronautica Militare, Centro Documentazione Umberto Nobile, Rome.

52. Amundsen, *My Life as an Explorer,* 155.

53. Ibid., 154.

54. Roald Amundsen, et al., *First Crossing of the Polar Sea* (New York: George H. Doran Co., 1927), 50. Subsequent references to *First Crossing of the Polar Sea* are annotated as *First Crossing.*

55. Bernon Prentice cable to Ellsworth, 25 March 1926, UB.

56. Contract, Aero Club and Nobile, 6 April 1926, UB.

57. Ellsworth speech at American embassy, Oslo, 10 April 1926; Amundsen and Ellsworth, *Air Pioneering,* 64.

58. Ellsworth cable to Clare Prentice.

59. *New York Times,* 7 March 1926.

60. Rockefeller letter to Fosdick, 19 March 1926, RAC.

61. Byrd letter to Bowman, 17 March 1926, AGS.

62. *New York Times,* 28 March 1926.

63. Byrd press release, 5 April 1926, RAC.

64. Ellsworth diary for the *Norge* expedition, 20 April 1926, AMNH.

65. Ibid., 28 April 1926.

66. Ibid.

67. Ibid., 29, 30 April 1926.

68. Byrd, *Skyward,* 174.

69. Amundsen, *My Life as an Explorer,* 167–68.

70. Byrd, *Skyward,* 175.

71. Amundsen, et al., *First Crossing.*

72. Amundsen, *My Life as an Explorer,* 168.

73. Byrd, *Skyward,* 176.

74. Ibid., 177.

75. Ibid., 179.

76. Ellsworth diary, 1 May 1926.

77. Amundsen, *New York Times,* 14 March 1926.

78. Amundsen, *My Life as an Explorer,* 169.

79. Ellsworth diary, 2 May 1926.

80. Ibid., 3 May 1926.

81. Ibid.

82. Ibid., 4 May 1926.

83. Amundsen, et al., *First Crossing,* 52.

84. Balchen, autobiographical notes, Accessional Microfilm, Record Group 401–97, Annex 1:7, NA.

85. Ibid., Annex 1:8.

86. Ibid., Annex 1:5, 6.

87. Ibid., Annex 2:26.

88. Ibid., Annex 2:27; and see Bryn letter, f.n. 43 supra.

89. Ellsworth diary, 3 May 1926.

90. Byrd, *Skyward,* 180–81.

91. Fosdick letter to Richardson, 26 January 1926, RAC.

92. Byrd telegram to Ford, 8 January 1926, EI.

93. Ibid.

94. Byrd telegram to Detroit Arctic Expedition, c/o Bowman, 9 January 1926, AGS.

95. Byrd letter to Bowman, 22 January 1926, AGS.

96. Byrd letter to Ford, 23 January 1926, EI.

97. Byrd letter to Bowman, 23 January 1926, AGS.

98. Byrd letter to Wilkins, 22 January 1926, Winston Ross papers, copy in Beekman Pool collection.

99. Byrd request to secretary of the navy, via chief of the Bureau of Aeronautics, 4 February 1926, NA.

100. Ibid.

101. Chief of the Bureau of Aeronautics, first endorsement on Byrd's request, 8 February 1926, NA.

102. Byrd letter to Bowman, 9 February 1926.

103. Bowman letter to Byrd, 8 February 1926, AGS.

104. Ibid.

105. Byrd letter to Amundsen, 23 February 1926, UB.
106. Arnesen dispatch to *Aftenposten,* 8 May 1926.
107. Amundsen, *My Life as an Explorer,* 169.
108. Ibid.
109. Ellsworth, *Beyond Horizons,* 205–206.
110. Herbert C. Ponting, British Antarctic Expedition, 1910–13, *The Times* (London), 17 December 1911.
111. Byrd letter to Saunders, 20 April 1932, NA.
112. Ellsworth, *Beyond Horizons,* 205.
113. Ellsworth diary, 9 May 1926.
114. Byrd, *Skyward,* 200–201.
115. Balchen, autobiographical notes, Annex 2:36.
116. *Christian Science Monitor,* 10 May 1926.
117. Balchen, autobiographical notes, Annex 2:37.
118. Byrd, *Skyward,* 197.
119. Finn Ronne, Captain, USNR, copy of notarized memorandum for the Record, Subject: Comments on Commander Richard E. Byrd's North Pole Flight, 8 March 1960. Beekman Pool collection, received from Mary Louise Ellsworth.
120. Gosta Liljequist, Swedish meteorologist, University of Uppsala, 1960, 598.
121. Ronne comments on Byrd's North Pole Flight, 8 March 1962.
122. Ibid., 3.
123. Byrd, *Skyward,* 201–203.
124. Dennis Rawlins, Preliminary [unedited] Report on Byrd 1925–1926 Data, Raimond Goerler's Discovery and Its Revelations, 4 May 1996, Re: Byrd 1926–1927 Diary, OSU.
125. Balchen typescript, "The Strange Enigma of Admiral Byrd," Microfilm, Record Group 401–59, 142, NA.

Chapter 5: First Crossing of the Polar Sea

1. *Aftenposten,* 11 May 1926.
2. Amundsen and Ellsworth, *Air Pioneering,* 85, 88ff.
3. Ellsworth diary, 11, 12 May 1926 (copied by J. D. Kimball), AMNH.
4. Ibid., 12 May 1926.
5. Ibid.
6. Amundsen, et al., *First Crossing,* 255, Finn Malmgren, "Weather and Weather Warnings During the Flight."
7. Amundsen, et al., *First Crossing,* 213, Hjalmar Riiser-Larsen, "The Navigation over the Polar Sea."
8. Ibid., 215.
9. Amundsen and Ellsworth, *Air Pioneering,* 100.
10. Ibid., 98.
11. Amundsen, et al., *First Crossing,* 218, Riiser-Larsen, "The Navigation over the Polar Sea."

12. Ellsworth diary, 13 May 1926; Ellsworth, *Beyond Horizons,* 226.

13. Amundsen and Ellsworth, *Air Pioneering,* 104.

14. Amundsen, et al., *First Crossing,* 146.

15. Ibid., 229, Riiser-Larsen, "The Navigation over the Polar Sea."

16. Ellsworth, *Beyond Horizons,* 227.

17. Ibid.

18. Umberto Nobile, *My Polar Flights,* trans. Frances Fleetwood (New York: G. P. Putnam's Sons, 1961), 81–82.

19. Ibid., 82.

20. Ellsworth telegram to Thommessen, 10 May 1926, UB.

21. Umberto Nobile letter to Ellsworth, 24 May 1926, Yale.

22. Ellsworth telegram to Thommessen, 29 May 1926.

23. Thommessen, Sverre, Bryn telegram to Ellsworth, 31 May 1926, UB.

24. Stibolt memorandum to Aero Club, 9 June 1926, trans. Lars O. Melemseter, UB.

25. Bryn telegram to Riiser-Larsen, 5 June 1926, trans. Lars O. Melemseter, UB.

26. Amundsen, *My Life as an Explorer,* 203.

27. Stibolt memorandum, 9 June 1926.

28. Quoted in special release for *La Prensa,* 9 June 1926, trans. Beekman Pool, UB.

29. Riiser-Larsen telegram to Thommessen, 11 June 1926, trans. Lars O. Melemseter, copy in Gustav S. Amundsen later memorandum to Ellsworth, 29 February 1928, UB.

30. Thommessen telegram to Riiser-Larsen, 11 June 1926, UB.

31. Amundsen, *My Life as an Explorer,* 208.

32. Ibid., 208–209.

33. De Martino letter to Nobile, 17 June 1926, trans. Dr. Gertrude Nobile, Museo Storico A. M. Sezione Documentazione, Rome.

34. Gertrude Nobile letter to author, 21 November 1982, explaining that de Martino's 17 June 1926 letter was important "because it confirms that who instigated Amundsen against Nobile was Ellsworth." Beekman Pool collection.

35. Nobile, *My Polar Flights,* 92.

36. Nobile, *La Tenda Rossa,* trans. A. Mondadori (Milan: Mondadori, 1970).

37. Ellsworth, *Beyond Horizons,* 230.

38. Ibid.

39. Lincoln Ellsworth, *New York Times,* 20 July 1926.

40. Woodruff speech, U.S. House of Representatives, 25 February 1927, U.S. Government Printing Office, Washington, D.C.

41. Ellsworth, *Beyond Horizons,* 235.

42. Ibid.

43. Amundsen and Ellsworth, *Air Pioneering,* 106.

44. Ibid., 107.

45. Amundsen, *My Life as an Explorer,* 176.

46. Ibid., 181.

47. Marie Curie letter to president of Czechoslovakia, 19 March 1926, trans. Beekman Pool, Musée Curie et des Archives de l'Institut du Radium.

48. Nobile, *My Polar Flights,* 53.

49. Bordry, director of Musée Curie et des Archives de l'Institut du Radium, letter to author, 2 November 1994, Beekman Pool collection.

50. Ellsworth, *Beyond Horizons,* 115.

51. "Polar Regions, The Polar Flights of Byrd and Amundsen," *The Geographical Review* 16 (October 1926), 662–64. As late as 1945 this uncertainty remained unresolved and the Arctic Institute of North America recommended mapping the continental shelf on the American side of the Polar Basin, as the only way of settling the question raised by Harris in 1911. See also, Arctic Institute of North America, "A Program of Desirable Scientific Investigations in Arctic North America," no. 1, Montreal (March 1946), 15, 16.

52. Ibid., 664.

53. Bowman letter to Byrd, 7 October 1926, OSU.

54. Riiser-Larsen, "Aircraft in Polar Exploration," *Great Norwegian Expeditions,* 184.

55. Francis Travelyan Miller, *Byrd's Great Adventure* (Philadelphia: John C. Winston Co., 1930), 335.

56. Ibid.

57. *New York Times,* 4 July 1926.

58. Ibid., 19 July 1926.

59. *New York American,* 20 July 1926; see also, *Aftenposten,* 20 July 1926.

60. *New York American,* 20 July 1926.

61. Ibid.

62. *New York Times,* 20 July 1926.

63. Ibid.

64. Amundsen, et al., *First Crossing,* 131.

65. Ibid.

66. *New York Times,* 20 July 1926.

67. Nobile cablegram to Aero Club, 20 July 1926 (copy received by author from Dr. Gertrude Nobile). No indication of source appears on the copy of this message nor on several others sent to the author by Dr. Nobile in the course of correspondence, 1982–85, regarding the relationship between her husband and Lincoln Ellsworth in those earlier years. Original letters from Dr. Nobile to author, 15 March, 2 April 1982; 2 February, 18, 20 March 1985; copies of author's letters to Dr. Nobile, 15 February, 5, 26 March 1982; 2 February 1985, Beekman Pool collection.

68. Ellsworth telegram to Nobile, 23 July 1926 (copy received by author from Dr. Nobile, 9 April 1985), Beekman Pool collection.

69. Ellsworth second telegram to Nobile, 23 July 1926 (copy from Dr. Nobile), Beekman Pool collection.

70. Nobile telegram to Ellsworth, 23 July 1926, NA.

71. *New York Times,* (July) 1926.

72. Dr. Nobile letter to author, 20 March 1985, Beekman Pool collection. Accompanying the letter was a copy of her husband's letter to A. S. Tresnikov, 18 January 1974.

73. *Aftenposten,* 24 July 1926, trans. Lars O. Melemseter, folder 480B, clipping 369, UB.

74. Ibid.

75. Ove Vangensten, legation secretary, Rome, telegram to Thommessen, 25 July 1926, trans. Lars O. Melemseter, UB.

76. Amundsen radiogram to Ellsworth, 25 July 1926, Yale.

77. *Aftenposten,* 28 July 1926, trans. Lars O. Melemseter, folder 480B, clipping 375, UB.

78. Amundsen radiogram to Ellsworth, 30 July 1926, Yale.

79. Ellsworth letter to Byrd, 25 July 1926, OSU.

80. Byrd letter to Ellsworth, 30 July 1926, OSU.

81. Ellsworth radiogram to Amundsen, 3 August 1926, UB.

82. Amundsen radiogram to Ellsworth, 3 August 1926, UB.

83. Ellsworth telegram to Amundsen, 4 August 1926, UB.

84. Ellsworth telegram to Amundsen, 10 August 1926.

85. Per Skjoldberg letter to Thommessen, 14 August 1926, trans. Lars O. Melemseter, UB.

86. Bryn cablegram to Thommessen, 10 August 1926, trans. Lars O. Melemseter, UB.

87. Internews telegram to *Aftenposten,* 15 August 1926, Norsk Polarinstitutt.

88. Ellsworth telegram to Thommessen, 15 August 1926, UB. A message from Thommessen's associate, Bjoern, characterized the obvious unreality of Ellsworth's disavowal with the words, "The farce is complete." Bjoern telegram to Thommessen, 16 August 1926, trans. Lars O. Melemseter, UB.

89. Ellsworth telegram to *Aftenposten,* 15 August 1926, Norsk Polarsinstitutt.

90. *New York Herald Tribune,* European edition, 16 August 1926, UB.

91. Thommessen letter to Sverre and Bryn, 22 August 1926, trans. Lars O. Melemseter, UB.

92. Bernon Prentice, Chairman, American Advisory Committee, telegrams to Ambassador Henry Prather Fletcher, American embassy, Rome; Salvatore Cortesi, Associated Press, Rome; Comm. Felice Cacciapuoti, Florence; 3 September 1926, Yale.

93. Vangensten telegram to Thommessen, 15 September 1926, trans. Lars O. Melemseter, UB.

94. Amundsen letter to Ellsworth, 16 October 1926, Yale.

95. Ellsworth cable to Amundsen, 4 September 1926, UB.

96. Ellsworth cable to Amundsen, 5 September 1926, UB.

97. Ellsworth letter to Byrd, 10 September 1926, OSU.

98. Byrd letter to Ellsworth, 13 September 1926, OSU.

99. Byrd letter to Bowman, 25 September 1926, AGS.

100. Byrd letter to Ellsworth, 27 September 1926.

101. *Ellsworth Family,* vol. 2, 41.

102. Bowman letter to Ellsworth, 15 November 1926, JHL.

103. Ibid.

104. *Ellsworth Family,* vol. 2, 42.

105. Ibid., 41.

106. Ibid., 42–46.

107. Roald Amundsen and Lincoln Ellsworth, cablegram to Aero Club, 2 Decem-

ber 1926, JHL. See also six-page memo of Amundsen's attorney, E. W. Nansen, 8 October 1926, analyzing quarrel with Aero Club about authorship of book, lecturing, and other matters.

108. Riiser-Larsen letter to Ellsworth, 6 December 1926, Yale.

109. Amundsen, *My Life as an Explorer,* 270–77, Riiser-Larsen.

110. Ibid., 222.

111. Estratto dal Notiziario N. 14 del Dicembre 1926 dell'Addeto Aeronutico Presso L'Ambasciata d'Italia a Washington.

112. Bowman letter to Ellsworth, 16 February 1927, JHL.

113. George H. Wilkins, *Flying the Arctic* (New York: Grosset & Dunlap, 1928), 144, 155–71.

114. Bowman letter to Miller, *Detroit News,* 25 April 1927, AGS.

115. Ellsworth letter to Grosvenor, 25 July 1927, NGS.

116. Bowman letter to Wilkins, 2 September 1927, AGS.

117. Ellsworth letter to Grosvenor, 31 October 1927, NA.

118. Roald Amundsen, "The *Rows* Aboard the *Norge,*" *World's Work* 14 (August 1927), 389–404.

119. Nobile, *My Polar Flights,* 91.

120. Nobile letter to Ellsworth, 20 October 1927, NA.

121. Ellsworth letter to Nobile, two unfinished drafts (n.s.), NA.

122. Ellsworth letter to Nobile, 17 November 1927, NA.

123. Ellsworth letter to Amundsen, 18 November 1927, Beekman Pool collection.

124. Amundsen letter to Ellsworth, 1927, Beekman Pool collection.

125. Amundsen letter to Ellsworth, 1927, Beekman Pool collection.

126. Ellsworth letter to Amundsen, May 1928, Beekman Pool collection.

Chapter 6: This Hero Business

1. Ellsworth letter to Byrd, 21 May 1928, OSU.

2. Ellsworth telegram to Amundsen, 29 September 1926, UB.

3. Ellsworth cable to Amundsen, 8 October 1926, UB.

4. Ellsworth letter to Byrd, 5 May 1928, OSU.

5. Minutes, American Scenic and Historic Preservation Society, 11 March 1927, 11, New York Public Library.

6. Kunz letter to Bingham, 7 March 1927, OSU; referred to in Hiram Bingham letter to Kunz, 15 September 1927, Stef.

7. De Martino letter to Kunz, 23 August 1927, Stef.

8. Ellsworth letter to Byrd, 17 August 1927, OSU.

9. *New York Herald Tribune,* European edition, reporting award by the Protective Society for Animals, in Rome, 16 August 1926.

10. Ellsworth letter to Byrd, 17 August 1927, OSU.

11. Bingham letter to Kunz, 15 September 1927, Stef.

12. Bingham letter to Kunz, 23 September 1927, Stef.

13. Byrd, *Skyward,* 140. Promoted to lieutenant commander by special act of Congress.

14. Disbrow letter to Kunz, 21 October 1927, Stef.

15. Byrd letter to Kunz, 10 November 1927, Yale.

16. Byrd, *Skyward,* 294.

17. Woodruff speech in U.S. House of Representatives, 27 February 1927, U.S. Government Printing Office, 2.

18. Ibid., 11.

19. Senate Bill 815, 6 December 1927, U.S. Senate Archives.

20. Dawes letter to Ellsworth, 20 December 1927, OSU.

21. Byrd letter to Prentice, 23 December 1927, OSU.

22. Ellsworth telegrams to Byrd, 22, 25 January 1928, OSU.

23. Ellsworth letter to Byrd, 13 February 1928, OSU.

24. Byrd letter to Bingham, 13 March 1928, OSU.

25. Clark letter to McVeigh, 28 March 1928, 4–6, OSU.

26. Ellsworth letter to Byrd, 2 April 1928, OSU.

27. Byrd letter to Robinson, 2 April 1928, SIA.

28. *New York Times,* 25 May 1928, 1:2; Paul Emile Victor, *Man and the Conquest of the Poles* (New York: Simon and Schuster, 1963), 243.

29. Davide Giudici (special news correspondent on board the *Krassin*), *The Tragedy of the Italia* (New York: D. Appleton & Co., 1929), 132.

30. Ibid., 28.

31. Ibid., 29.

32. Nobile, *Ali sul Polo,* ed. U. Mursia, Milan, 1975, 234–35.

33. Amundsen radiogram to Ellsworth, 31 May 1928, Stef.

34. Ellsworth cable to Fletcher, *New York Times,* 1 June 1928.

35. 70th Congress, Private Bill No. 287, 29 May 1928.

36. Ellsworth telegram to Byrd, 30 May 1928, OSU.

37. Ellsworth letter to Clark, 5 June 1928, Stef.

38. Maurice Parijanine, *The Krassin,* trans. Lawrence Brown (New York: Macaulay Company, 1929), 36–37.

39. Giudici, *Tragedy of the Italia,* 23–24.

40. *New York Times,* 2 July 1928.

41. Nobile, *Ali sul Polo,* 234.

42. Ellsworth cablegram to American legation, Oslo, 30 June, *New York Times,* 1 July 1928.

43. *New York Times,* 3 July 1928.

44. Clark letter to McVeigh, 24 July 1928, Stef.

45. *Cleveland Plain Dealer,* 14 July 1928, Stef.

46. *New York Times,* 24 July 1928, 10:6.

47. *New York Times,* 2 September 1928.

48. "Roald Amundsen, a Tribute," *Ellsworth Family,* vol. 2, 92–94; reprinted from the *New York Times,* September 1928.

49. Lawrence Brown, trans. *The Krassin,* by Parijanine, 216ff.

50. Mowinckel radiogram to Ellsworth, 14 December 1928, Stef.

51. Froisland radiogram to Ellsworth, 14 December 1928, Stef.

52. Guidici, *Tragedy of the Italia,* 134.

53. Ibid., 134–36.

54. François Behounek, *New York Times,* 29 July 1928, 1, 2.

55. Amundsen, *My Life as an Explorer,* 178.

56. Bowman letter to Hooper, December 1928.

57. Einar Lundborg, *The Arctic Rescue: How Nobile Was Saved* (New York: Viking Press, 1929), 221.

58. Dawes letter to Ellsworth, 21 April 1928, OSU.

59. Dawes telegram to Byrd, 28 April 1928, OSU.

60. Cone letter to Abbott, 13 April 1928, SIA.

61. Cone memorandum to Abbott, 19 April 1928, SIA.

62. Abbott letter to Dawes, 7 May 1928, OSU.

63. Abbott radiogram to Byrd, 12 December 1929, SIA.

Chapter 7: Friends in Need

1. Frank J. Butler (in charge of J. W. Ellsworth estate account in Ohio office) letter to Lincoln Ellsworth, 29 December 1928, Stef.

2. Bowman letter to Ellsworth (three typed pages), 9 January 1929, JHL.

3. Bowman letter to Clark, 9 January 1929, AGS.

4. Clark letter to Ellsworth, 19 January 1929, Stef.

5. Ellsworth telegram to Clark, 24 January 1929, Stef.

6. Ellsworth telegram to Fay, 24 January 1929, UB.

7. Osborn letter to Clark, 12 March 1929, Stef.

8. Clark letter to Osborn, 12 March 1929, Stef.

9. Ellsworth letter to Clark, 12 March 1929, Stef.

10. Ellsworth letter to Clare Neilson, 31 May 1929, Nielson family papers.

11. David Dietz, Scripps Howard Newspapers, 28 May 1929.

12. Ellsworth letter to Clare Neilson, 31 May 1929.

13. Mary Louise Ellsworth, taped interview with author, 23 August 1978.

14. William A. Shaw, Editor of Calendar of Treasury Records at H.B.M. Records Office, p. 38, Lenzburg Castle, Agrau, H. R. Sauerlander & Co., 1907.

15. Mary Louise Ellsworth conversation with author, 16 March 1982.

16. Ellsworth, *Beyond Horizons,* 12, 13.

17. Shaw, Calendar Treasury Records, 16.

18. Ellsworth letter to Clark, 28 June 1929, Stef.

19. Ibid.

20. Roald Amundsen, *The North West Passage* (Archibald Constable and Company, Limited, London, 1908), vol. 1: 97, 8; vol. 2: 78.

21. Mary Louise Ellsworth conversation with author, 21 September 1978.

22. Ellsworth letter to Clark, 28 June 1929, Stef.

23. Kathleen Mortimer letter to author, 16 May 1983.

24. Ellsworth handwritten note, n.d., NA.

25. Mary Louise Ellsworth, taped interview with author, 23 August 1978.

26. Ellsworth letter to Gertrude Gavin (Mrs. Michael), 5 December 1929, Beekman Pool collection.

27. *Ellsworth Family,* vol. 2: 45, 50; Accession 2370, Dept. of Geology, AMNH, 27 March 1930.

Chapter 8: Plans and Diversions

1. Wilkins letters to Bowman, 11–18 June 1930, AGS.
2. Wilkins letter to Bowman, 18 January 1931, AGS.
3. Bowman telegram to Wilkins, 19 January 1931, AGS.
4. Wilkins telegram to Bowman, 20 January 1931, AGS.
5. Clark letter to Ellsworth, 29 January 1931, Stef.
6. Ellsworth note to Frank Butler (in charge of J. W. Ellsworth's estate account in Ohio office), 30 January 1931, Stef.
7. Press release signed by Wilkins and Ellsworth, 30 January 1931, Stef.
8. Ellsworth letter to Wilkins, 1 February 1931, David Larson collection.
9. Clark letter to Bowman, 12 February 1931, Stef. In several conversations with the author, Marley Ross, a close friend of Wilkins, indicated that the bond between Ellsworth and Wilkins was greatly influenced by the streak of mysticism shared by the two men.
10. Bowman letter to Ellsworth, 3 February 1931 (re: upcoming meeting with Clark, Joerg, Balchen, et al.), Stef.
11. Clark memorandum for files 26 October 1936, from pencil notes of 10 February 1931 luncheon meeting, Stef.
12. Ellsworth letter to Clark, 22 February 1931, Stef.
13. Clark handwritten memo of 10 February 1931 meeting, supra, 4, Stef.
14. Wilkins-Ellsworth cable to Gunnar Isachsen, 21 February 1931, Stef.
15. Ellsworth letter to Clark, 22 February 1931, Stef.
16. Ellsworth letter to Wilkins, 26 February 1931, D. Larson collection.
17. Ibid.
18. Ibid.
19. Ellsworth letter to Wilkins, 5 February 1931, D. Larson collection.
20. Bowman letter to Sverdrup, with enclosed three-page outline of the Ellsworth Antarctic Expedition, 9 March 1931, AGS.
21. Correspondence with Norwegian ship owners Lars Christensen, Gunnar Isachsen, Thor Dahl, and the Association of Whaling Companies, 6 March–2 May 1931, Stef., and 6 March–15 June 1931, AGS.
22. Sverdrup letter to Bowman, 25 March 1931, AGS.
23. Ellsworth telegram to Clark, 2 March 1931.
24. Engraved invitation from Wilkins to Ellsworth to christening ceremony of submarine *Nautilus,* Stef.
25. Ellsworth letter to Wilkins, 31 March 1931, D. Larson collection.
26. Admiral Hugh Rodman, quoted in *Knoxville News-Sentinel,* 17 April 1931; and see letter to Director of the American Geographical Society, 5 June 1931, AGS.

27. Ellsworth cablegrams, 1 May 1931 to Riiser-Larsen and 9 May 1931 to Lars Christensen, AGS.

28. Riiser-Larsen letter to Ellsworth, 12 May 1931, AGS.

29. Ellsworth radiogram to Wilkins, 4 June 1931, AGS.

30. Wilkins letter to Ellsworth, 4 June 1931, NA.

31. Wilkins letter to Clark, 4 June 1931, NA.

32. Bowman letter to Under Secretary of State William R. Castle, 5 June 1931, NA.

33. Robert Cushman Murphy letter to S. R. Darnley, Chairman of the "Discovery Committee," 25 June 1931, AGS.

34. Hearst newspapers, 6 June 1931.

35. *New York American,* 31 May 1931.

36. Ibid.

37. Hearst newspapers, 6 June 1931.

38. Wilkins-Ellsworth Trans-Arctic Submarine Expedition Official Diary, 11–22 June 1931, OSU.

39. Ibid., 22 July, 9 August.

40. Universerv, Fleet London, 10 August 1931, OSU.

41. H. U. Sverdrup and F. M. Soule, "Scientific results of the *Nautilus* expedition of 1931," Massachusetts Institute of Technology, Meteorological Papers, vol. 2, no. 1, 1933; Waldo Lyon, "The Submarine and the Arctic Ocean," *Polar Record,* vol. 2, no. 75, 1963, 699–700.

42. Wilkins dispatch, WRH NYC or Universerv Fleet London Direct or through other stations, 4 September 1931, OSU.

43. Wilkins, press release, September 1931.

44. Wilkins, *Under the North Pole* (New York: Brewer Warren & Putnam, 1931), Preface, v.

45. Waldo Lyon (U.S. Navy Electronics Laboratory, San Diego, Calif., September 1963), *Polar Record* 11, 700.

46. Stefansson, *The Northward Course of Empire* (New York: Macmillan Co., 1924), 189–99.

47. Wilkins, *Under the North Pole,* 3.

48. Memorandum enclosed with Wilkins letter to Bowman, 6 May 1930, AGS.

49. Hearst newspapers, 6 June 1931.

50. Joerg telegram to Bowman, 26 June 1931, AGS.

51. Bowman telegram to Joerg, 26 June 1931, AGS.

52. Eckener cable to Von Meister, 30 June 1931, JHL.

53. Bowman cable to Ellsworth, 14 July 1931, AGS.

54. Prospective Plan for Proposed Antarctic Expedition via S.S. *Volendam* to be presented to Lincoln Ellsworth by Balchen and Thorne by 3 August, JHL.

55. Ellsworth cablegram to Bowman, 15 July 1931.

56. Ernst Lehmann, *Zeppelin, The Story of Lighter-Than-Air Craft* (New York: Longman, Green & Co., 1937), 310.

57. Ellsworth, *Beyond Horizons,* 248.

58. Ibid.

59. HQ. USAFHRC film roll, declassified 20 June 1990, Film Index 1179, #1007535, Roll No. 30913, 10 August 1931.

60. Ibid.

61. Ibid.

62. Ellsworth telegram to Byrd, 19 November 1931, OSU.

63. Byrd letter to Ellsworth, 15 December 1931, OSU.

64. Ellsworth letter to Byrd, 18 December 1931, OSU.

65. Byrd letter to Ellsworth, 22 December 1931, OSU.

66. Ellsworth letter to Byrd, 28 December 1931, OSU.

67. Byrd letter to Ellsworth, 29 December 1931, OSU.

68. Ellsworth letter to Balchen, 18 April 1932, NA.

69. *New York Herald Tribune,* 18 April 1932.

70. Byrd letter to Saunders, 20 April 1932, NA.

71. Ford letter to Rockefeller, 30 September 1927, RAC.

72. Byrd letter to Saunders, 20 April 1932, NA.

73. Balchen, autobiographical notes, Accessional Microfilm, Record Group 401–97, Annex 2, 266, 142, NA.

74. Byrd, *Skyward,* 201–203.

75. This information was seen by the author in a microfilm, AFSHRC Index 1161-1007466, 1933, 5 (the microfilm was thereafter withdrawn by Byrd's wife Audry).

76. Ellsworth letter to Balchen, 18 May 1932, Stef.

77. Byrd to Ellsworth, 21 May 1932, OSU.

78. Mary Louise Ellsworth, taped interview with author, 18 November 1984.

79. Ellsworth, *Beyond Horizons,* 257.

80. Mary Louise Ellsworth conversation with author, 24 August 1978.

81. Mary Louise Ellsworth conversation with author, 24 August 1978, author's memo.

82. Mary Louise Ellsworth phone conversation with author, 12 November 1978.

83. Mary Louise Ellsworth letter to Lincoln Ellsworth, 11 November 1932, Beekman Pool collection.

84. Balchen, autobiographical notes, Accessional Microfilm, Record Group 401–97, 267, NA.

85. Mary Louise Ellsworth letter to Lincoln Ellsworth, 13 November 1932, Beekman Pool collection.

86. Mary Louise Ellsworth letter to Lincoln Ellsworth, 19 November 1932, Beekman Pool collection.

87. Mary Louise Ellsworth letter to Lincoln Ellsworth, 13 November 1932, 2, Beekman Pool collection.

88. Mary Louise Ellsworth letter to Lincoln Ellsworth, 25 November 1932, Beekman Pool collection.

89. Ellsworth letter to Clare Neilson, 15 December 1932, Nielson family papers.

Chapter 9: Antarctica—Maiden Voyage

1. Ellsworth, *Beyond Horizons,* 253.
2. Ibid., 246; John P. Clum, mayor of Tombstone, Arizona, and the editor of *Epitaph,* its newspaper, described vividly the flight that brought fame to Lincoln's hero ". . . who never feared anyone who found him in the open," and ". . . who confronted and killed three members of a gang of stage robbers, murderers and all around crooks and criminals who had come into town with the declared intention of killing the chief of police," *Arizona Historical Review* 12 (October 1929).
3. Map, proposed route of Ellsworth Trans-Antarctic Expedition, n.d., AGS.
4. Ellsworth, *Beyond Horizons,* 256.
5. American Geographical Society, memorandum, Ellsworth Trans-Antarctic Flight Expedition, n.d., AGS.
6. American Geographical Society, press release, Ellsworth Trans-Antarctic Flight Expedition, n.d., AGS.
7. Ellsworth, *Beyond Horizons,* 282.
8. Ibid.
9. Balchen journal, 24 February–11 April 1933, Index 1179, Microfilm Strip 1007525, declassified, HQ USAF, Washington, D.C.
10. Balchen journal, 15 April 1933, Index 1179, Microfilm Strip 1007525, declassified, HQ USAF, Washington, D.C.
11. Ellsworth, *Beyond Horizons,* 253.
12. Mary Louise Ellsworth interview with author, 18 May 1981.
13. Mary Louise Ellsworth interview with author, 24 March 1984.
14. Ellsworth, *Beyond Horizons,* 254.
15. Balchen, autobiographical notes, Accessional Microfilm, Record Group 401–97, 269, NA.
16. Byrd letter to Bowman, 14 July 1933, AGS.
17. Byrd letter to Bowman, 8 August 1933, AGS.
18. *Polar Record* 7 (7 January 1934), 85.
19. Byrd letter to Bowman, 8 August 1933, AGS.
20. Balchen letter to Emmy Balchen, trans. Lars O. Melemseter, 8 August 1933, Dr. Fred Goldberg collection.
21. Balchen letter to Emmy Balchen, 11 September 1933.
22. Magnus Olsen, *Saga of the White Horizon* (Lymington, Eng.: Nautical Publishing Co., 1972), 114.
23. Balchen letter to Emmy Balchen, 29 October 1933.
24. Balchen letter to Emmy Balchen, 5 November 1933.
25. Ibid.
26. Balchen letter to Emmy Balchen, 14 November 1933.
27. Balchen letter to Emmy Balchen, 4 December 1933.
28. Ellsworth letters from shipboard to various suppliers, 1 December 1933, OSU.
29. Wilkins dispatch to *New York Times,* 5 December 1933, NA.
30. Ellsworth dispatch to *New York Times,* 8 December 1933, NA.
31. Ellsworth, *Beyond Horizons,* 263.

32. Wilkins dispatch to *New York Times,* 4 January 1934, NA.

33. Olsen, *Saga of the White Horizon,* 99–100.

34. Ibid., 101–102.

35. Ibid., 108.

36. Ibid., 104.

37. Ibid., 109.

38. Ellsworth, *Beyond Horizons,* 267.

39. Ibid., 268.

40. Balchen letter to Emmy Balchen, 18 February 1934.

41. Balchen, autobiographical notes, Accessional Microfilm, Record Group 401–97, 282, NA.

42. Balchen letter to Emmy Balchen, 13 February 1934, Dr. Fred Goldberg collection.

43. Balchen letter to Emmy Balchen, 19 April 1934.

44. Ellsworth, *Beyond Horizons,* 287–88.

45. Balchen letter to Emmy Balchen, 17 August 1934.

46. Ellsworth dispatch to *New York Times,* 15 October 1934.

47. Ellsworth, *Beyond Horizons,* 276–77.

48. Ellsworth dispatch to *New York Times,* 30 October 1934, NA.

49. Ellsworth, *Beyond Horizons,* 278.

50. Ellsworth dispatch to *New York Times,* 5 December 1934.

51. Ellsworth dispatch to *New York Times,* 13 December 1934.

52. Ellsworth address to American Polar Society, 5 December 1944.

53. Ellsworth, *Exploring Today* (New York: Dodd, Mead & Co., 1935), 103.

54. Michael O. Woodburne, "Newly Discovered Land Mammal from Antarctica," *Antarctic Journal* 17 (1982 review), 64–65.

55. Ellsworth, *Beyond Horizons,* 289.

56. Ellsworth dispatch to *New York Times,* 18 December 1934.

57. Balchen, autobiographical notes, Accessional Microfilm, Record Group 401–97, 272, NA.

58. Ellsworth, *Exploring Today,* 50.

59. Wilkins radiogram to Bowman, 29 December 1934, AGS.

60. Ellsworth dispatch to *New York Times,* 30 December 1934.

61. Balchen, Index 1179, Microfilm Strip 1007525, roll. no. 30913 (declassified 20 June 1990), Bolling Air Force Base, Washington, D.C. 20332, copy in Beekman Pool collection.

62. Wilkins message to Stefansson for information of Bowman, 3 January 1935, AGS.

63. Ellsworth, *Beyond Horizons,* 292.

64. Ibid.

65. Balchen, autobiographical notes, Accessional Microfilm, Record Group 401–97, 294, NA.

66. Ellsworth, *Beyond Horizons,* 292.

67. Balchen, autobiographical notes, Accessional Microfilm, Record Group 401–97, 295, NA.

68. Ellsworth, *Beyond Horizons,* 294.

69. Ibid., 298.
70. Ellsworth dispatch to *New York Times,* 5 January 1935.
71. Ellsworth dispatch to *New York Times,* 9 January 1935.
72. Ellsworth dispatch to *New York Times,* 10 January 1935.
73. Ibid.
74. Ellsworth dispatch, 18 January 1935, NA.
75. Ellsworth radiogram to Bowman, 15 January 1935, NA.
76. Balchen letter to Emmy Balchen, trans. Lars O. Melemseter, 5 February 1935, Dr. Fred Goldberg collection.

Chapter 10: A Job to Do
1. Wilkins letter to Aksel Holm, 5 April 1935, OSU.
2. Ibid.
3. Wilkins letter to Balchen, 26 March 1935, AAF Index 1179, Film Roll no. 30.
4. Hollick-Kenyon letter to Ellsworth, 5 April 1935, Stef.
5. Lymburner letter to Ellsworth Trans-Antarctic Expedition, 27 April 1935, Stef.
6. Wilkins letter to Lymburner, 6 May 1935, Stef.
7. *Montreal Star,* 10 May 1935.
8. Ellsworth, *Beyond Horizons,* 297.
9. *New York Times,* 10 May 1935.
10. Lymburner, taped interview with author, 22 February 1985, Beekman Pool collection.
11. Lymburner letter to his wife, 10 September 1935, Lymburner family papers.
12. Ibid.
13. Leonard Chapple letter to author, 9 February 1983, Beekman Pool collection.
14. Lymburner letter to his wife, 10 September 1935.
15. Lymburner, taped interview with author, 22 February 1985.
16. Ellsworth, *Beyond Horizons,* 305. Despite such foresight, the flight worked far from smoothly, due to unforeseen variables: ground speed estimated too high; difficulty measuring drift over featureless snow; accident with sextant; radio failure.
17. Ibid., 308.
18. Ibid., 356–57.
19. Herbert Hollick-Kenyon flight log, Ellsworth Trans-Antarctic Flight, 20 November 1935, 3, Hollick-Kenyon family papers.
20. Ibid.
21. Ellsworth, *Beyond Horizons.*
22. Notebook carried on Ellsworth Trans-Antarctic Flight, 1935, to pass messages between pilot and navigator, NA.
23. Hollick-Kenyon log, 21 November 1935, 7.
24. Ibid., 9.
25. Ellsworth, *Beyond Horizons,* 313.
26. Hollick-Kenyon log, 21 November 1935, 9.
27. Pilot/navigator notebook, 4.

28. Ibid., 5.

29. Ibid., 6.

30. Hollick-Kenyon log, 21 November 1935, 12.

31. Ellsworth, *Beyond Horizons,* 316.

32. Pilot/navigator notebook, 7.

33. Hollick-Kenyon log, 23 November 1935, 17.

34. Hollick-Kenyon message to *Wyatt Earp* radio log, 1325, 23 November 1935. "On board M.S. *Wyatt Earp*" messages received from the wireless on *Polar Star* during flight 23 November, NA.

35. Hollick-Kenyon log, 23 November 1935, 19.

36. Notes from Ellsworth's diary, Trans-Antarctic Flight, 23 November–15 December 1935, OSU; typescript signed H. W. (Hubert Wilkins). From the wording and format of this document, and the need while in flight to continuously scan upcoming terrain for significant features, it seems unlikely that Ellsworth kept much of a written record, and that Wilkins, ever methodical, filled the gap by assembling these notes and identifying the source with his initials.

37. Wireless messages from *Polar Star* to *Wyatt Earp,* 23 November 1935.

38. Hollick-Kenyon log, 23 November 1935, 20.

39. Ellsworth diary, Trans-Antarctic Flight, 23 November 1935.

40. W. L. G. Joerg, "The Cartographical Results of Ellsworth's Trans-Antarctic Flight of 1935," *Geographical Review* 27 (July 1937), 430–44, and map. See also, "The Topographical Results of Ellsworth's Trans-Antarctic Flight of 1935," *Geographical Review* 26 (July 1936), 454–62.

41. Pilot/navigator notebook, 10.

42. *Wyatt Earp* radio log, 23 November 1935, 17, 18.

43. Hollick-Kenyon log, 23 November 1935, 21.

44. Pilot/navigator notebook, 12.

45. Hollick-Kenyon log, 23 November 1935, 23.

46. Ellsworth diary, Trans-Antarctic Flight, 23 November–15 December 1935, signed H. W., OSU.

47. Ellsworth, "Ellsworth's Own Diary," *Journal of the American Museum of Natural History* 37 (May 1936), 401–3.

48. Hollick-Kenyon log, 23 November 1935, 25–26.

49. Ellsworth, *Beyond Horizons,* 325.

50. Hollick-Kenyon log, 24 November 1935, 27.

51. Ellsworth, *Beyond Horizons,* 325. Both Ellsworth's diary and Hollick-Kenyon's flight log refer to dropping the American flag. Ellsworth's account of the flight, written several years later (*Beyond Horizons,* 325), refers to raising the flag while in a camp.

52. Hollick-Kenyon log, 24 November 1935, 27.

53. Glin Bennett, *Beyond Endurance: Survival at the Extremes* (New York: St. Martin's/Marek, 1983), 178.

54. Hollick-Kenyon log, 27 November 1935, 32.

55. Ellsworth diary, Trans-Antarctic Flight, 30 November 1935.

56. Hollick-Kenyon log, 30 November 1935, 37.

57. Ellsworth, *Beyond Horizons,* 330.

58. Ellsworth diary, Trans-Antarctic Flight, 1 December 1935.

59. Ibid.

60. Ellsworth, *Beyond Horizons,* 330.

61. Hollick-Kenyon log, 3 December 1935, 39.

62. Hollick-Kenyon log, 4 December 1935, 41.

63. Ellsworth diary, Trans-Antarctic Flight, 4 December 1935.

64. Hollick-Kenyon log, 5 December 1935, 46.

65. Ellsworth diary, Trans-Antarctic Flight, 5 December 1935.

66. Hollick-Kenyon log, 8 December 1935, 48.

67. Hollick-Kenyon log, 9 December 1935, 49.

68. Ellsworth, *Beyond Horizons,* 339.

69. Hollick-Kenyon log, 10 December 1935, 53.

70. Ellsworth, *Beyond Horizons,* 341.

71. Hollick-Kenyon log, 15 December 1935, 71.

72. Ellsworth diary, Trans-Antarctic Flight, 15 December 1935.

73. Ellsworth, *Beyond Horizons,* 345.

74. Hollick-Kenyon log, 17 December 1935, 73.

75. Ibid., 74–81.

76. Ibid., 73.

77. Ellsworth, *Beyond Horizons,* 317, 345.

78. Ibid., 347.

79. Hollick-Kenyon log, 87.

80. Ibid., 82–83.

81. Ellsworth, *Beyond Horizons,* 350–51.

82. Ibid., 351.

83. Mrs. Hollick-Kenyon, telephone conversation with author, 3 March 1983.

84. News clipping, 7 January 1936, Hollick-Kenyon family scrapbook.

85. Officer on *Discovery II,* letters to Sally Douglas, 31 October 1970, Beekman Pool collection.

86. Lowell Thomas, *New York Herald Tribune,* 6 March 1938.

87. Ellsworth diary, Trans-Antarctic Flight, 14 January 1936, OSU.

88. E. R. Douglas (group captain, royal Australian air force) report kept on board RRS *Discovery II,* on expedition to aid Lincoln Ellsworth and Herbert Hollick-Kenyon, January and February 1936, 12, Douglas family papers. Subsequent references to the report are annotated as Douglas report.

89. Ibid., 14.

90. Mary Louise Ellsworth, statement to author, 23 August 1978.

91. Ellsworth, *Beyond Horizons,* 352.

92. Douglas report, 16.

93. Ibid., 17.

94. Ellsworth, *Beyond Horizons,* 355–63.

95. On board MS *Wyatt Earp,* message received from the *Polar Star* during flight

23 November 1935, Appendix B, 18, NA.

96. Douglas report, 22.

97. Ibid., 24.

98. F. D. Ommanney letter to Sally Douglas, daughter of E. R. Douglas, 31 October 1970, copy in Douglas family papers.

99. Sally Douglas letter to Mary Louise Ellsworth, 29 December 1970, Beekman Pool collection.

100. Byrd telegram to Prentice, 29 November 1935, OSU.

101. Byrd letter to Arthur Hayes Sulzberger, 11 December 1935, OSU.

102. Byrd letter to Sulzberger, 12 December 1935, OSU.

103. Byrd letter to Prentice, 12 December 1935, OSU.

104. Byrd to Prentice, a second letter, 13 December 1935, OSU.

105. Byrd letter to Prentice, 13 December 1935, OSU.

106. Prentice letter to Byrd, 8 January 1936, OSU; Wilkins radiogram asking Prentice to thank Byrd for "fine offers," n.d., OSU; Ellsworth radiogram to Byrd, 22 January 1936, OSU.

107. Stefansson, *Polar Times* 2 (January 1936), 8 (quoting statement to *New York Times,* 18 January 1935).

108. Byrd telegram to Ellsworth, 30 December 1936, OSU.

109. Ellsworth, *Beyond Horizons,* 318.

110. *New York Times,* editorial, 24 January 1936.

111. Ellsworth, *Beyond Horizons,* 362.

Chapter 11: Claiming Antarctica

1. Duke of Windsor, *A King's Story* (New York: G. P. Putnam's Sons, 1951), 353.

2. Mary Louise Ellsworth, taped interview with author at her home, Carlyle Hotel, New York, N.Y., 23 August 1978. Tape in Beekman Pool collection.

3. Ibid.

4. Lincoln Ellsworth, "Antarctic Lures Ellsworth Again," copyright *New York Times* and NANA, Inc., *Polar Times* 6 (March 1938), 6.

5. Wilkins letter to Ellsworth, 17 February 1937, OSU.

6. Ibid.

7. Wilkins letter to John K. Northrup, 15 May 1937, OSU.

8. Ibid.

9. Northrup letter to Wilkins, 25 May 1937, OSU.

10. Wilkins letter to Hollick-Kenyon, 27 May 1937, OSU.

11. Hollick-Kenyon cable to Wilkins, 1 June 1937, OSU.

12. Ellsworth cable to Wilkins, 4 June 1937, Winston Ross collection.

13. Lincoln Ellsworth, "Ellsworth Plans Antarctic Flight," copyright NANA, Inc., *Polar Times* 5 (October 1937), 21.

14. Ellsworth telegram to Wilkins, 10 June 1937, David Larson collection.

15. Hollick-Kenyon letter to Wilkins, 9 June 1937, OSU.

16. Wilkins letter to Ellsworth, 10 June 1937, OSU.

17. Ellsworth telegram to Wilkins, 2 July 1937, David Larson collection.

18. Ellsworth telegram to Wilkins, 11 July 1937, David Larson collection.

19. Ellsworth wireless to Wilkins, 21 July 1937, quoted by Wilkins in letter to Charles McVeigh, 31 July 1937, OSU.

20. Ellsworth wireless to Wilkins, 22 July 1937, quoted by Wilkins in letter to McVeigh, 31 July 1937.

21. Ellsworth letter to Wilkins, 31 July 1937, OSU.

22. Wilkins letter to Ellsworth, 31 July 1937, OSU. Climaxing years of preparation, a Soviet airplane had landed at the North Pole on 21 May 1937, and established a permanent weather and scientific station. A month later the Soviets had announced a government plan to establish several "North Polar" camps at more remote locations.

23. *Polar Times* 5 (October 1937), 9; and *Polar Times* 6 (March 1938), 7.

24. *Polar Times* 6 (March 1938), 7.

25. Photostat of commission, 27 September 1937, Beekman Pool collection.

26. Probabilities of Outbreak of War, PSF container 499, Documents H. Naval Attaché London, vol. 1, 17 March 1936 to 30 August 1939, NA.

27. John Toland, *Adolf Hitler* (Garden City, N.Y.: John Toland, 1976), 397.

28. Probabilities of Outbreak of War, PSF container 499, Documents H. Naval Attaché London, vol. 1, 17 March 1936 to 30 August 1939, supra, NA.

29. "Vast Antarctic Area Claimed by Germany," *Polar Times* 8 (March 1939), 6; and *Polar Times* 10 (March 1940), 14.

30. Ellsworth radiogram to Wilkins, 7 May 1938, Winston Ross collection.

31. Wilkins letter to Ellsworth, 9 May 1938, Winston Ross collection.

32. Wilkins letter to Ellsworth, 25 May 1938, Winston Ross collection.

33. Ellsworth cablegram to Wilkins, 29 May 1938, Winston Ross collection.

34. Wilkins letter to Ellsworth, 1 June 1938, Winston Ross collection.

35. Ellsworth letter to Grosvenor and John Oliver La Gorce, 25 June 1938, NGS.

36. La Gorce radiogram to Grosvenor, describing Ellsworth's letter, 28 June 1938, NGS.

37. *New York Times,* 8 July 1938, 19.

38. Ellsworth cable to Wilkins, 7 September 1938, David Larson collection.

39. Ellsworth wireless to Wilkins, 30 September 1938, David Larson collection.

40. Ellsworth wireless to Wilkins, 7 October 1938, David Larson collection.

41. Ellsworth wireless to Wilkins, with scribbled notation of Wilkins' reply, n.d.

42. S. W. Boggs to acting secretary of state, 11 August 1930, 800.014 Antarctic/32, NA.

43. Memorandum, American Policy Relating to the Polar Regions, Department of State, Division of European Affairs, 28 July 1938 (declassified 4 April 1984), 2, NA.

44. Ibid., 2.

45. Mikhail Vodopyanoff, quoted from "A New Year's Dream," *Pravda,* 1 January 1938, in *Polar Times* 6 (March 1938), 6.

46. Memorandum, American Policy, 14 (see endnote 43).

47. Ibid., 12.

48. Secretary of State Cordell Hull letter to American Consul James Orr Denby, Cape Town, 30 August 1938, 031.11 Ellsworth Antarctic Expedition/89, declassified 2 April 1954, NA.

49. Ibid.

50. Denby letter to secretary of state, 1 October 1938, 031.11 Ellsworth Antarctic Expedition/94, declassified 11 March 1954, NA.

51. Ibid., 2.

52. State Department telegram to American consul, Cape Town, 22 October 1938, Claims 800.014 (129) Doc. File, NA.

53. Arthur L. Richards letter to secretary of state, 7 November 1938 (declassified 11 March 1954), 031.11 Ellsworth Antarctic Expedition/95, NA.

54. Lincoln Ellsworth, W.H.D. press dispatch, Cape Town, 29 October 1938, Winston Ross collection (now OSU).

55. Ellsworth, W.H.D. press dispatch, latitude 55 S., longitude 75 E., 21 November 1938, 1, 2, OSU.

56. Sir Hubert Wilkins' Report of the Ellsworth Antarctic Flight Expedition, 1938–39, to the Minister, Department of External Affairs, Commonwealth of Australia, 1, 2. Winston Ross collection (now OSU).

57. Ellsworth, W.H.D. press dispatch, 3 January 1939, OSU.

58. Ibid.

59. Ellsworth, W.H.D. press dispatch, 5 January 1939.

60. Ellsworth radiogram to Mary Louise Ellsworth, 5 January 1939, Beekman Pool collection.

61. Ellsworth, W.H.D. press dispatch, 7 January 1939.

62. Wilkins' report to the Minister, 1938–39 (supra), 5, 6, OSU.

63. Ibid., 6.

64. W.H.D. press dispatch, 7 January 1939. Reference to the possible presence of valuable minerals may have been a reason why declassification of an early document (see endnote 50) was delayed until 1984, far longer than other contemporary documents relating to such events.

65. Wilkins, report to the Minister, 8, 9 January 1939.

66. Ellsworth, W.H.D. press dispatch, 11 January 1939, 2, 3.

67. Wilkins, report to the Minister, 1938–39, 8, 9.

68. W.H.D. press dispatch, 11 January 1939, 5, 6.

69. *Washington Star,* 12 January 1939.

70. Lymburner, taped interview with author, 22 February 1985, Beekman Pool collection.

71. Ellsworth, and footnote in Wilkins' report, 10.

72. Balchen letter to Emmy Balchen, 5 November 1933.

73. Wilkins radio dispatch to secretary, Department of External Affairs, Canberra, Australia, 12 January 1939 (declassified 7 April 1984), Department of State, Division of European Affairs, 800.014 Antarctica.

74. Sumner Welles letter to Franklin D. Roosevelt, 6 January 1939 (declassified 4 April 1984), 800.014, Antarctic, US/LW, NA.

75. Ibid.

76. Roosevelt memorandum to Welles, 7 January 1939, NAC 800.015, Item 135, NA.

77. Hugh S. Cumming Jr. memorandum of 12 January conversation, United States

Claims in the Antarctic, 17 January 1939 (declassified 5 April 1984), 800.014 Antarctic/151, US/LW, NA.

78. Cumming memorandum of conversation, United States Claims in the Antarctic, 20 January 1939, 800.014 Antarctic/152, NA.

79. Memorandum to U.S. secretary of state, United States Claims in the Antarctic, 17 January 1939, 800.014 Antarctic/143, NA.

80. Cumming memorandum of conversation, United States Claims in the Antarctic, 28 January 1939 (declassified 5 April 1984), 800.014 Antarctic/154, US/LW, NA.

81. *Polar Times* 8 (March 1939), quoting Associated Press, Sydney, Australia, 8 February 1939.

82. Ibid., quoting Associated Press, Melbourne, Australia, 13 February 1939.

83. Cordell Hull to Franklin D. Roosevelt, 13 February 1939, Territorial Claims 800.014, NA.

84. Sydney, Australia, 28 February news clip, *Polar Times* 8 (March 1939), 1.

85. Kojiro Hiyoshi, Chairman Nobeoka Agriculture Association news clip, 28 February 1939, *Polar Times* 8 (March 1939), 6.

86. *Polar Times* 8 (March 1939), 6.

87. Halvdan Koht, Norwegian state government resolution, 14 January 1939, *Polar Times* 8 (March 1939).

88. Pierrepont Moffatt memorandum of conversation, 3 March 1939, NA.

89. Moffatt, 15 April 1939, NAC 800.014.

90. Ellsworth letter to Hull, 17 April 1939, 031.11-107 and 111, Ellsworth Antarctic Expedition, NA.

91. *New York Herald Tribune,* 18 April 1939.

92. State Department memorandum, 18 April 1939, Department of State 800.014 Antarctic, NA.

93. Ellsworth cablegram to Wilkins, 19 April 1939, David Larson collection.

94. Ellsworth letter to Hull, 25 May 1939, 800.014, Antarctica/194, NA.

95. Unsigned communication 13 June 1939 addressed to R. Walton Moore, who sent original to the president the following day. Document file, Department of State 800.014 Antarctic/188, NA.

96. Ibid.

97. *Petermann's Geographische Mitteilungen,* 85 #6, June 1939, trans. State Department Division, 800.014 (item 236), NA.

98. State Department memorandum to Senator James F. Byrnes, 21 June 1939, 800.014, Antarctic/202, NA.

99. German newspaper clipping, 25 July 1939, State Department Division 800.014 (item 234), NA.

100. Dr. Johannes Georgi, trans., Section 6, "Zcor Frage der Nomengeburg in der Antarktis," *Petermann's Geographische Mitteilungen* 95 (German National Archives, 1951).

101. Cumming memorandum of conversation, 17 July 1939, 800.014 Antarctic/200, NA.

102. Roosevelt memorandum to secretary of state, 28 July 1939, 800.014, Box 4521, NA.

103. Roosevelt memorandum for under secretary of state, 5 August 1939, 800.014 Antarctic/236 1/4 and 237 1/4, NA.

104. Boggs memorandum to Cumming, 12 August 1939, quoting an unnamed British military magazine, 800.014 Antarctic/252, US/LW, NA.

105. Editorial from *Diario Comercial,* San Pedro Sula, Honduras, 17 August 1939, 800.014 Antarctica/257, NA.

106. See endnote 26, supra.

107. Ellsworth telegram to Wilkins, 11 August 1939, NA.

108. Roosevelt to Byrd, 25 November 1939, State Department Division 800.014 (item 321A), NA.

109. Lieutenant Commander Lincoln Ellsworth, USNR, address made at the tenth anniversary meeting of The American Polar Society, 4 December 1944.

Chapter 12: Dreams Only

1. Lincoln Ellsworth and Toriboro Mejia Xesspe, "Investigation of the Architectural Ruins in the Crater of El Misti, Peru," typescript, n.d., 4, Beekman Pool collection.

2. Ibid., 5.

3. Ibid., 8.

4. Ellsworth telegram to Clark, 22 September 1942, original source unknown, copy in Beekman Pool collection.

5. Ibid.

6. Ellsworth letter to Wilkins, 25 May 1943, Winston Ross collection, copy in Beekman Pool collection.

7. Ellsworth letter to Clark, 25 May 1943.

8. Mary Louise Ellsworth statement to author, 21 September 1978.

9. Mary Louise Ellsworth statement to author, date unrecorded.

10. Clark letter to Wilkins, 16 January 1948, Stef.

11. Press release, American Polar Society, 5 December 1944, Beekman Pool collection.

12. Ibid.

13. Wilkins letter to Ellsworth, 6 April 1946, David Larson collection.

14. Wilkins letter to Clark, 10 September 1947, Stef.

15. Wilkins letter to Mrs. Harold Clark, 4 October 1947, Stef.

16. Ellsworth radiogram to Wilkins, 23 January 1948, David Larson collection.

17. Mary Louise Ellsworth statement to author, 6 May 1984, Beekman Pool collection.

18. Clark letter to John A. Lyon, 14 December 1948.

19. Horace W. Foster letter to John H. Hallowell, 18 February 1949, Stef.

20. Ellsworth letter to Clark, 27 April 1948, original source unknown, copy in Beekman Pool collection.

21. Wilkins letter to McVeigh, 17 April 1949.

22. Wilkins letter to Ellsworth, 17 April 1949.

23. Marion Goff interview with author, June 1949.

24. Ibid.

25. Mary Louise Ellsworth letter to Clark, 15 January 1950, Stef.

26. Mary Louise Ellsworth letter to Clark, 8 August 1950.

27. Mary Louise Ellsworth letter to author, 15 July 1984, Beekman Pool collection.

Epilogue

1. Aeronautic Achievements, Air Pioneering in the Arctic, *The Two Polar Flights of Amundsen and Ellsworth* (New York: National Americana Society: 1929), 124.

2. "Americans in Antarctica," American Geographical Society, Special Publication no. 39 (Burlington, Vt.: Lane Press, 1971), 365–66.

3. "Report of Working Group on Cartography" at Special Meeting on Antarctic Research, Cambridge, U.K., 29 August–2 September 1960, NA.

4. Harold E. Saunders, "Memorandum for Members of the Advisory Committee on Antarctic Names, January 11, 1961," NA.

See also, Fred G. Alberts, ed., *Geographical Names of the Antarctic,* 251 (Washington, D.C.: National Science Foundation). "A major group of mountains, 200 miles long and 30 miles wide, which trend NNW-SSE and rise from the relatively featureless snow plain that borders the western margin of the Ronne Ice Shelf. They are bisected by Minnesota Glacier to form the northern Sentinel Range and the southern Heritage Range. The former is by far the higher and more spectacular with Vinson Massif (5,140 m.) constituting the highest point on the continent. The mountains were discovered on November 23, 1935 by Lincoln Ellsworth in the course of a trans-Antarctic flight from Dundee Island to the Ross Ice Shelf. He gave the descriptive name Sentinel Range. The mountains were mapped in detail by USGS from ground surveys and U.S. Navy aerial photography, 1958–66. When it became evident that the mountains comprise two distinct ranges, the US-ACAN restricted the application of Sentinel Range to the high northern one and gave the name Heritage Range to the southern one; the Committee recommended the name of the discoverer for this entire group of mountains."

5. On 14 September 1988, in Washington, D.C., the U.S. Postal Service issued a set of stamps commemorating these four men.

6. Bob Davis, *Wall Street Journal,* 27 December 1991, 34.

7. Raimond E. Goerler, ed., *To the Pole, The Diary and Notebook of Richard E. Byrd, 1925–1927* (Ohio State University Press, 1998). Also see Chapter Five, endnote 40, in *Polar Extremes.*

8. *New York Times,* 9 May 1996, 1.

Bibliography

ABBREVIATIONS

AGS — American Geographical Society Collection, Golda Meier Library, University of Wisconsin, Milwaukee, Wis.

AMNH — American Museum of Natural History, New York, N.Y.

EI — Edison Institute, Archives and Library, Dearborn, Mich.

FDRL — Franklin Delano Roosevelt Library, Hyde Park, N.Y.

HL — Houghton Library, Harvard University, Cambridge, Mass.

JHL — Johns Hopkins University Library, Eisenhower Library, Baltimore, Md.

MS–AM — Museo Storico–Aeronautica Militare, Rome, Archives: Gen. Umberto Nobile

NA — National Archives, Washington, D.C.

NGS — National Geographic Society, Washington, D.C.

OSU — Byrd Polar Research Center, Ohio State University, Columbus, Ohio

RAC — Rockefeller Archive Center, North Tarrytown, N.Y.

RGS — Royal Geographical Society, London

SPRI — Scott Polar Research Institute, Cambridge, U.K.

SIA — Smithsonian Institution Archives, Washington, D.C.

Stef. — Stefansson Collection, Dartmouth College Library, Hanover, N.H.

UB — Universitets Biblioteket i Oslo (University Library, Olso)

Yale — Yale University Library, New Haven, Conn.

BOOKS

Alberts, Fred G., ed. *Geographical Names of the Antarctic.* Washington, D.C.: National Science Foundation, 1981.

American Council of Learned Societies Staff, ed. *Dictionary of American Biography.* New York: Charles Scribner's Sons, 1981.

Amundsen, Roald. *The North West Passage.* London: Archibald Constable and Co., 1908.

———. *My Life as an Explorer.* Garden City, N.Y.: Doubleday, Doran & Co., 1928.

Amundsen, Roald, and Lincoln Ellsworth. *Air Pioneering in the Arctic: The Two Polar Flights of Roald Amundsen and Lincoln Ellsworth.* New York: National Americana Society, 1929.

Amundsen, Roald, and Lincoln Ellsworth, et al. *First Crossing of the Polar Sea.* New York: George H. Doran Co., 1927.

———. *Our Polar Flight.* New York: Dodd, Mead & Co., 1925.

Anderson, J. R. L. *The Ulysses Factor.* New York: Harcourt Brace Jovanovich, 1970.

Anderson, William R. *Nautilus 90 North.* Cleveland: World Publishing Co., 1950.

Auburn, F. M. *Antarctic Law and Politics.* Bloomington: Indiana University Press, 1982.

Balch, Edwin Swift. *The North Pole and Bradley Land.* Philadelphia: Campion & Co., 1913.

Balchen, Bernt. *Come North with Me: An Autobiography.* New York: E. P. Dutton & Co., 1958.

Barriault, Yvette. *Mythes et rites chez les Indiens Montagnais.* Quebec: La Société Historique de la C'te Nord, l'Imprimerie Laflamme Lt'e, 1971.

Bennett, Glin. *Beyond Endurance: Survival at the Extremes.* New York: St. Martin's/ Marek, 1983.

Berton, Pierre. *The Arctic Grail.* New York: Viking Press, 1988.

Blanchet, Guy. *Search in the North.* New York: St. Martin's Press, 1960.

Bohr, Niels Henrik David. *The Theory of Spectra and Atomic Constitution, Three Essays.* Cambridge, England: The University Press, 1922.

Boyd, Louise A. *The Fiord Region of Eastern Greenland.* New York: American Geographical Society, 1935.

Breasted, Charles. *Pioneer to the Past: The Story of James H. Breasted.* New York: Charles Scribner's Sons, 1947.

Brooks, Peter W. *Zeppelin: Rigid Airships, 1893–1940.* Washington, D.C.: Smithsonian Institution Press, 1992.

Bryce, George. *The Siege and Conquest of the North Pole.* London: Gibbings & Co., Ltd., 1910.

Byrd, Richard E. *Antarctic Discovery.* London: Putnam & Co., 1926.

———. *Skyward.* New York: G. P. Putnam's Sons, 1928.

Calvert, James. *Surface at the Pole.* New York: McGraw-Hill, 1960.

Campbell, Bruce. *Where the High Winds Blow.* New York: Charles Scribner's Sons, 1946.

Campbell, David G. *The Crystal Desert, Summer in Antarctica.* Boston, New York, London: Houghton Mifflin Co., 1992.

Chancellor, Paul. *The History of the Hill School, 1951–1976*. Pottstown, Penn.: The Hill School, 1976.

Cherry-Garrad, Apsley. *The Worst Journey in the World*. 2 vols. London: Constable & Co., 1992.

Constance, Arthur. *The Inexplicable Sky*. New York: Citadel Press, 1956.

Cook, Frederick A. *My Attainment of the Pole*. New York: Mitchell Kennerley, 1912.

Courteauld, Augustine, found by. *From the Ends of the Earth: An Anthology of Polar Writings*. London: Oxford University Press, 1958.

Cross, Wilbur. *Ghost Ship of the Pole*. New York: William Sloane Associates, 1960.

Cultra, Quen. *Queequeg's Odyssey*. Chicago: Chicago Review Press, 1977.

DeLong, Emma, ed. *The Voyage of the Jeanette*. Boston: Houghton Mifflin Co., 1884.

Eckener, Hugo. *My Zeppelins*. Trans. Douglas Robinson. London: Putnam & Co., 1958.

Edward VIII. *A King's Story, The Memoirs of the Duke of Windsor*. New York: G. P. Putnam & Sons, 1951.

Ellis, Frank H. *Canada's Flying Heritage*. Toronto: University of Toronto Press, 1980.

Ellsberg, Edward. *Hell on Ice: The Saga of the Jeanette*. New York: Dodd, Mead & Co., 1938.

Ellsworth, Lincoln. *Beyond Horizons*. Garden City, N.Y.: Doubleday, Doran & Co., 1938.

———. *Ellsworth and Related Families: A Genealogical Study with Biographical Notes*. Update arranged by Lincoln Ellsworth. New York: American Historical Co., 1948.

———. *Exploring Today*. New York: Dodd, Mead & Co., 1935.

———. *The Last Wild Buffalo Hunt*. New York: privately printed, 1916.

———. *Search*. New York: Brewer, Warren & Putnam, 1932.

Ferguson, Marilyn. *The Aquarian Conspiracy: Personal and Social Transformation in the 1980s*. Los Angeles: J. P. Tarcher, 1980.

Firor, John. *The Changing Atmosphere: A Global Challenge*. New Haven and London: Yale University Press, 1990.

Frantz, Marie Luise von. *Puer Eternus*. Santa Monica: Sigo Press, 1970.

Gary, M. *Glossary of Geology*. New York: French & European Publications, 1977.

Guidici, Davide. *The Tragedy of the* Italia. New York: D. Appleton & Co., 1929.

Glen, A. R. *Young Man in the Arctic*. London: Faber and Faber Ltd., 1935.

Glen, A. R., and N. A. C. Croft. *Under the Pole Star*. London: Methuen & Co., 1937.

Glines, Carroll Vane, ed. *Polar Aviation*. New York: Franklin Watts, 1964.

Gould, Laurence M. *The Polar Regions in Their Relation to Human Affairs (Bowman Memorial Lectures)*. New York: American Geographical Society, 1958.

Grierson, John. *Challenge to the Poles*. London: Shoe String, 1964.

Halder, von Nold. "Der 'Schlossherr' von Lenzburg." In *Lenzburger Neujahrs Blätten*. Aarau, Switzerland: Werner Krauss, 1937.

Hanson, Earl Parker. *Stefansson, Prophet of the North*. New York: Harper & Bros., 1941.

Hayes, J. Gordon. *The Conquest of the North Pole*. New York: Macmillan Co., 1934.

Henry, Thomas Robert. *The White Continent: The Story of Antarctica.* New York: William Sloane Associates, 1951.

Herbert, Wally. *The Noose of Laurels: Robert E. Peary and the Race to the North Pole.* New York: Atheneum, 1989.

Heyerdahl, Thor, Soren Richter, and H. J. Riiser-Larsen. *Great Norwegian Expeditions.* Oslo: Dreyers Forlag, n.d.

Hind, Henry Youle. *Explorations in the Interior of the Labrador Peninsula.* London: Longman, Green, Roberts & Green, 1863.

Hobbs, William Herbert. *Explorers of the Antarctic.* New York: House of Field, 1941.

Howarth, David. *The Sledge Patrol.* New York: Macmillan Co., 1957.

Hunt, Harrison J., and Ruth Hunt Thompson. *North to the Horizon: Arctic Doctor and Hunter 1913–1917.* Camden, Maine: Down East Books, 1980.

Huntford, Roland. *Scott and Amundsen: The Race to the South Pole.* New York: G. P. Putnam's Sons, 1980.

Jackson, Donald Dale, and Editors of Time-Life Books. *The Explorers.* Alexandria, Va.: Time-Life Books, 1982.

Joerg, W. L. G., ed. *Problems of Polar Research.* New York: American Geographical Society Special Publication No. 7. Worcester, Mass.: Commonwealth Press, 1928.

Kane, Elisha Kent. *Arctic Explorations in the Years 1853, '54, '55.* 2 vols. Philadelphia: Childs & Peterson, 1856.

Kiley, Dan. *The Peter Pan Syndrome.* New York: Dodd, Mead & Co., 1983.

Kingery, W. David, ed. *Ice and Snow.* Cambridge: MIT Press, 1962.

Lake, Simon. *The Submarine in War and Peace.* Philadelphia: Lippincott, 1918.

Lake, Stuart. *Wyatt Earp, Frontier Marshal.* Boston and New York: Houghton Mifflin Co., 1931.

Lehmann, Ernst. *Zeppelin, The Story of Lighter-Than-Air Craft.* New York: Longman, Green & Co., 1937.

Levin, Bernard. *Enthusiasm.* New York: Crown Publishers, 1984.

Liddell Hart, Adrian. *Strange Company.* London: Weidenfeld and Nicolson, 1953.

Lindsay, Martin. *Three Got Through.* London: Falcon Press, 1946.

Lundborg, Einar. *The Arctic Rescue: How Nobile Was Saved.* New York: Viking Press, 1929.

Martin, Lawrence. "The Antarctic Sphere of Interest." In *New Congress of the World.* New York: Macmillan Co., 1949.

Mason, Theodore K. *Two Against the Ice.* New York: Dodd, Mead & Co., 1982.

McKay, Ernest A. *A World to Conquer: The Epic Story of the First Around-the-World Flight.* New York: Arco Publishing, 1981.

McKee, Alexander. *Ice Crash.* New York: St. Martin's Press, 1979.

McLean, John. *Notes of a Twenty-Five Years' Service in the Hudson Bay Territory.* London: Richard Bentley, 1849.

Miller, Francis Trevelyan. *Byrd's Great Adventure.* Philadelphia: John C. Winston Co., 1930.

Mirsky, Jeannette. *To the Arctic! The Story of Northern Exploration from Earliest Times to the Present.* New York: Allan Wingate, 1949.

Mittelholtzer, Walter. *By Airplane Towards the North Pole.* Trans. Eden and Cedar Paul. London: Allen & Unwin, 1925.

Montague, Richard. *Oceans, Poles and Airmen.* New York: Random House, 1971.

Nansen, Fridtjof. *Farthest North.* New York: Harper & Bros., 1897.

———. *In Northern Mists.* Trans. Arthur G. Chater. New York: Frederick A. Stokes Co., 1911.

National Americana Society. *The Ellsworth Family in Two Volumes.* vol. 1: James W. Ellsworth, His Life and Ancestry. New York: National Americana Society, 1930; vol. 2: Lincoln Ellsworth. Howard Eldred Kershner, ed. New York: National Americana Society, 1931.

Nielson, Thor. *The Zeppelin Story: The Life of Hugo Eckener.* London: Wingate, 1955.

Nobile, Umberto. *Addio Malyghin.* Milan: Mondadori, 1948.

———. *Ali Sul Polo.* Ed. U. Mursia. Trans. Esther Brooks. Milan: Mursia, 1975.

———. *My Five Years with Soviet Airships.* Trans. Frances Fleetwood. Akron, Ohio: Lighter-Than-Air Society, 1987.

———. *My Polar Flights.* Trans. Frances Fleetwood. New York: G. P. Putnam's Sons, 1961.

———. *La Tenda Rossa (The Red Tent).* Trans. A. Mondadori. Milan: Mondadori, 1970.

———. *Publicazioni di Umberto Nobile (1915–1978).* Rome: Tip, Editrice Nationale, n.d.

———. *With the* Italia *to the North Pole.* London: Allen & Unwin, 1930.

Noyes, Alfred. *Watchers of the Sky.* New York: Frederick A. Stokes Co., 1922.

Olsen, Magnus. *Saga of the White Horizon.* Lymington, Eng.: Nautical Publishing Co., 1972.

Papanin, Ivan. *Life on an Ice Floe.* New York: Julian Messner, 1939.

Parijanine, Maurice. *The Krassin.* Trans. Lawrence Brown. New York: Macauley Co., 1929.

Partridge, Bellamy. *Amundsen, The Splendid Norseman.* New York: Frederick A. Stokes Co., 1929.

Peary, Robert E. *Nearest the Pole.* New York: Doubleday, Page & Co., 1907.

Perkins, John. *To the Ends of the Earth.* New York: Pantheon Books, 1981.

Pettijohn, F. J. A. *A Century of Geology at Johns Hopkins University.* Baltimore: Gateway Press, 1988.

Phipps, Lutwidge. *The Journal of a Voyage Undertaken by Order of His Present Majesty for Making Discoveries Towards the North Pole.* London: F. Newberry, 1774.

Ponting, Herbert G. *The Great White South.* London: Duckworth, 1932.

Prentiss, Henry Mellen. *The Great Polar Current. Polar Papers, Delong—Nansen—Peary.* New York: Frederick A. Stokes Co., 1897.

Pyne, Stephen J. *The Ice: A Journey to Antarctica.* Iowa City: University of Iowa Press, 1986.

Rawlins, Dennis. *Peary at the Pole, Fact or Fiction?* Washington, D.C.: Robert B. Luce, 1973.

Riiser-Larsen, H. J. *Great Norwegian Expeditions.* Oslo: Dreyers Forlag, special edition for American-Scandinavian Foundation, N.Y., n.d.

Robinson, Bradley. *Dark Companion.* London: Hodder & Stoughton, 1948.

Rodgers, Eugene. *Beyond the Barrier: The Story of Byrd's First Expedition to Antarctica.* Annapolis, Md.: Naval Institute Press, 1990.

Roosevelt, Theodore. *Ranch Life and the Hunting-Trail.* New York: Century Co., 1888.

Rose, Lisle A. *Assault on Eternity.* Annapolis, Md.: Naval Institute Press, 1980.

Scott, J. M. *Portrait of an Ice Cap.* London: Chatto & Windus, 1953.

Scott, R. F. *Scott's Last Expedition: The Personal Journals of Captain R. F. Scott, R.N., C.V.O., on His Journey to the South Pole.* New York: Dodd, Mead & Co., 1923.

Shackleton, E. H. *The Heart of the Antarctics.* Philadelphia: Lippincott, 1909.

Shapley, Deborah. *The Seventh Continent: Antarctica in a Resource Age.* Baltimore, Md.: Resources for the Future, Inc., dist. Johns Hopkins University Press, 1985.

Simpson, C. J. W. *North Ice.* London: Hodder & Stoughton, 1957.

Smith, Page. *A People's History of the United States. Vol. 6: The Rise of Industrial America.* New York: McGraw-Hill, 1987.

Stefansson, Vilhjalmur. *The Adventure of Wrangel Island.* New York: Macmillan Co., 1925.

———. *The Northward Course of Empire.* New York: Macmillan Co., 1924.

———. *Unsolved Mysteries of the Arctic.* New York: Macmillan Co., 1938.

Stewart, John. *Antarctica: An Encyclopedia.* Jefferson, N.C., and London: McFarland & Co., Inc., 1990.

Stolp, Gertrude Nobile. *Bibliographia di Umberto Nobile.* Florence: L. S. Olschki, 1984.

Sverdrup, Otto. *New Land: Four Years in the Arctic Regions.* 2 vols. Trans. Ethel Harriet Hearn. London: Longman, Green & Co., 1904.

Thomas, Lowell. *Sir Hubert Wilkins, His Life of Adventures.* New York: McGraw-Hill, 1961.

Toland, John. *Adolf Hitler.* Garden City, N.Y.: Doubleday, 1976.

———. *The Great Dirigible: Their Triumphs and Disasters.* New York: Dover Publications, 1972.

Vaeth, J. Gordon. *Graf Zeppelin: The Adventures of an Aerial Globe Trotter.* New York: Harper & Bros., 1958.

Van Dyke, Henry. *A Biography.* New York: Harper & Bros., 1935.

———. *The Gospel for an Age of Doubt.* New York: Macmillan Co., 1898.

———. *The Grand Canyon.* New York: Charles Scribner's Sons, 1914.

———. *The Poems of Henry Van Dyke.* New York: Charles Scribner's Sons, 1911.

Verne, Jules. *Twenty Thousand Leagues Under the Sea.* London: Everymans Library, 1905.

Victor, Paul Emile. *Man and the Conquest of the Poles.* New York: Simon & Schuster, 1963.

Wallace, Dillon. *The Lure of the Labrador Wild.* New York: Fleming H. Revell Co., 1905.

Weems, John Edward. *Race for the Pole.* New York: Henry Holt, 1960.

Wilkins, Capt. George H. *Flying the Arctic.* New York: Grosset & Dunlap, 1928.

Wilkins, Sir Hubert. *Under the North Pole.* New York: Brewer, Warren & Putnam, 1931.

Williams, Henry Smith. *The Historian's History of the World.* London: Encyclopedia Britannica, 1926.

Wilson, Clifford, ed. *North of 55´.* Toronto: Ryerson Press, 1954.

Wright, Helen. *Explorer of the Universe: A Biography of George Ellery Hale.* New York: E. P. Dutton & Co., 1966.

Wright, John Kirtland. *Geography in the Making.* New York: American Geographical Society, 1952.

PERIODICALS, BULLETINS, PAMPHLETS, AND SPECIAL PUBLICATIONS

"Aide to Ellsworth Hurt in Shift of Ice." *Polar Times* no. 8 (March 1939): 2–3.

Amundsen, Roald. "Amundsen Answers His Critics." *World's Work* 13 (July 1927): 281–93.

———. "The Rows Aboard the Norge." *World's Work* 14 (August 1927): 389–404.

Amundsen, Roald, and Lincoln Ellsworth. "The Hop-Off, Radiograms of the Amundsen-Ellsworth Polar Flight, 1925." Messages to the press sent from Spitsbergen before and after the flight. Pamphlet. New York: Walter Hyams & Co., 1925.

"Amundsen's Polar Flight." *Geographical Journal* 66 (July 1925): 48–53.

Anderson, Peter J. "Richard Evelyn Byrd—Polar Explorer." *Iron Worker* 28 (Autumn 1974): 2–13.

"Antarctic Lures Ellsworth Again." *Polar Times* no. 6 (March 1938): 6.

The Arctic Institute of North America. *A Program of Desirable Scientific Investigations in Arctic North America.* Bulletin No. 1. Montreal: The Arctic Institute of North America, March 1946.

Arikaynen, Alexander I., and Oleg A. Kossov. "Toward Peace and Security in the Arctic: Cooperation Between the Soviet Union and the United States." *Northern Notes* (November 1989): 1, 58–70.

Aurousseau, M. "The Treatment of Antarctic Names." *Geographical Review* 38 (July 1948): 487–90.

"Australia Rejects Wilkins Proposal." *Polar Times* no. 9 (November 1939): 10.

"Australians Dispute Ellsworth's Claims." *Polar Times* no. 8 (March 1939): 4.

Bartlett, H. T. "Rigid Airships." *United States Naval Institute Proceedings* (1924): 161–72.

Bertrand, Kenneth J. "Americans in Antarctica." In American Geographical Society Special Publication No. 39. Burlington, Vt.: Lane Press, 1971.

Binney, George. "Amundsen's Polar Flight." Reviews of Lincoln Ellsworth, *My Polar Flight,* and Roald Amundsen, Lincoln Ellsworth, and other members of the expedition, *Our Polar Flight. Geographical Journal* 67 (March 1926): 253–59.

Bouton, Katherine. "A Reporter at Large South of 60 Degrees South." *New Yorker* (23 March 1981): 42–122.

Byrd, Lieutenant Commander Richard E. "Byrd Hails Flight of Ellsworth and Aide; Explorers Here and Abroad Add Praise." *Polar Times* no. 2 (January 1936): 8.

———. "This Hero Business." *Ladies' Home Journal* 44 (January 1927): 21, 113–14.

Cortesi, Salvatore. "An Historic Italian Villa." Pamphlet. Rome: Tip, Editrice Nationale, n.d.

Downs, Winfield S. "Lincoln Ellsworth, Civil Engineer and Explorer." *Americana Illustrated* 21 (January 1927): 1–92.

Douglas, Vice Admiral Sir Percy. "Mr. Ellsworth and the Discovery II." *Polar Record* no. 12 (July 1936): 166–72.

Ellsworth, Lincoln. "Arctic Flying Experiences by Airplane and Airship." In W. L. G. Joerg, ed., *Problems of Polar Research*. American Geographical Society Special Publication No. 7. Worcester, Mass.: Commonwealth Press, 1928.

————. "At the North Pole." *Yale Review* 16 (1927): 739–49.

————. "Ellsworth, in the 'Roaring Forties,' Heads Ship for Kerguelen Isles." *Polar Times* no. 8 (March 1939): 4.

————. "Ellsworth in Flight Over the Antarctic." *Polar Times* no. 8 (March 1939): 1–2.

————. "Ellsworth Found Antarctic 'Spine' of Mountain Peaks." *Polar Times* no. 2 (January 1936): 4–5.

————. "Ellsworth Is Forced Back Again But Finds High Mountain Range." *Polar Times* no. 2 (January 1936): 9.

————. "Ellsworth Lauds Flight Equipment." *Polar Times* no. 2. (January 1936): 2.

————. "Ellsworth Tells Expedition Plans." *Polar Times* no. 7 (October 1938): 2.

————. "Ellsworth's Own Diary." *Natural History* 37 (May 1936): 400–404.

————. "Ellsworth's Transantarctic Flight: Antarctica." *American Geographical Society Special Bulletin* 39: 365–66.

————. "Explorers Fight Fire on Their Ship." *Polar Times* no. 8 (March 1939): 5.

————. "The First Crossing of Antarctica." *Geographical Journal* 89 (March 1937): 193–213.

————. "Fortune and Misfortune in Antarctica." *Natural History* 35 (May 1935): 397–402.

————. "My Flight Across Antarctica." *National Geographic* 70 (July 1936): 1–35.

————. "My Four Antarctic Explorations." *National Geographic* 76 (July 1939): 129–38.

————. "North to 88 and the First Crossing of the Polar Sea." *Natural History* 27 (May–June 1927): 275–89.

————. "To Antarctica Again." *Natural History* 34 (July–August 1934): 332–44.

————. "What's the Use?" *Americana Illustrated* 21 (January 1927): 91.

Ellsworth, Lincoln, and Edward H. Smith. "Report of the Preliminary Results of the Aereoarctic Expedition with 'Graf Zeppelin,' 1931." *Geographical Review* 22 (January 1932): 61–82.

"Ellsworth Antarctic Expedition 1933–34." *Polar Record* no. 5 (January 1933): 52–55; no. 6 (July 1933): 123–26; no. 7 (January 1934): 81–87.

"Ellsworth Antarctic Expedition 1934–35." *Polar Record* no. 9 (January 1935): 66–68.

"Ellsworth Antarctic Expedition 1935–36." *Polar Record* no. 11 (January 1936): 101–103.

"Ellsworth Gets Hubbard Medal." *Polar Times* no. 3 (June 1936): 8.

"Ellsworth Lands on Unvisited Isle; Finds Group off Antarctic Barrier." *Polar Times* no. 8 (March 1939): 3.

"Ellsworth Plane Is Put Aboard Ship." *Polar Times* no. 2 (January 1936): 7.

"Ellsworth Plans Antarctic Flight." *Polar Times* no. 5 (October 1937): 21.

"Ellsworth Plans South Pole Camp." *Polar Times* no. 8 (March 1939): 1–2.

"Ellsworth's Data Awaited for Map." *Polar Times* no. 2 (January 1936): 8.

"Ellsworth Tells the Story of Flight Across Antarctic." *Polar Times* no. 2 (January 1936): 1–2.

"Explorer Becomes Only Man to Span Both the Polar Regions." *Polar Times* no. 2 (January 1936): 1.

Georgi, Johannes, trans. "Zur Frage der Namengebung in der Antarktis." *Petermanns Geographische Mitteilungen* 95 (1951, 2. Quartalshott.): 6. NA.

"Geographical Medal Goes to Ellsworth." *Polar Times* no. 2 (January 1936): 8.

"The German Antarctic Expedition of 1938–39." *Polar Times* no. 10 (March 1940): 14.

Harris, R. A. "Arctic Tides." Pamphlet. Washington, D.C.: Government Printing Office, 1911.

———. "Some Indications of Land in the Vicinity of the North Pole." *National Geographic* 15 (June 1904): 255–61.

———. "Undiscovered Land in the Arctic Ocean." *American Museum of Natural History Journal* 13 (February 1913): 57–61.

Hill, L. C. "Ellsworth Antarctic Relief Expedition." Report by Capt. L. C. Hill, Commanding Officer of the Royal Research Ship Discovery II, 1936. Pamphlet. Canberra, Australia: L. F. Johnson, 1936.

Hobbs, William Herbert. "American Antarctic Discoveries, 1819–1940." *Polar Times* no. 17 (December 1943): 20–22.

Holland, G. J. "The First Crossing of the Polar Sea." *Americana Illustrated* 21 (January 1927): 63–92.

Hope, E. R. "Geotectonics of the Arctic Ocean and the Great Arctic Magnetic Anomaly." *Journal of Geophysical Research* 64, no. 4 (April 1959): 408–23.

Howgate, Henry W. "Polar Colonization: Memorial to Congress and Action of Scientific and Commercial Association." Pamphlet. Washington, D.C.: Beresford, 1878.

"The Italia Disaster." *Geographical Journal* 76 (September 1930): 257–59.

Jackson, Donald Dale. "Lincoln Ellsworth, the Forgotten Hero of Polar Exploration." *Smithsonian* 21 (October 1990): 171–88.

Joerg, W. L. G. "Brief History of Polar Exploration Since the Introduction of Flying." American Geographical Society Special Publication No. 11, second revised edition. New York, 1930.

———. "The Cartographical Results of Ellsworth's Trans-Antarctic Flight of 1935." *Geographical Review* 27 (July 1937): 430–44.

———. "The Topographical Results of Ellsworth's Trans-Antarctic Flight of 1935." *Geographical Review* 26 (July 1936): 454–62.

Keller, F. M. "North to Eighty-eight Degrees." *Americana Illustrated* 21 (January 1927): 24–62.

Liljequist, Gosta H., University of Uppsala, *Interavia* 15 (1960): 589.

MacMillan, Donald B. "Why Go North?" *American Mercury* 34 (February 1935): 202–208.

Melville, Commodore George W. "A Proposed System of Drift Casks to Determine the Direction of the Circumpolar Currents." Bulletin of the Geographical Society of Philadelphia (April 1898).

Miller, O. M. "Air Navigation Methods in the Polar Regions." In W. L. G. Joerg, ed. *Problems of Polar Research*. American Geographical Society Special Publication No. 7. Worcester, Mass.: Commonwealth Press, 1928.

Mitchell, Barbara, and Jon Tinker. "Antarctica and Its Resources." Pamphlet. Earthscan. London: International Institute for Environmental Development, 1980.

Nansen, F. "The Oceanographic Problems of the Still Unknown Arctic Regions." In W. L. G. Joerg, ed. *Problems of Polar Research*. American Geographical Society Special Publication No. 7, Worcester, Mass.: Commonwealth Press, 1928: 3–14.

Nordenskjold, Otto, and Ludwig Mecking. "The Geography of the Polar Regions." American Geographical Society Special Publication No. 8. New York, 1928.

"Obituary. Lincoln Ellsworth 1880–1951." *Journal of the Arctic Institute of North America* 4 (1951): 151.

Official Name Decisions Gazeteer No. 14-3, June 1969, 58, shows latitude and longitude of four major features named Ellsworth. NA.

Owen, Russell. "Ellsworth Fills In a Gap in Antarctica." *Polar Times* no. 2 (January 1936): 5–6.

"Perils of Antarctic Flight Recounted by Ellsworth." *Polar Times* no. 2 (January 1936): 2–4.

"Plans for Mr. Lincoln Ellsworth's Antarctic Expedition, 1934." *Polar Record* no. 8 (July 1934): 147.

"Polar Dreams, Polar Nightmares: The Quests of Lincoln Ellsworth." *Ohio Historical Society, Timeline* 5 (December 1988): 14–27; 6 (January 1989).

"The Polar Flights." *Geographical Journal* 68 (July 1926): 62–72.

Poulter, Thomas C. "Byrd's Courage Tested By His Solitary Vigil." *Polar Times* no. 1 (June 1935): 6.

Roberts, Brian. "Chronological List of Antarctic Expeditions." *Polar Record* 9 (September 1958): 191–239. (See esp. p. 210, re: Byrd's third expedition, 1939–41.)

"Secret Nazi Base in Arctic Erased." *Polar Times* no. 7 (December 1943): 13.

Shaw, William A., ed. "Lenzburg Castle." Pamphlet. Aarau, Switzerland: H. R. Sauerlander & Co., 1907.

"The Ship That Found the Long-Missing Ellsworth and His Pilot." *The Illustrated London News* 98 (25 January 1936): 137–39.

Stephenson, Alfred, and Arthur R. Hinks. "Diagram Relating the Discoveries of Wilkins and Ellsworth to Those of the British Graham Land Expeditions." *Geographical Journal* 96 (September 1940): back of map, opp. p. 282.

Svarlien, Oscar. "The Sector Principle in Law and Practice." *Polar Record* 10 (September 1960): 248–63.

Sverdrup, Harald Ulrik. "Dynamics of Tides on the North Siberian Shelf." *Geosys. Publikasjoner* 4, no. 5.

Sverdrup, Harald Ulrik, with F. M. Soule. "Scientific Results of the Nautilus Expedition." Cambridge, Mass.: MIT Meteorological Papers 2 (1933): 1.

Thiel, Edward. "Antarctica, One Continent or Two?" *Polar Record* 10 (January 1961): 335–48.

U.S. Department of the Interior. "Geographic Names of Antarctica." Special Publication No. 86 (May 1947): 161.

————. "Geographic Names of Antarctica." Supplement to Gazeteer #14 (January 1963): 12.

Waring, J. F. "James W. Ellsworth and the Refounding of the Western Reserve Academy." Pamphlet. Hudson, Ohio: Western Reserve Academy, 1961.

"Weddell Sector." *Polar Record* 1 (January 1931): 24–26.

Wilkins, Capt. Sir Hubert. "The Wilkins-Hearst Antarctic Expedition, 1928–1929." *Geographical Review* 19 (July 1929): 353–76.

Woodburne, Michael O. "Newly Discovered Land Mammal from Antarctica." *Antarctic Journal* 17 (1982 review): 64–66.

Woolf, S. J. "Ellsworth Looks to the Frozen South." *The New York Times Magazine* 29 (May 1932).

Wrigley, J. M. "The Polar Flights of Byrd and Amundsen." *Geographical Review* 16 (October 1926): Polar Regions, 662–64.

"Wyatt Earp Party Balked by Crevasse." *Polar Times* no. 2 (January 1936): 7.

DIARIES, LOGS, MEMORANDA, REPORTS

Amundsen, Roald
  Diary, 7 October 1924–21 May 1925. Trans. for *Polar Extremes* by Lars O. Melemseter. UB. Dagbok Fra Polflyvningen 1925, 22 May–15 June 1925. Trans. for *Polar Extremes* by Erik J. Friis, former editor and publisher of the Scandinavian-American Bulletin. UB.
  Diary, Kings Bay to Alaska, 1926 *Norge* flight. UB.
Balchen, Bernt
  Dictated notes covering major events in his life from youth to 1934. Microfilm Accessional Record Group 401-97, NA.
  Memo book: "The Ellsworth Transarctic Expedition Started April 1932." OSU.
  Diary 1933, film rolls, OSU.
  Diaries/records, 1926–35, microfilm rolls 30908, 30913, 30917, HQ USAF HRC, Maxwell Air Force Base, Alabama. Duplicates in Beekman Pool collection.
  Rejection of Byrd's claim that he reached the North Pole. AAF microfilm Index 1161, 044, 45, 62, formerly at HQ USAF HRC/AD, Maxwell Air Force Base, then withdrawn by family in 1975 and copyrighted. See also, Air Force Classification Numbers: 1007465, Ellsworth Antarctic Expedition, 1931–35 1007529, Test Flights for Ellsworth Expedition, Jan.–Dec. 1933 vol. 1 1007530,

Ellsworth Expedition Diary, 1934, vol. 2 1007531, Ellsworth Expedition 1935, vol. 3 1007523, Ellsworth Expedition, Plans, Diary 13–23 April 1932 1007578 & 1007579, Personal Correspondence re: Ellsworth Expeditions "The Strange Enigma of Admiral Byrd," typescript. RG401/59, NA.

Balchen, Bess

Richard Byrd's 1926 North Pole Fiasco, Internet 15 pages, story based on Bess's diaries at the time. E-mail address kikut@acadia.net, ACADIA, December 1998 copyright.

Byrd, Admiral Richard E.

Polar Times, vol. 2, no. 8, 1996, 9–13. Five pages are dedicated to presenting both sides of the controversy: "Did Admiral Byrd make it to the North Pole?"

Clark, Harold

Memorandum re: proposed flight by Amundsen from Alaska to Spitsbergen, 1922–23, 13 December 1928. Stef. Confidential report of investigation relative to Roald Amundsen, made through the Credit Department of the Chase National Bank, 10 February 1925. Stef.

Douglas, Flight Lieutenant E.

Diary kept on board *Discovery II*, 23 December 1935–15 February 1936. The Dominion Museum, Wellington, N.Z.

Report on relief flight to Mr. Lincoln Ellsworth and Mr. Hollick-Kenyon per R.R.S. *Discovery II*, January 1936, Government of the Commonwealth of Australia.

Ellsworth, Lincoln

"A Diary of a Few Wanderings Written in Abstract Moments," 12 May–7 October 1905 (on survey for goldmine, Alaska). NA.

Diary and notes, 1906, Grand Trunk Pacific Railway survey. NA.

Journal, 14 July–23 October 1909, Vancouver to Edmonton.

Philosophical writings. NA.

"Astronomy Notes—1920."

"Nature and Religion," 1923–24.

"News from the Stars," 1921.

"Wonder of the Universe," 1924.

Diary for Amundsen-Ellsworth Expedition, 1925. AMNH.

Diary for the 1926 *Norge* expedition. AMNH.

Diary, Trans-Antarctic Flight, 23 November–15 December 1935; Little America, 15 December–15 January 1936 (signed with no explanation, H.W.). OSU.

Notebook, 107 pp., 25 May–13 June 1925. NA.

Notebook used to exchange messages during antarctic flight, 1935. NA.

Commission of Lincoln Ellsworth as Lieutenant in the Naval Reserve, United States Navy, 27 September 1937.

Investigation of the Architectural Ruins in the Crater of El Misti, Peru (Ellsworth El Misti Expedition, 1941). Ellsworth family papers.

"Operation of Military Aircraft in Polar Regions: Report on Study on Conditions." NA.

Ferguson, H. L.
  Diary, "Over the Andes, Colombia," 1909, Lincoln Ellsworth, H. L. Ferguson.
    Ferguson family papers.
Hill, L. C.
  "Ellsworth Antarctic Relief Expedition," Report by Capt. L. C. Hill, Com-
    manding Officer of the Royal Research Ship Discovery II. Canberra, Aus-
    tralia: Commonwealth Government Printer, 21 May 1936.
Hollick-Kenyon, Herbert
  Flight Log, 1935, Ellsworth Transantarctic Flight. Hollick-Kenyon family papers.
  Scrapbook loaned to author by Hollick-Kenyon's widow. Hollick-Kenyon family
    papers.
Hull, Cordell
  Department of State, Report to Roosevelt, 13 February 1939 re: Territorial claims,
    800.014. NA.
(Labrador) Corp. Ltd.
  Background information. Montreal: (Labrador) Corp. Ltd., n.d., Beekman Pool
    collection.
PSF Container 499. Probability of Outbreak of War.
  Documents, Naval attaché London. Vol. I: 17 March 1936–30 August 1939. NA.
Northern Quebec and Labrador Journals and Correspondence, 1819–85. The Hud-
    son's Bay Record Society, vol. 24. London, 1963.
Pool, Beekman H.
  Diary, Labrador crossing, 1930. Beekman Pool collection.
Rawlins, Dennis
  "Preliminary (unedited) Report on Byrd 1925–1926 Data: Raimond Goerler's
    Discovery and Its Revelations." Baltimore, Md.: D. Rawlins, 4 May 1996.
Ronne, Finn
  "Memorandum for the record, Subject: Comments on Commander Richard E.
    Byrd's North Pole Flight," 22 February 1960, sworn to before notary public 8
    March 1960 (copy received by Mary Louise Ellsworth from Finn Ronne).
    Beekman Pool collection.
  Letter to Mary Louise Ellsworth, 26 March 1971, stating that Byrd never reached
    the North Pole. Beekman Pool collection.
Saunders, Harold E., Chairman, Advisory Committee on Antarctic Names
  Memorandum concerning proposed name change for Ellsworth Highland, 18
    November 1960, Dept. of Navy, Bureau of Ships (Code 106). NA.
  Memorandum for members of Advisory Committee on Antarctic Names, Tenta-
    tive Draft of Division for Ellsworth Mountains, 11 January 1961. NA.
South Polar Chart #1240, engraved by Malby & Sons, 232.13 British Hydrographic
    Office, with pencil notation "Captain's property." Ellsworth's transantarctic
    flight course, times, and positions of landings, and named features have been
    clearly printed, with a major notation: "American flag raised and area between
    meridians 80′ and 120′ west longitude named JAMES W. ELLSWORTH LAND."

Beekman Pool collection. This was given to Ellsworth by Captain L. C. Hill, commander of the Royal Research Ship *Discovery II.*

Texaco, Inc.

"Antarctic Adventure." The Texaco Star, No. 1. White Plains, N.Y.: Texaco, Inc., 1936.

Texas Co., The "Ellsworth Antarctic Expedition." The Texas Co. Public Relations Report, 1932.

U.S. Department of State Memoranda and communications (many originally classified) between Sumner Welles, Franklin D. Roosevelt, Senator James F. Byrnes, Cordell Hull, and others, January 1939, regarding Lincoln Ellsworth's 1938–1939 expedition and claims in Antarctica. Territorial Claims, 800.014 Antarctic. NA.

U.S. Navy

"United States Naval Aviation, 1910–1980, Prepared at the Direction of the Deputy Chief of Naval Operations (Air Warfare) and the Commander, Naval Air Systems Command," 1981. Copy, Beekman Pool collection.

Wilkins, Sir Hubert

Official Diary Wilkins-Ellsworth Trans-Arctic Submarine Expedition, 1931. OSU.

Copy of message typed on board MS *Wyatt Earp*, Dundee Island, 26 November 1935. SPRI.

Report of the Ellsworth Antarctic Flight Expedition, 1938–39. OSU.

PUBLIC ADDRESSES

Clark, Harold T., secretary of the Cleveland Museum of Natural History. "Episodes of the Amundsen-Ellsworth Arctic Flights" address given at the Amundsen Memorial Day Services held at the museum, Cleveland, Ohio, 14 December 1928.

Dietrichson, Lieutenant Lief R. Lecture re: flight. Universitets Biblioteket, Oslo, 31 October 1925.

Ellsworth, Lincoln. Address at the tenth-anniversary meeting of the American Polar Society, New York, 5 December 1944.

———. "Ellsworth Antarctic Flight, 1936." Speech delivered at the Royal Geographical Society, London, 1936.

———. Lectures. Melbourne, Australia, 19 February 1936; Sydney, Australia, 2 March 1936. Microfilm 401-36, Ellsworth AV 1 and 3, NA.

Joerg, W. L. G. "Demonstration of the Peninsularity of Palmer Land, Antarctica, Through Ellsworth's Flight of 1935." Paper read 23 February 1940, Symposium on Polar Exploration. *Proceedings of the American Philosophical Society for Promoting Useful Knowledge* 82 (June 1940): 821–32.

PERSONAL COMMUNICATIONS

Balchen, Bernt. Letters to his wife, 1934–35. Dr. Fred Goldberg collection.

Douglas, Flight Lieutenant E. R. Manuscript letter to Mary Louise Ellsworth, 12 March 1984. Beekman Pool collection.

Douglas, Sally (daughter of Flight Lieutenant E. R. Douglas). Conversations and correspondence with author, 1980s.

Ellsworth, Lincoln. Labrador wilderness journey with author, June–September 1930. Author's visit at Schloss Lenzburg, August 1931, and continuing relationship until 1951.

    Letters to Clare Neilson (niece), 1920s–1930s. Ellsworth family papers.

    Letters to Clare Prentice (sister), 1920s–1930s. Ellsworth family papers.

Ellsworth, Mary Louise. Letters to author, 1952–88.

    Taped interview, 23 August 1978.

    Conversations with author, identified by contemporaneous memoranda, 1951–88.

Lymburner, J. B. ("Red"). Taped interview, 22 February 1985.

Moran, G. R. (from Byrd's office). Letters to author, 1979, indicating anxiety about writers with axes to grind.

Neilson, Clare (niece of Lincoln Ellsworth). Telephone conversations, 1980–95.

Nobile, Gertrude (widow of General Umberto Nobile). Correspondence with author, 1982–85.

Ommanney, F. D. Letter to Sally Douglas, 31 October 1970. Douglas family papers.

Ross, Winston (secretary and friend of Sir Hubert Wilkins). Conversations with author, 30 September–2 October 1983.

Saunders, Harold E. (Chairman, Advisory Committee on Antarctic Names). Letter to Mrs. Lincoln Ellsworth, 9 January 1961. Dept. of Navy, Bureau of Ships (Code 106). NA.

Index

Great Britain. *See also* Australia
 land claims, 226, 231
  Ross Dependency Claim, 235
Green, Fitzhugh, 88
Greenland, 30, 63, 79, 88, 251
Grosvenor, Gilbert H., 120, 133
Grouitch, Mabel Dunlop, 19
Gruening, Ernest, 238
Guilbaud, René, 136
guns, 24, 39

H
Haakon VII, 43
Hamilton River, 14, 15
Hansen, Godfred, 146
Harmsworth Island, 159
Harriman, W. Averell, 147
Harris Land, 34. *See also* Crocker Land
Harris, R.A., 33
Heard Island, 235
Hearst Land, 240
Hearst newspapers, 155, 157
Heimdal, 68, 89–90
Henson, Matthew, 26
Herschel, John Frederick William, 38
Hill, J.J., 13
Hill, L.C., 209
Hill School, 22, 24
Hitler, Adolf, 224
HMS *Cornwall,* 241
Hobby, 47, 68, 87
Hobe Sound, 220
Hollick-Kenyon, Herbert, 190–213, 221,
 222, 253
Hollick-Kenyon Plateau, 200
Holm, Aksel, 189
Holmboe, Jorgen, 177, 186
Holth, Baard, 174
home, 39, 142, 143–147, 219, 242
Honduras, 240
Hooper, F.H., 138
Hoover, Herbert, 213
Horgen, Emil, 99
Hot Springs, 142
Höver, John, 86
Hubbard, Leonidas, 14, 15
Hudson (OH), family farm, 20, 28–29, 42,
 142, 245
Hudson's Bay, 32
Hull, Cordell, 227, 236, 237

I
Inness, George, 21
Irene, 42
Isachsen, Gunnar, 152
Italian government, 80–98, 105, 122, 130, 135

J
James W. Ellsworth Fjord, 187
James W. Ellsworth Land, 185, 194, 200,
 234, 240, 243, 252
Japan, land claims, 236–237
Jay Hawker expedition, 152, 241
Joerg, W.L.G., 98, 151, 197, 198
Johns Hopkins University, 220
Josephine Ford, 90, 91, 92
*Journal of the American Museum of Natural
 History,* 198

K
Kenya, 226
King William Island, 146
Kings Bay, 47, 69
Knut Skaaluren, 87, 89
Koht, Halvdan, 237
Kougarok, 26
Krassin, 135
Kredittkassen, 104
Kunz, George, 129, 130, 131

L
Labrador canoe trip, 13, 14–17
Lackawanna Steel Company, 28
Lady Franklin Bay, 68
Lake Menihek, 16
Langley Medal, 133, 139–140
Larsen, Helene, 46, 72, 143
Lawrence, Kitty Lanier, 147–148
League of Nations, 224
Lehmann, Ernst A., 159
Leica, 163, 194, 197
Lenzburg, 143–147, 159, 163, 190
Levanevsky, Sigismund, 223–224
Liljequist, Gösta, 97
Lincoln Ellsworth, 70
Lincoln Ellsworth Fund, 244
Lindbergh, Charles, 133
Little America, 158, 177, 192, 202, 203, 204,
 235, 236
 Ellsworth at, 205–208
Little Church Around the Corner, 174
Lomonosov Range, 123
Lure of the Labrador Wild, The (Wallace), 14
Lusitania, 35

About the Author

Although a graduate of Harvard and Columbia Law School, Beekman Pool has always been more at home in the wilderness than in city streets. While still in college, he met Lincoln Ellsworth, whose approach to life was much like his. Although a generation separated them, they became close friends, journeying together up the wildest untouched river of northern Labrador. Pool has been a traveler in both Polar worlds, and a writer and lecturer on the life and art of the Canadian Inuit. Until his death in 1951, Ellsworth remained his friend and fellow enthusiast of the world of ice and snow. In World War II, Beekman Pool served at an 8th Army bomber base in England, both as service pilot and intelligence officer. He and his wife, Elizabeth, live in New Hampshire with their dog, Lincoln.